*Refiguring*
ENGLISH
STUDIES

Refiguring English Studies provides a forum for scholarship on English studies as a discipline, a profession, and a vocation. To that end, the series publishes historical work that considers the ways in which English studies has constructed itself and its objects of study; investigations of the relationships among its constituent parts as conceived in both disciplinary and institutional terms; and examinations of the role the discipline has played or should play in the larger society and public policy. In addition, the series seeks to feature studies that, by their form or focus, challenge our notions about how the written "work" of English can or should be done and to feature writings that represent the professional lives of the discipline's members in both traditional and nontraditional settings. The series also includes scholarship that considers the discipline's possible futures or that draws upon work in other disciplines to shed light on developments in English studies.

**Volumes in the Series**

David B. Downing, editor, *Changing Classroom Practices: Resources for Literary and Cultural Studies* (1994)

Jed Rasula, *The American Poetry Wax Museum: Reality Effects, 1940–1990* (1995)

James A. Berlin, *Rhetorics, Poetics, and Cultures: Refiguring College English Studies* (1996)

Robin Varnum, *Fencing with Words: A History of Writing Instruction at Amherst College during the Era of Theodore Baird, 1938–1966* (1996)

Jane Maher, *Mina P. Shaughnessy: Her Life and Work* (1997)

Michael Blitz and C. Mark Hurlbert, *Letters for the Living: Teaching Writing in a Violent Age* (1998)

Bruce Horner and Min-Zhan Lu, *Representing the "Other": Basic Writers and the Teaching of Basic Writing* (1999)

Stephen M. North, with Barbara A. Chepaitis, David Coogan, Lâle Davidson, Ron MacLean, Cindy L. Parrish, Jonathan Post, and Beth Weatherby, *Refiguring the Ph.D. in English Studies: Writing, Doctoral Education, and the Fusion-Based Curriculum* (2000)

Stephen Parks, *Class Politics: The Movement for the Students' Right to Their Own Language* (2000)

Charles M. Anderson and Marian M. MacCurdy, *Writing and Healing: Toward an Informed Practice* (2000)

Anne J. Herrington and Marcia Curtis, *Persons in Process: Four Stories of Writing and Personal Development in College* (2000)

Amy Lee, *Composing Critical Pedagogies: Teaching Writing as Revision* (2000)

Derek Owens, *Composition and Sustainability: Teaching for a Threatened Generation* (2001)

# *Thank You!*

*We're glad to help you and hope you find our publications useful. If you would like to request a catalog, or have a catalog sent to a friend or colleague, simply e-mail the name and address to orders@ncte.org, or call 877-369-6283.*

## Claims

If there is a problem with your shipment, please notify the NCTE Customer Service Department. We do request that you make your claim within 3 months of placing your order.

## Returns

**Individuals:** You will receive a refund/adjustment for the purchase price of any book returned in salable condition within 30 days of purchase.

**Bookstores:** Please mail or fax a request for permission to return books and include the title, quantity, and the 12-digit NCTE invoice number.

## Questions

Please contact the NCTE Customer Service Department at 877-369-6283 or 217-328-3870 with questions or concerns about your order. You may also e-mail your inquiry to orders@ncte.org.

## Customer Service

Phone: 877-369-6283
Fax: 217-328-9645
E-mail: orders@ncte.org
Web: www.ncte.org

National Council of Teachers of English
1111 W. Kenyon Road
Urbana, IL 61801-1096

# Radical Departures

## Composition and Progressive Pedagogy

CHRIS W. GALLAGHER
*University of Nebraska–Lincoln*

National Council of Teachers of English
1111 W. Kenyon Road, Urbana, Illinois 61801-1096

An earlier version of Intralude 3 and Chapter 3 was published as "'Just Give Them What They Need': Transforming the Transformative Intellectual." *Composition Studies* 28.2 (2000): 61–83.

Intralude 5 was first performed as a panel at the 2000 Conference on College Composition and Communication Convention. It appears with the generous permission of my fellow panelists: Amy Lee, Steve North, Shari Stenberg, and Krista Stock.

Some of the ideas in Chapter 5 first appeared in "Review: Remodeling English Studies." *College English* 63.6 (2001): 780–89.

Staff Editor: Bonny Graham
Interior Design: Jenny Jensen Greenleaf
Cover Design: Barbara Yale-Read

NCTE Stock Number: 38160-3050
ISSN 1073-9637

©2002 by the National Council of Teachers of English.

Library of Congress Cataloging-in-Publication Data
Gallagher, Chris W.
    Radical departures : composition and progressive pedagogy / Chris
W. Gallagher.
        p. cm. — (Refiguring English studies, ISSN 1073-9637)
    Includes bibliographical references (p. ) and index.
    ISBN 0-8141-3816-0
        1. English language—Composition and exercises—Study and teaching.
    2. English language—Rhetoric—Study and teaching. 3. Report writing—
    Study and teaching. I. Title. II. Series.
    PE1404 .G355 2002
    808'.042'0712—dc21
                                                                    2001056295

*I dedicate this book to my literacy sponsors:*

To my parents, Daniel and Maureen, who offered me my first lesson in critical literacy by driving me to a courthouse, paying a fee they surely couldn't afford, and allowing me to rename myself. May they see the legacy of that lesson, as well as their love of language, reflected in these pages.

To my brother, Jamey, whose writing I find inspiring. May he find in these pages some evidence that academic writing, too, can be worthwhile—and readable.

To Kathy Cain and Al DeCiccio, who invited me into their writing center and into their profession. May they find nothing in these pages to make them regret it.

To Cy Knoblauch and Judy Fetterley, who taught me that some conversations never end but only get richer. May they see in these pages a contribution to discussions begun long ago.

To Lil Brannon, who knows how to support by challenging. May she find these pages supportive of and challenging to her own thinking.

To Amy Lee and Shari Stenberg, true "critical colleagues" for whom I will always write first. May they see *our* ideas represented in these pages.

To Debbie Minter, whose generosity as a reader and a teacher I can neither match nor repay. May she see her always-generative response work honored in this final-draft-for-now.

To Peter Gray and Stephen Foley, who have supported and energized my thinking about things that matter. May they see their commitment to creative teaching and learning reflected in these pages.

To Steve North, whose good humor (curmudgeonly reputation aside) and professional example guide me. May he find in these pages an example of "making trouble elsewhere" that he can live with.

To Kurt Austin and Bonny Graham, who saw this project through the editorial process with patience and good counsel. May they see their light-handed but steady influence in these pages.

To NCTE's reviewers, and especially Ellen Cushman, whose advice helped me shape and sharpen the book. May they see their wisdom reflected in changes I have made, and mine in the changes I have not. . . .

To the "transformative intellectuals"—students and teachers—with whom I have been fortunate enough to work in New Hampshire, Massachusetts, New York, and Nebraska. And especially to Krista Stock, the best kind of writer: "the learning kind." May they find much of what they have taught me in these pages.

And, above all, to Molly, Cady, and Erin, who give me a reason to write—and to get up in the morning. May these pages in some small measure begin to repay the considerable sacrifices they have made for it.

This project was supported by a Summer Research Grant from the University of Nebraska–Lincoln Research Council.

# CONTENTS

# Introduction

M y coming to Composition and Rhetoric was not, so far as I
know, unusual. Trained in literary scholarship and critical
theory, but without a Ph.D., I found myself teaching five sections
of first-year composition a semester. That first year as an "adjunct"
was not good. As diligently as I "corrected" student narratives,
descriptions, compare-and-contrast essays, cause-and-effect papers,
and so forth, the students seemed intent on *not* learning the basics
of composition.

But then, at the end of that long year, a thought occurred to
me: perhaps the difficulties I was experiencing in the classroom
lay not in what I had supposed to be my inexplicable misfortune
in attracting the dullest students in each of my three colleges, but
rather in my own ignorance about my job. I headed for the library stacks of one of the schools in hopes of gleaning some practical advice on how to teach writing.

As it turned out, I found more in those stacks than recipes
for good practice. I found what seemed to me then—and seems
to me now—an intellectually vital, pedagogically oriented, stu-
dent-sensitive, and politically charged field of study. In short, I
found just what I had lacked: a sense of purpose to my teaching,
an intellectual and political frame for understanding why one
might choose to devote one's professional life to teaching writing.

In a way, this book began that day in the library stacks of
that small college. Now, several years later, I find myself wanting
to write for the kind of person I was then: someone new to the
teaching and study of writing; someone ready to take seriously
the responsibilities and pleasures of teaching writing in this political age; someone who wants to know more about how and
why the teaching and study of writing have taken their sometimes vexed place in the academy and in our culture. So although
I hope that teachers and scholars already "in" Composition and

Rhetoric will find this book interesting and instructive, I have written it with those who are new to the teaching and study of writing at the front of my mind.

One of the (many) peculiarities of our field is that one can find one's way "into" it in a number of ways—sometimes without even knowing it. We are granted a teaching assistantship to teach first-year writing; we are assigned by our small school to teach a rhetoric course; we enroll, out of curiosity, in a graduate (and sometimes, these days, an undergraduate) course called Composition Theory; we are assigned, as graduate students or new faculty, to work in a writing center; we develop a scholarly interest in the writing of our students; we find ourselves working with colleagues in a National Writing Project site; we are asked to participate in a P–12 (prekindergarten through twelfth grade) writing initiative—the list could go on. One of the primary aims of this book is to introduce the work of Composition and Rhetoric to teachers and scholars who find themselves somehow involved in (if not yet or fully "in") Composition and Rhetoric so that they might situate themselves in relation to it. Specifically, I hope that readers will find in these pages

- an *introduction* to the history and development of composition as an institutional practice and Composition and Rhetoric as a field of study; [1]

- an *exploration* of the many possibilities offered by work in composition/Composition and Rhetoric today; and, perhaps most important,

- an *invitation* both to develop a broad, politically informed vision of where the field has been and is, and to participate in its (ongoing) remaking.

Developing a politically informed vision of the field is important because in one way or another, the teaching of composition and the field of Composition and Rhetoric have always been infused with political visions. I may have been wrong, when I first read the professional literature, to think that it provided a *single* political frame. (I often wonder if I began reading in the "critical literacy" school of Bs—Berlin, Berthoff, Bizzell, Brodkey—or if I was simply more attuned to "critical pedagogy" through my prior, if spotty,

reading in the radical education of Freire, Giroux, and McLaren.)
But nothing in my subsequent research or experience has contra-
dicted the idea that "progressive politics" (variously defined, to be
sure) have always played a crucial role in how writing has been
taught and studied in U.S. secondary and postsecondary schools.

In fact, when I returned to the university to pursue my doc-
torate (working my way "into" Composition and Rhetoric), my
courses in composition theory, research in composition, history
of rhetoric, and composition pedagogy did little to challenge the
notion that Composition and Rhetoric is a decidedly political—
and indeed, a politically "progressive" (in the sense of being left
leaning)—enterprise. We were introduced to texts whose names
suggested as much: *The Politics of Writing Instruction: Postsecondary, Left Margins, Composition and Resistance, Pedagogy in
the Age of Politics, Pedagogy Is Politics*. And if any doubt lin-
gered about the political orientation of the field, we were introduced to its "shaping voices": Bakhtin, Dewey, Marx, Volosinov,
Raymond Williams, and other luminaries of the left.

My point here is not to raise the specter of left-leaning, con-
version-oriented graduate education (à la Welch, "Resisting").
On the contrary, although it did seem to me that left politics
came with the territory of Composition and Rhetoric, those were
politics, in general terms, to which I subscribed, and I found—
and find—it laudable that so many in the field devote themselves
to what I consider humane social visions. Rather, I mention the
politics of this graduate program because it seems to me that
compositionists would do well to attend carefully to the politics
of the stories we tell about ourselves. Specifically, we—those of
us already in the field as well as those who would join our ranks—
need to study the historical and contemporary relationships between our work and "progressivism" in its various forms. This
book is an effort in that direction.

## Composing Composition

In search of what Susan Miller calls a "respectable past," compositionists have reached as far back as the ancient rhetoricians *(Textual)*. But we have also marked our birth as recently as 1963 (North,

*The Making of Knowledge*), or even the early 1980s (Zebroski). We might cite as our moment of conception the 1880s, the decade that saw the beginning of required first-year composition, or 1949, the year the Conference on College Composition and Communication was created. But wherever we mark our origins, we tend to tell the story of Composition and Rhetoric as "progressive" in two senses. First, we typically fashion ourselves as politically progressive—again, generally left leaning. Second, in a related move, we tend to trace our evolution as a march out of the benighted past into the enlightened present. Louise Wetherbee Phelps calls this archetypal story "the path taken" ("Paths"). We might cast this story as a family saga: in the beginning were the current-tradition-alists—those great-grandparents no one wants to talk about—who presided over the "Dark Ages" of composition (Connors, *Composition-Rhetoric*). They reigned for many years, securing composition's place as the ugly stepchild of English studies, with their reductive emphasis on formal correctness and linguistic propriety. But then along came communications-minded folk—our heroic grandparents—who offered first-year composition some measure of academic legitimacy by showing that even first-year college students are engaged in complicated linguistic behaviors. Out of this short-lived marriage between composition and communications grew an organization, a journal, a conference, some studies, some books—the makings of a real academic discipline. Then came our parents, the new rhetoricians, who put us on even surer footing by reconnecting us with a very old intellectual tradition. We even began to develop graduate programs. Next came our older siblings, those process-oriented folks, expressivists and cognitivists alike, liberal champions of the writer's, and the student's, voice. (Like most youngsters, we look up to our older siblings even as we look down on them.) And then there's us: the social epistemics, those on the other side of the "social turn" (Trimbur, "Taking"), who seek to "empower" students through critical literacy and democratic citizenship.[2]

Of course, this story is a caricature; the categories themselves are too convenient to be accurate, and the teleology is blatantly false. In fact, as Phelps ("Paths") shows, this story substitutes a teleology for a taxonomy—namely, the rhetorical taxonomy James

Berlin develops in his landmark "Rhetoric and Ideology in the Writing Class," and then extends in *Rhetoric and Reality*. This substitution distorts our complicated history by placing different "rhetorics" (each of which has, it is true, garnered more interest than others at particular historical moments) on a strict time line.[3] Although we can point to certain moments of left-wing activism in the field (see Parks), the political and institutional history of composition and Composition and Rhetoric is of course more complicated than this triumphalist story would allow. For instance, although many of our historians have held that early composition (in the last quarter of the nineteenth century and first quarter of the twentieth) was largely *regressive* (Berlin, *Writing Instruction*; Connors, "Rise"; Crowley, *Composition*; S. Miller, *Textual*), we also know that it was informed by the ideas and practices of *progressive* education (Applebee; Berlin, *Rhetoric*). And yet only recently have we seen significant departures in our histories from our own "progressive" narrative.[4] What this book hopes to add to this historical record is a significantly detailed portrait of how modern composition emerged at the end of the nineteenth and the beginning of the twentieth centuries as a complex, often self-contradictory "progressive" reform. Moreover, I hope to show how various visions and versions of "progressivism" continue to inform the development of Composition and Rhetoric.[5]

## Composing Progressivism

Obviously, as my use of quotation marks suggests, at stake here is how we define *progressive*. If Bruce Horner is right that the word *traditional* (as in, say, "current-traditional") is often unreflectively used—in Composition and Rhetoric and elsewhere—as a term of derogation, it is equally true that the word *progressive* is often used unreflectively as a term of approbation. These two terms—one denoting a move backward, into the past, and the other suggesting a move forward, into the future—exist in a binary that disparages the past and assumes that we are on that grand march toward a far better future. In this commonsense formulation, to be traditional is to be "stuck in the past," unaware or unwilling to accede to the undeniable improvements of time. Conversely, to be progressive is to be forward-looking, innovative, enlightened.

At the same time, there is a strange irony at work in how our field understands "progressivism." For many in Composition and Rhetoric, *progressive* has come to connote a weak-kneed and naive liberalism—and is thus viewed as passé and, yes, traditional. It is a political position that we have "moved past" (see, for instance, Murphy). While educational progressives of the early twentieth century (including John Dewey, whose work figures prominently in this book) were often derided as Bolsheviks, and in fact drew on Marxist thought, the term "progressive" is sometimes used today to *distinguish* nonradical thinkers from the more properly radical.

In the end, "progressivism" has been assigned every position along the political spectrum. Although this book will not offer a full-fledged history of educational progressivism—one that pins down its politics once and for all—it does study its political, pedagogical, institutional, and disciplinary effects on composition/ Composition and Rhetoric. This seems especially timely given concerns expressed by some compositionists that, despite claims that we have "moved beyond" progressivism, we may not be as radical as we think and that, in fact, radical ideas may have been lost in the evolution of our field (Connors, *Composition-Rhetoric;* Crowley, *Composition;* Horner; Villanueva; several essays in Gilyard, *Race*).

Indeed, even within the progressive education "movement" of the late nineteenth and early twentieth centuries there was little consensus about what *progressive* meant. One of the aims of this book is to show that a wealth of contradictory reforms and pedagogies has been proposed under the banner of progressivism. But I hope also to show that it may be fruitful to reframe and reclaim one branch of educational progressivism all but forgotten today. David Tyack calls this branch "pedagogical progressivism" to distinguish it from "administrative progressivism." This brand of progressive education derives primarily from the work of John Dewey.

Like progressivism, its most well-known proponent has been assigned to every position on the political spectrum, from raving

Bolshevik to sell-out conservative. Today, although he is often cited—fleetingly—by "radical" scholars, only self-identified "liberal" *opponents* of radical pedagogy seem prepared to claim Dewey as their own (see Fishman; Fishman and McCarthy, *John Dewey,* "Teaching"). In my view—and this will become clear enough—Dewey's ideas about education are far more radical than they are represented to be by his foes and friends alike. While my project here is not to defend Dewey's political reputation, I do want to suggest that those of us who are interested in democratic education and social justice do ourselves a disservice by writing off Dewey's thinking as insufficiently radical.

Dewey's ideas about progress itself provide a place to start. For Dewey, progress was neither natural nor inevitable; indeed, as World War I raged, Dewey reminded his readers that progress is "a responsibility and not . . . an endowment" ("Progress" 238). It must be earned through "deliberate human foresight and socially constructive work" (237). Moreover, only "socially constructive work" that expanded democratic possibilities deserved the honorific. Working for progress meant helping to build a just society in which opportunities and resources were widely and fairly distributed and in which experiences and ideas were freely circulated ("Need"). But while he held that progressive work expanded democratic possibilities, Dewey did not believe there was a point at which progress would be achieved or complete. Rather, he saw progress as a process, an "end-in-view," rather than a product, a "fixed end" (*Democracy,* "Nature"). Education could participate in this process, but only if it were understood as "a constant reorganizing or reconstructing of experience" (*Democracy* 76) rather than rote memorization and "skills-and-drills."

I suspect this last notion will be familiar to many readers. Although many compositionists, myself included, believe that Dewey exhibited excessive faith in the schools as a lever of social progress, we are also drawn to this social vision and believe that education *can* be an important site of work in the world (Knoblauch and Brannon, "Pedagogy"). Our field also has strong historical ties to Dewey's brand of progressivism, and I argue in this book that Composition and Rhetoric is uniquely positioned—by history and temperament—to participate in a reclamation of pedagogical progressivism. But first, as I show, we need to develop a new kind of disciplinarity, one that radically departs from academic business as usual by placing a sophisticated understanding and practice of pedagogy at the center of our work.

## Composing Pedagogy

But isn't Composition and Rhetoric already a pedagogy-centered enterprise? Some scholars have even argued that our field is *too* pedagogical, not focused enough on "theory building" or on literacy practices outside of the academy or the schools (e.g., Olson; Dobrin). First, I do not believe that a sophisticated understanding of pedagogy either severs it from theory building or confines it to educational institutions. Rather, I propose that we understand pedagogy as *the reflexive inquiry that teachers and learners undertake together.* Under this formulation, pedagogy is theory producing, rather than theory applying, and it may well take place outside of sanctioned institutional relationships (which is why I prefer the terms "teacher" and "learner" to, say, "professor" and "student"). I'm not interested in offering another version of the familiar lament that compositionists sacrifice teaching in favor of theory. In fact, there is no shortage of discussions about teaching in Composition and Rhetoric. My point, rather, is that this very binary—teaching/theory—is the problem, because it risks sacrificing a complex understanding of pedagogy as shared knowledge building. When I worry that Composition and Rhetoric is not sufficiently pedagogy-centered, then, I am not suggesting that we have abandoned attention to teaching; rather, I am exploring the way in which we *understand* teaching (and learning) in the first place. Similarly, far from suggesting that we don't pay enough attention to college composition classrooms, I argue that we unnecessarily narrow our purview by confining our focus to first-year writing or even postsecondary writing curricula.

Put simply, pedagogy is what happens when people seek to produce knowledge together. Understood as reflexive inquiry, pedagogy is the antithesis of administrative progressivism, with its emphasis on standardization, external control, and skill instruction. At the heart of reflexive inquiry is a "turning back," as

Donna Qualley has it, to attend to *how* we make meaning and arrive at beliefs (21)—or what Sullivan and Porter, echoing Bourdieu, call "epistemological vigilance" (5). And as Qualley suggests, reflexivity involves engagement with others; this kind of inquiry does not produce the kind of "confessional and apologetic" self-consciousness that Cushman and Monberg warn is often characteristic of reflexivity (170). In fact, reflexive inquiry actively disrupts "navel gazing" by highlighting the situated relations between the learner and those with or about whom he or she learns. Pedagogy is always a form of collective action.

In a pedagogy-centered discipline, pedagogy *produces* disciplinary knowledge. Reflexive inquiry begins with the assumption that teachers and learners collaborate in the construction of their objects of study. As Dewey held, the subject matter *matters* only to the extent that teachers and learners can engage it, use it, and ultimately reconstruct it. This idea was the cornerstone of Deweyan pedagogical progressivism, as it is the cornerstone of my understanding of pedagogy, which invites teachers and learners to take stock together of how they construct knowledge, how they make meaning.

So, to return to the question of whether Composition and Rhetoric is already a pedagogy-centered discipline, I think the answer is yes and no. As I show in Chapter 1, our field does in fact have historical ties to pedagogical progressivism, and it has undeniably produced a fair amount of scholarship that falls under the rubric of pedagogy, as defined here. I aim to highlight and honor this work in this book. At the same time, I hope to show how this work has been limited both by external factors and by the ways in which the field has been organized. As I demonstrate in Chapter 2, a latter-day administrative progressivism continues to constrain the development and effectivity of pedagogical progressivism in Composition and Rhetoric. In Chapters 3 and 4, I argue that the field's responses to our contemporary form of administrative progressivism—namely, our alliance with critical pedagogy and our pursuit of traditional disciplinarity—have moved us further away from our roots in pedagogical progressivism. Finally, in Chapters 5 and 6, I show how college writing curricula and "outreach" work have been limited as a result of those external pressures and the field's responses to them.

# Composing *Radical Departures*

Far from offering merely a negative critique of the field, however, this book offers a (guardedly) hopeful message. *Radical Departures* is organized into two parts, each consisting of three chapters and accompanying "intraludes" (more on the latter below). Part I analyzes various visions and versions of progressivism in Composition and Rhetoric's past and present. Part II works—in a hopeful, but I trust not naive, way—to reframe and reclaim "pedagogical progressivism" for the field's future.

Chapter 1 explores how progressive education was imagined by English teachers, and especially composition teachers, in the schools and universities of the Progressive Era—a time that would prove crucial to the shaping of our field. Drawing chiefly on the first two decades of *English Journal,* the self-identified "progressive" publication of the National Council of Teachers of English, I show that modern composition was born in a cauldron of competing "progressive" agendas. While pedagogical progressives saw composition as an opportunity to practice child-centered pedagogy and to argue for inclusive, democratic educational and social reform, administrative progressives saw composition as a chance to practice skills-and-drills instruction and to argue for top-down, bureaucratic, "efficient" educational and social reform. In fact, first-year composition, established in the 1880s, was quickly enlisted in "the cult of efficiency" (Callahan). At the same time, the new U.S. university—itself decidedly corporate-minded and "administratively progressive"—was being formed in the image of the German research university. This confluence of events would shape the future of composition, and Composition and Rhetoric, down to the present day.

In fact, I show in Chapter 2 that a latter-day form of administrative progressivism—which some have dubbed the "conservative restoration" (Shor, *Culture*)—continues to shape our work. This chapter aims to avoid simple stories about "winners" and "losers" in the history of educational reform while confronting the reality that the ideological and material forces that conspired against pedagogical progressivism in the Progressive Era still condition (but never fully determine) the possibilities for pedagogical and literacy work. This is evident in what I call the "reincorporation of the schools," as well as in the two postsecondary examples I cite: Linda Brodkey's "Troubles at Texas" and the struggles over basic writing in the City University of New York (CUNY) system. For although we have continued to gain institutional legitimacy (and resources) as an academic field, compositionists find it difficult to gain a voice in public struggles over literacy and teaching. Indeed, our "disciplining" constrains the field's political effectivity by involving it in an academic economy that positions some of us (compositionists) as academic researchers, and others of us (writing teachers, often "adjuncts" or TAs) as "mere" workers.

Chapter 3 argues that while we have turned to our newest "progressivism"—critical pedagogy—as a means of resisting latter-day administrative progressivism, this alliance has had the ironic effect of exacerbating these academic class-based conflicts by privileging a "critical tradition" over pedagogy as I have posed it—the reflexive inquiry that teachers and learners undertake together. Mainstream critical pedagogy, unlike pedagogical progressivism, removes pedagogy from its center, replacing it with often decontextualized social visions. It attempts to theorize pedagogy *for* or *around* teachers and students, rather than *with* them. In response, Chapter 3 begins the recuperative project that is at the heart of Part II by rethinking critical pedagogy's notion of the "transformative intellectual" and by introducing the concept of "institutional literacy." These ideas—both unpacked further in later chapters—allow us to respect everyday moments of resistance by teachers and learners, rather than encouraging us to stage (or wait for others to stage) a grand gesture of antihegemonic transformation. They write students and teachers back into the pedagogical act, reminding us that pedagogy is a collaborative and reflexive process that cannot be scripted by a remote expert, whether that expert is a "regressive" bureaucrat or a "progressive" theorist.

Chapter 4 extends the exploration, begun in Chapters 2 and 3, of Composition and Rhetoric's vexed place in the American academy. It inquires into the field's ambivalence about traditional disciplinarity and ties this ambivalence to the curricular anomaly of the universally required course, part of the legacy of administrative progressivism. It also asks, "What visions and versions of 'progress' are represented in our ambivalent confrontations with academic disciplinarity?" In the end, I argue that Composition and Rhetoric's strange institutional position, though not ideal, does offer productive possibilities for being both inside and outside traditional academic and disciplinary regimes. It may even allow us to rethink disciplinarity by putting pedagogy at its center, and by refusing to continue to think of Composition and Rhetoric as a strictly postsecondary enterprise. I end the chapter by beginning to map out what a pedagogy-centered discipline might look like, and by describing a two-pronged approach to rethinking our work in pedagogically progressive terms. This approach involves developing (1) pedagogy-centered curricula and (2) pedagogy-centered outreach.

Chapter 5 asks the question, "What does 'pedagogy-centered curricula' mean, and what would they look like?" First, I show that one feature of the legacy of the rapprochement between the German research university and the corporate-minded U.S. university has been the "teaching our passions" tradition, in which curriculum is organized not around pedagogy but around professors' specialized knowledges. Recent work in the field, however, points toward new models of curriculum (and, by extension, disciplinarity). Specifically, it seeks to create diverse curricula that involve students more actively in disciplinary knowledge making. This work, along with Dewey's curricular thinking, allows me to clear some space for pedagogy-centered curricula.

Chapter 6 follows much the same pattern as Chapter 5. The driving question here is, "What would pedagogy-centered *outreach* mean, and what would it look like?" I begin by sketching the historical forces that have encouraged and discouraged alliances between writing teachers in the schools and writing teachers in the universities in an effort to determine why and how Composition and Rhetoric has not made working with teachers a visible, integral component of its work in recent years. I then draw on recent work in the field that refuses the missionary model of "public service" in favor of more collegial, nonhierarchical outreach work. I apply these ideas specifically to working with public school teachers, who have traditionally been our allies but with whom in recent years we have not sought democratic alliances—in part because compositionists have been so interested in gaining academic legitimacy in the academy. I argue that, along with reimagining postsecondary writing curricula, pedagogy-centered outreach projects hold our best hope for enacting a different kind of disciplinarity—one that reframes and reclaims pedagogical progressivism.

## Composing the Composition of *Radical Departures*

Although scholarship alone cannot exert sufficient pressure to change how disciplinarity is practiced, I do believe that it can contribute to interrogating academic systems that are often taken for granted. My admittedly modest and frankly exploratory contribution to this effort here is to try to demonstrate the interaction of scholarship, teaching, and outreach in my own professional life by offering a kind of working portfolio of projects that I have been involved in as a teacher, scholar, and public school advocate. Taken together, these representations—which I term "intraludes"—offer a (still developing) narrative portrait of my work in a range of sites with a variety of "transformative intellectuals."

I risk what one reviewer has called the "cute coinage" of *intralude* because I want to preserve the idea of interrupting that *inter*lude suggests, but I also want to indicate that the narratives are *within*—part of—the arguments and claims made, rather than simply *between* the chapters.[6] Most of the material for these narratives was derived from ethnographic and teacher research techniques: note taking, textual and artifact analysis, interviews. The intraludes are narrative representations, however, presented mostly in collage form. I make this discursive choice not because I don't value other forms of research, but because this form is consistent with the aims of this project, which seeks to provide rich narrative material for teachers and researchers to engage with, rather than replicable "results" from a series of experiments on students (and other) subjects. The collage form allows me to represent moments of teaching and learning in ways that traditional scholarly discourse does not, and so while some readers may object to the "creative" form in a book that purports to be "scholarly," I hope that more readers will read the narratives for how they "*disrupt* my arguments . . . talk back to my beliefs, their possibilities, their limitations" (Welch, *Getting* 179).

As I developed the intraludes, I heard in the back of my head the insistent voices of many graduate students I have taught: "All right, critiques and questions are all well and good. But what are we supposed to *do* now? How does this help us think about what to do in our comp courses Monday morning?" While I sympathize with this familiar sentiment, I don't believe—as I tell these students—that such questions serve developing teachers very well. As I have suggested, pedagogy cannot be "given" by "experts" to "practitioners." Thus, while I am cognizant of my responsibility to offer representations of the kind of work that I believe is true to the spirit of pedagogical progressivism, I am not about to offer a series of lessons that this inquiry makes available to classroom teachers. Readers looking for examples will, I hope, find what they are looking for in the intraludes. Those looking for models will, I'm afraid, be disappointed.

Pedagogical progressivism, after all, offers no simple recipes for good practice. In fact, at the heart of this Deweyan enterprise is the idea that pedagogy cannot be designed from outside the shared inquiry it names. To be sure, I could fill this book with course artifacts: syllabi, prompts, student writing, responses to those texts, and the like. But in the final analysis, this project is less concerned with what to do in class on Monday morning than with promoting an understanding of pedagogy as a process of shared and reflexive inquiry that must be co-constructed by those who engage in it.

# I

# VISIONS AND VERSIONS OF "PROGRESSIVISM"

# On Doing History

*I pull the journals down . . . again. They are dusty, which only further complicates their color ambiguity (they fall vaguely in the brown-tan-green nexus; perhaps there is a word for the color these once were; surely there is not a word for the color they are now). They are, I see, just where I left them: I discern traces of my last visit (this is my index card; this one is still pushed back too far; this may be my fingerprint). They are heavy, as always; delicate, as ever; frayed, of course.*

*And—this is the word that strikes me every time—they are dank. Stale smelling. Yet dry to the touch: brittle-dry.*

*Two at a time, no more: they are heavy, delicate, frayed.*

---

It's about listening. Sarah Orne Jewett writes about "an ear made delicate by listening" (qtd. in Pryse 49). That's what historians' ears ought to be: delicate. How else to hear a conversation so faint, a conversation not meant for you, though it is in a sense about you? (We don't write for those who come after us, but our subject is what we hope we will help them to be.)

This is why it's an exercise in humility, doing history. It's relearning, sometimes unlearning, the present. Not only in the how-we-got-here sense, but also in the how-we-*are*-here sense. Because we *will* see ourselves in their words; this is the way we read.

Who did they hope we would be? (And who *are* we, after all?) What did they make possible for us? What did they make *im*possible? And what will we do with what they left us? Doing history is an act of intimacy.

---

As a teacher, a writer, a graduate student in search of a project (i.e., a fledgling researcher), I want to know: what has been said about what I think I might want to say?

First time through, I'm reading for the conversation. Who's speaking? What are they saying? What are the main lines of inquiry or argument? How are these positioned in relation to one another? The reading is slow, arduous at times. I take quick notes, not entirely sure what I'm looking for, trying to remember my framing questions:

- What did *progressivism* mean to these English teachers?
- How many self-identified as progressive, and why?
- What were the alternatives to progressivism at the time?

The questions are no more specific than that. I think of this as a virtue—I will find what I find—but as my notebook fills with only the vaguest of notes, I begin to wonder.

---

Humility: trying not to fall into what Stephen North calls "chrono-centrism" (*Making*). The idea that the past has been one grand march to the glorious present. The idea that every day, in every way, we're getting better: quicker, smarter, more humane. Nothing makes an ear callous like this chron-ic dysfunction.

So I learn how to listen. But for what? The Real Story (How It Was back then)? A Telling Story (what they tell us)? Or A Story to Tell (here's a story . . . )?

A story, at any rate. A story about a conversation.

Others have read and written other stories of this conversation; others have thought other conversations more worthy of storytelling. This is as it should be; we *should* have different stories to tell. But I stand by this story of this conversation. It's not, after all, easily come by, and it's not a product of either fertile imagination or unmitigated bias (though it's perhaps helped along at moments by a bit of each). And so I'll argue for it, and provide textual evidence for it, not only because it's hard-won, but also because I want this story to enter our conversation.

———————

History is not, most of us (today, in this conversation) would agree, an objective rendering of facts, a telling of the One True Story. But neither is it a pure fiction (though it might borrow literary techniques from fiction). The historian of postmodernity is liberated from the responsibility to tell The Truth, the Whole Truth, and Nothing but the Truth, but that's not to say that he or she doesn't have responsibilities. The first and definitive responsibility of the historian is to develop a delicate ear.

———————

It's an act of imagination, an act of good faith, an act of generosity. It's not uncritical—reverse chrono-centrism—but it's patient. It is the way I try—but too often fail—to read student texts, to read all texts.

———————

Second time through, a dissertation writer now, I'm reading for the issues: What are the lines of inquiry or argument relevant to the issues I'm focusing on? Who tends to be most interested in these issues? What kinds of alliances emerge around these issues?

I have been away from this windowless, almost airless basement for close to a year. I've been thinking about the conversation, how I simply can't hear all of it at once (seventeen volumes of *English Journal*; ten issues per volume; maybe 1,020 articles). I think about my own interests, the issues that sustain me, the issues on which I'd like to get an early "progressive" take. Political teaching, political writing, assessment. What did these mean then? I read to find out, my eyes scanning faster. I move through the volumes more quickly now, with my new filter. My notes, though, are more detailed; I am more likely to stop, to linger. But now, at least I know why.

----

A solitary pursuit, this: I never see another soul down here. It's lonely, pulling down these journals (two at a time, no more) and spending another long afternoon. I think of the image I once had of The Researcher (culled from countless movie portrayals): rumpled, frumpy, nasty old thing oblivious to all but his (always *his*) precious old books, repositories of some Forgotten Lore. A version of the romantic writer, no doubt. Driven by a thirst for Knowledge, he sequesters himself from The World, sacrificing All for his Quest. A man to be pitied, perhaps, but also a man to be admired: he toils for us, the poor, ordinary folk who don't Know.

And here I sit, not yet thirty years old: the right gender and race, but in every other way (or so I hope) a figure unbefitting that image. For me, finally, this is not an act of sequestration, but rather, like all acts of literacy, one of intimacy. The voices in my head emerge not from some divine madness, some inner demon, but rather from the pages of these heavy, delicate, frayed journals and from my colleagues, who are here with me: *Read this way*, they tell me, *and write that way. We know this already*, they say, *but we don't know that. Ignore this*, they teach me, *but pay attention to that.*

----

The work is, at times, dreadfully dull: reading for patterns, collecting data. At times, I think, *They're not speaking to me after all. Their formality; their air of show-and-tell; above all their storylessness—surely I am not the posterity for which they recorded their words.*

And then: a lovely image; a generous comment about a student; a novel (to me) idea; a familiar (to me) idea; a—praise be—story. I stop, I linger. I am hoping to get through this volume and the next by 5 P.M. (does The Researcher ever have a daughter to pick up, a dinner to get started?), but I stop, I linger, I listen. This voice—the voice, inevitably, of a caring teacher—draws me, and I listen. I thrill at this voice of the past, speaking so well and so kindly and in a way that I can hear. I remember why I'm listening—and why I'm teaching.

And then, it's back to reading for patterns, back to collecting data.

---

Third time through, a book writer, I'm reading for positions. Why did people take the positions they did on these issues? What was taken for granted about these issues? What was left unexplored? What allowed people to say what they did about these issues?

A professor now, I sit in a new windowless, almost airless basement in a new university, halfway across the country. Much of the drafting is done, but there's work to do yet. I'm still not getting at the whys, the what's-at-stake-for-whom questions. So I move through the volumes again, for what I promise myself will be the last time, taking even more extensive notes, focusing in great depth on fewer texts. I am well into my third notebook now, but I have my frame: this is filling-in, fleshing-out work.

---

It's an act, after all, of motivated, selective listening. And then: representing. Howard Zinn explains the historian's dilemma by comparing it to that of a cartographer, who must "first flatten and distort the shape of the earth, then choose out of the bewildering mass of geographic information those things needed for the purpose of this or that particular map" (8). But while the cartographer's dilemma is largely technical, Zinn claims, the historian's is mainly ideological: "it is released into a world of contending interests, where any chosen emphasis supports (whether the historian means to or not) some kind of interest, whether economic or political or racial or national or sexual" (8). (I could quibble here: both the historian's and the cartographer's tasks are technical *and* ideological—but, point mostly taken.)

So what is a historian to do? Kathleen Welsch helps me think about this:

> [H]istorians are more than storytellers who invite listeners to sit at separate fires to learn separate tales of the past. They are also teachers. It is the historian's responsibility to teach us a variety of ways to read the past, to engage in historical debate, to position narratives in relation to each other so as to gain critical perspective, to draw conclusions on and consider implications of opposing historical projects, and to create constructive tension that moves us forward in our inquiry. Critically drawing in—not just drawing on—the work of fellow historians is what North claims transforms "what would be merely stories" into "his-tory" (82), a complex and critical web of storytelling. (122)

The historian's dilemma is the teacher's dilemma—one I know well. And so, for me, the historian's goals must be the teacher's goals:

- ◆ Be aware and reflexive (but not confessional or apologetic) about my agenda. Make that still developing agenda part of what is studied.

- ◆ Be aware and reflexive (but not confessional or apologetic) about my positions. Researcher, writer, professor, white heterosexual male—these matter; they affect what I can hear and how I represent what I (think I) hear.

- ◆ Leave that agenda, and those positions, open to critique and revision. Remember that they are, always, under construction, in process. Listen and engage with others—what can they teach me about my subject?

----

Is it history or is it historiography?
Is it criticism or is it scholarship?
(See Connors, *Composition-Rhetoric*.)
Answer: yes.

----

As I read, I think of what John Dewey says of the past in *Democracy and Education*: while we should read it—and write it—as a "present resource," it should never be merely a model for the present. A past recapitulated is a present unrealized and a future forestalled. History should not make of culture "an ornament and solace; a refuge and an asylum" (75); it should make it a vital, ongoing process, a resource for the present imagination.

Their words ring strangely familiar: critical thinking, democratic education, active learning, community projects. And: the basics, skills-and-drills, teaching to the test. Here *we* are, I think. And yet I know they are not us, nor we them.

Don't listen for salvation, I remind myself.
Don't listen for condemnation, either.
Don't listen for some transportable tradition.
Don't listen for The Answer, The Way.
Don't listen for the Moral, the Not-This-Way.
Listen for retrospection: thinking back.
Listen for suggestion: thinking now.
Listen for imagination: thinking forward.
Listen for reconstruction: building again.
Listen for something to reframe,
        something to reclaim.

# CHAPTER ONE

# Composition as a
# Progressive Enterprise

Many histories of our field point to the Progressive Era (and specifically 1875–1925) as formative years in the evolution of composition (Applebee; Berlin, *Rhetoric;* Brereton; Connors, *Composition-Rhetoric;* Crowley, *Composition;* Kitzhaber; S. Miller, *Textual*). And yet, strangely, only Applebee and Berlin consider the influence of "progressive education" on the formation of modern composition. (Even Brereton, who claims that modern composition was "shaped by the reform impulses that pervaded late nineteenth- and early-twentieth-century America during the Progressive Era" [3], fails to consider progressive education itself as a formative influence on the emergence and early development of composition.) Moreover, neither Berlin nor Applebee takes a hard look at "the progressive movement" as it developed outside of English. Specifically, these historians make little of the fact that there never was a single, unified "progressive education movement," preferring instead to speak of progressivism as a monolithic, self-contradictory entity.[1]

This chapter places the emergence of modern composition in the context of progressive education by listening to how early practitioners of composition in the universities and schools represent their work ("composition" during the Progressive Era was by definition a cross-institutional enterprise). I also consider how the nascent National Council of Teachers of English and its first journal, *English Journal*, participated in "progressive" educational movements, and how those larger movements shaped the emergence and early development of modern composition. In adding this set of conversations to the historical record, I hope to prompt certain questions: What has it meant, and what might it mean, for composition to be "progressive"? What kind of work has been, and might be, accomplished (and suppressed) under the banner of "progressivism"? Why does the idea of progressivism have such staying power, especially in Composition and Rhetoric? In other words, I am interested in studying not only how different visions and versions of "progress(ivism)" have informed who we were and are, but also who we might become.

## A Tale of Two Progressivisms

Any attempt to account for educational progressivism as it emerged in the late nineteenth and early twentieth centuries must confront the claim by leading historians—Cremin, Reese, and Tyack, for instance—that progressive education was never a single, unified movement, but rather two distinct movements. These historians acknowledge that a mind-boggling array of contradictory reforms was proposed under the banner of progressivism; an incomplete list would include child-centered pedagogy, standardized tests and curricula, tracking, reliance on "experts," classroom experiments, creative arts, and industrial education. But they attribute this fact not to a lack of focus in a single group, but rather to competition between two groups who took the same name.

It is important to note that both groups of progressives developed in response to the profound social unrest of the late nineteenth century. The nation was undergoing rapid and frightening changes: a series of depressions struck between the 1870s and 1890s; the railroad, industrial interests, and vast migration to the cities conspired to threaten the agrarian economy and rural life; huge corporations consolidated their near-monopolistic power (Carnegie in steel; Rockefeller in oil); and violent strikes broke out in a number of states. This period also saw a dramatic increase in the number of students at all educational levels—largely as a result of massive waves of immigration.[2] All levels of education were beginning to serve groups of students who had traditionally been denied access to education by virtue of their gender, race, or class. In higher education, the Morrill Land Grant Acts of 1862 and especially of 1890, which included special provisions for African American institutions; the move toward coeducation;

the replacement of the old U.S. college by the new U.S. university; and the beginnings of the democratization of postsecondary education conspired to change the nature of college life (Connors, *Composition-Rhetoric*; Gordon; Gilyard, "African American"; Hobbs; North, *Refiguring*; Royster and Williams). At the same time, U.S. businessmen began to criticize the public schools in the wake of the unveiling of the Russian system of "technical instruction" at the Philadelphia Exposition of 1876 (Cremin 21). Although it would be a decade before Joseph Meyer Rice raised fears of educational crisis to a fever pitch with his scathing critiques of public schools in *The Forum*, the ferment had begun as the United States entered the last quarter of the nineteenth century. The idea that mass public education would inevitably lead to national progress had been ruptured. The underside of universal education, which Horace Mann had advertised less than half a century earlier as "the great equalizer," was beginning to show.[3] If U.S. education were to live up to the great expectations of Mann and his fellow reformers, it would need to be made "truly progressive" (Cremin).

All early progressives shared an abiding faith that education could serve as a lever for social progress. The fundamental differences between the two main groups, however, hinged on their answer to the question, Progress toward *what*? The first group, which David Tyack dubs the "pedagogical progressives," sought to put the schools in service of democracy and social justice. For this group, education was crucial in the realization of a more equitable, more democratic society, and a great deal of attention was paid to how teaching and learning were enacted in classrooms and communities. In contrast, "administrative progressives" (Cremin) sought to put schools in the service of industrialization and urbanization, placing most of their emphasis on "efficient" management. If pedagogical progressives sought to protect and expand democracy in the face of encroachment by the vagaries of industrial capitalism, this latter group sought to grease the wheels of what Alan Trachtenberg calls the "incorporation of America" by bringing about the incorporation of the schools.[4]

This fundamental distinction emerges clearly when we consider how prominent members of these groups believed schools should be run. For pedagogical progressives, the primary aims of education were to cultivate in students an active, reflective approach to their own learning, and to encourage the study and practice of living well with others. At the Cook County Normal School in Chicago, for instance, Francis W. Parker set up an "embryonic democracy" in which students took up both humanistic pursuits (including the creative arts) and practical studies (with emphasis on laboratory learning). In both fields, the object was to help students reflect critically, as individuals and as group members. For instance, students at Cook County wrote, edited, and produced their own readers, which replaced textbooks and primers. Reading and writing skills, according to Cremin, were "combined as elements of communication, to be studied within the context of actual conversation and writing" (132). In the age of skills-and-drills instruction, Parker sought to help teachers and students reflect critically on what it meant to engage in these social practices.[5]

Although John Dewey dubbed Parker the "father of progressive education," it was Dewey's educational thinking that would become most influential for pedagogical progressives. Dewey decried the authoritarian skills-and-drills methods of traditional education, with its emphasis on rote memorization and passive learning of already-worked-out subject matter. He insisted that "[t]he child is already intensely active, and the question of education is the question of taking hold of his activities, of giving them direction" (*School* 36). The point of education, Dewey urged, is to engage students in social practices, not to pour "knowledge into a mental and moral hole which awaits filling" (*Democracy* 51). For Dewey, as for other pedagogical progressives, education was practice *in* democratic living, not practice *for* it. Teachers and students worked together to foster mutually facilitated learning.

This helps explain Dewey's often misunderstood maxim that education "is its own end" (*Democracy* 50). Although critics have used this line to support the argument that Dewey's educational philosophy was ultimately severed from social change, it is in fact consistent with Dewey's insistence that education can be a lever for democratic reconstruction. Consider Dewey's definition of education: "the educational process is one of continual reorganizing, reconstructing, transforming" (50). The notion of change—both personal and social—is *intrinsic* to education. According to Dewey, pedagogy "must progressively realize present possibilities, and thus make individuals better fitted to cope with later requirements" (56). Pedagogy, in other words, does not simply train students for the future—for the world of work, for instance—but rather engages them in a variety of "present possibilities" *within the present social context.*

Inspired by Dewey's educational philosophy and pedagogical practice, pedagogical progressives, much of whose work is chronicled in John and Evelyn Dewey's *Schools of To-morrow,* sought change from the inside out: true educational and social change, as they understood it, began in classrooms during the pedagogical process. From "Mrs. Johnson's" Fairhope school in Alabama to the Gary Plan in Indiana (see Cohen and Mohl), all of the pedagogical experiments the Deweys studied emerged from a belief that revitalizing the schools meant nothing less than revitalizing the communities of which they were a crucial part (Dewey and Dewey 174–75).

The chief problem with educational reform, according to Dewey, was that it was being put in the hands of outside "experts," including businessmen and administrators with no educational backgrounds, rather than in the hands of teachers (*Democracy,* "Relation"). This group of elite professionals—who, ironically, also worked in the name of "progressivism"—were remarkably successful in aligning the schools with corporate practices and ideology. As educational historian Joel Spring observes, the early twentieth century saw schooling increasingly organized around the imperative "to improve human capital as a means of economic growth" (153). And leading the way were school administrators: "between 1900 and 1924, school administration rapidly professionalized around . . . values of cost efficiency and school management" (250). Their success was captured in a 1920s report on progressivism: "'in the struggle between quantitative administrative efficiency and qualitative educational goals . . . the big guns are all on the side of the heavily concentrated controls behind the former'" (qtd. in Tyack 198).

The administrative progressives were not necessarily school administrators per se. In fact, as David Tyack makes clear, administrative progressivism was led by efficiency experts, corporate leaders, and other professionals from the world of business. These professionals, spurred on by muckraking journalists who routinely excoriated the schools for their inefficiency, set about corporatizing the schools by setting up school boards on the model of boards of directors; by calling on efficiency experts to run time-motion analyses on teachers; by subjecting students to standardized curriculum and tests—in short, by running schools as if they were competitive businesses. Callahan summarizes:

> The procedure for bringing about a more businesslike organization and operation of the schools was fairly well standardized from 1900 to 1925. It consisted of making unfavorable comparisons between the schools and business enterprise, of applying business-industrial criteria (e.g., economy and efficiency) to education, and of suggesting that business and industrial practices be adopted by educators. (6)

Administrative progressives' willingness to subordinate teaching and learning to the tyranny of the bottom line derived from their cherished belief that schools should assist in the ineluctable progress toward urbanization and industrialization. In the midst of radical social changes, and in light of the pride with which U.S. society viewed its recent industrialization, it is perhaps not surprising that school reformers looked to industry and business for models after which to fashion the schools: "The division of labor in the factory, the punctuality of the railroad, the chain of command and coordination in modern businesses—these aroused a sense of wonder and excitement in men and women seeking to systematize the schools" (Tyack 28). Some reformers imagined students as factory workers churning out products, and teachers as their overseers. More often, the teacher was viewed as the factory worker and the student was considered the product. In 1917, for instance, F. E. Shapleigh offered this analogy:

> The school is a factory. The child is the raw material. The finished product is the child who graduates. We have not yet learned how to manufacture this product economically. No industrial corporation could succeed if managed according to the wasteful methods which prevail in the ordinary school system. (qtd. in Callahan 176)[6]

The transformation of the schools into factories and corporations paved the way for a number of reforms: the use of Frederick Taylor's scientific management techniques in the schools and the concomitant shifting of power from teachers to outside "experts"; heavy reliance on "objective," standardized tests; the development and implementation of prepackaged, standardized curricula; the tracking of students based on results of those tests; more stringent work conditions for teachers (larger classes, higher accountability); and many more. In short, teachers' work was to a large extent conditioned by the constraints imposed by administrative progressives; indeed, the work of a teacher became largely to execute and measure the effects of the mandates of these "experts."

## The Emergence of Modern Composition and NCTE

It was in this complex context that modern composition was born. As many historians have noted, modern composition was a product of the hysteria caused by the failure of over half of the young men who took Harvard's 1874 written entrance exam (Applebee; Berlin, *Writing;* Connors, *Composition-Rhetoric;* Crowley, *Composition;* Kitzhaber). When results of the examination became known, a national literacy scandal was declared, and the schools were pronounced ineffective and inefficient. (It was assumed that the public schools could only be in worse shape than the elite preparatory schools from which many of the Harvard examinees hailed.) Presuming that schools would not remedy the dire situation in short order, many reformers—including A. S. Hill of Harvard—agreed that the colleges and universities were forced to make (presumably temporary) provisions for the woefully underprepared students who would continue to darken their doors. This was the beginning of required first-year composition, that curious phenomenon that has stubbornly retained its place in the American academy despite its century-long status as one of the few (and often the only) required courses in increasingly elective college curricula.

Of course, the schools, too—and especially the high schools—were pressured to improve. By the 1890s, many rural and urban schools were in disrepair. The former provided teachers with drastically inadequate training; the latter were becoming terribly overcrowded. The Harvard exams made evident how inefficient even the "best" schools really were, according to many businessmen. Muckraking journalists working for popular magazines such as *McClure's* and *Saturday Evening Post* also fanned the flames of educational crisis (Callahan). Not to be outdone, higher education joined the fray. One "progressive" reform during the late nineteenth century was a movement—led by elite eastern universities and formalized in the work of the 1892 Committee of Ten—for uniform college entrance requirements and standardized high school reading lists. It was thought that the postsecondary institutions could thus put pressure on high schools to raise their standards and produce a more suitable student "product."

Not surprisingly, secondary schools resented being placed under the thumb of the colleges (Applebee; Hook). Out of this tension between secondary and postsecondary schools emerged the National Council of Teachers of English (1911), along with its official journal, *English Journal* (1912). Although its mandate would grow thereafter, the immediate catalyst for the formation of this initially Chicago– and New York–based group was the domination of the high schools by the colleges.[7] Fred Newton Scott, who launched a Ph.D. program in rhetoric at Michigan and who insisted that a "system by which colleges could exert control over secondary school requirements was 'feudal'" (qtd. in Hook 12), was elected its first president.

Under Scott's leadership, the young NCTE was successful in expanding its membership. As early as 1913, editor James Hosic could write the following in response to the impression that *English Journal (EJ)* was read almost exclusively by high school teachers:

> A large number of our subscribers are college professors, some of them heads of departments in the largest universities. The normal schools are also well represented, and many elementary-school teachers and principals are on the list, as well as city superintendents and state school officers. It may be worthwhile to add that practically all of the large libraries . . . receive the magazine and that there are subscribers in such far off lands as Turkey, Australia, Japan, the Philippines, and New South Wales, to say nothing

of Germany, England, and Canada. Of course every state in the
Union is represented. (qtd. in Hook 56)

A brief look at who wrote for *EJ* during its early years provides another index of NCTE's quick growth. During *EJ's* first
ten years, between 20 percent and 42 percent of the submissions
came from either Chicago or New York.[8] This is unsurprising
when we consider that NCTE held its annual convention in one
of those two cities every year but one (1919, Boston) during its
first decade. As early as 1915, however, twenty-five states were
represented by writers in *EJ*. At no point during the first ten years
were fewer than sixteen states represented by the writers. Perhaps even more interesting is the healthy balance of representation among colleges and schools in *EJ* during its first decade.[9]
Although submissions from schools generally outweighed submissions from colleges, college representation never fell below
30 percent of total contributions and school representation never
rose above 60 percent.

While the early NCTE was becoming increasingly diverse in
geographical and institutional terms, we must recognize its limitations as well. Despite the rapid growth of postsecondary education for African Americans as a result of the second Morrill
Act, for instance, few articles were published by writers from
what Royster and Williams call "historically African American
institutions" (566). Similarly, though this period saw a dramatic
rise in the number of women attending both secondary and
postsecondary education (Gordon; Hobbs), and though *EJ* did
publish a number of articles by women teaching in all-female
schools, I count only two articles from 1912 to 1929 that pay
explicit attention to the role of gender in education (Marsh;
Yeomans). The others take up generic topics such as "How We
Use Our School Library" (Keyes), "Entrance Literature and the
Ancient Classics" (Shackford), or "Inspiration in Freshman Composition" (Magee).[10]

In short, the early NCTE was both admirably "progressive,"
promoting educational change through national, cross-institutional dialogue, *and* decidedly mainstream, representing the interests of a primarily white, male-identified constituency. We might
consider it a typical liberal organization—it worked for change

but without radically disrupting the status quo. The very first editorial comment to appear in *EJ* makes this orientation clear enough:

> The *Journal* is progressive. . . . [W]e are eager to move forward
> . . . . Nevertheless, we believe in sound methods of investigation
> and testing. The American educational world is at present quite
> too much of a mob, ready to crowd after any leader sufficiently
> stentorian. After all, the burden of proof rests upon the new.
> (Hosic, "Policy" 375)

Thus, the journal offers a developing portrait of "progressive" English during the Progressive Era (see also Hatfield, "Nominal"). It also provides a record of what we might consider a two-decade-long experiment in trying to establish cross-institutional dialogue (in 1928, *EJ* began to publish a separate college edition). Finally, unlike its disciplinary counterparts—*PMLA, Modern Language Notes*, or *Modern Philology*, for instance—*EJ* was pedagogical in focus: it provided a forum not only for theoretical and historical research, but also for teacher narratives and classroom experiments in literature and—significantly, for our purposes—in composition. All of these factors make *EJ* a useful resource for historical inquiry into how progressivism was figured in English, including composition, classrooms during the Progressive Era. While a single periodical can never offer a complete and definitive picture, this one offers us valuable insight into how many English teachers, and especially composition teachers, envisioned and tried to enact "progressive education."

## Modern Composition as Pedagogical Progressivism

As the editorial comment above suggests, the young NCTE and its journal were not necessarily supportive of *pedagogical* progressivism. After all, it is likely that one of the "sufficiently stentorian" educational leaders that the editors of *EJ* had in mind was John Dewey, who had yet to publish his magnum opus (*Democracy and Education*, 1916), but who had spoken loudly with the publication of a series of lectures under the title *School and*

*Society* (1899), the influential study *The Child and the Curriculum* (1902), pamphlets such as "My Pedagogic Creed" (1897), and a slew of essays in education journals such as the *Elementary School Record* and *University Record*. By the time NCTE was formed in 1911, Dewey's ideas were widely circulated and had already influenced education at all levels.

At the same time, we do see in the pages of *EJ* a good deal of attention (albeit sporadic and unorganized) to Dewey's educational philosophy and to what James Berlin calls a "rhetoric of public discourse" (*Rhetoric*) or "democratic literacy" *(Rhetorics)*. These teachers, who often designated their approach "the social view" or "the social conception," sought to teach writing in the service of democratic citizenship. They believed that students should be encouraged to inquire into the most pressing political issues of the day.[11] In this view, the goal of education was to prepare students for democratic citizenship by encouraging literacy as a means to social awareness and involvement (Carter; Gaston; Gibbs; Hansen). And more than that, helping students to participate in public discourse meant opening up the possibility of participating in the reconstruction of the social order (Fries; Ruud). These educators focused on the creation of a classroom environment that facilitated the development of the individual intellect and the realization of social responsibility. Thus, composition teachers took up and designed a number of pedagogical innovations—including collaborative projects, student contracts, and self-directed learning—in the name of democratic progressivism (see, for instance, Clark; Douglas; Glaser; Hargrave; Hatfield, "Not," "Project"; Keyes).

Like the teachers showcased in the Deweys' *Schools of Tomorrow,* some English teachers sought to place pedagogy at the center of school and community reform. One high school teacher, for example, wrote in 1914 about the need to make educational projects "real" and responsive to the needs of the particular school and community in which students worked. E. H. Kemper McComb, a high school teacher, used Deweyan language to exhort his fellow teachers: "Lay firm hold of the fundamental idea that education is life itself; give your pupils problems that grow out of the social conditions of your schools; show them how to solve these problems in a natural way that prevails outside the school walls" (415). By way of example, McComb reflected on how his seniors collaborated to develop a program for Fire Prevention Week, a project that required them to write for multiple audiences and purposes, and that asked them to use their developing literacies to engage the local community.

In fact, in the 1910s and early 1920s, we see in the pages of *EJ* a movement for what John D. Cooke called "Community English." In the high schools and in first-year composition, students were often asked to organize themselves as a small community, often on the model of "societies" that proceeded by parliamentary law. Community English asked students to engage directly the community of which the school was a part; it was an early version of what we today call community service learning. Cooke, for instance, asked his high school students to write letters, give speeches, conduct public debates, hold pageants, and the like. Student inquiry into the community was viewed not only as a rich learning experience, but also as an opportunity for community development. Through such projects, students would become more informed and more involved in their local place.

Community English shows that, at least in some locales, composition during the early years of the twentieth century was not simply the intellectual backwater that some of our historians have claimed. Indeed, Robert Connors has marked the period from roughly 1900 to 1930 as "the Dark Ages of composition" (*Composition-Rhetoric* 99). According to Connors, this period saw composition become almost completely severed from its roots in rhetorical theory, giving over instead to the canon of concepts—the modes of discourse, the methods of exposition, the levels of style, the select-narrow-expand invention system—that we now associate with "current-traditional rhetoric" (13). Connors's reliance on textbooks, however, leads him to speculate about classroom practice in ways that contradict many of the representations of teaching in *EJ*. Though writing teachers struggled with how to enact Dewey's pedagogical principles, many of them devoted themselves to student-centered, project-oriented, community-based classroom practices. The first two decades of *EJ* demonstrate that the teaching of English, and specifically composition, was a complicated affair.

## Modern Composition as Administrative Progressivism

At the same time, it is fair to say that this kind of pedagogical progressivism was not the dominant approach to composition in the schools or in the first-year college course during the Progressive Era.[12] Taken as a whole, composition was neither student-centered nor committed to social reconstruction. But if composition did "devolve" during the Progressive Era, as Connors suggests, I believe it is too simple to attribute this devolution to "the badly prepared and reactionary nature of the audience for textbooks after 1900: the writing teachers" (*Composition-Rhetoric* 99). Given the working conditions of these teachers, Connors's argument seems reasonable enough; then, as today, good teaching in the universally required course was almost certainly accomplished despite working conditions that seem cruelly designed to thwart such work. But these working conditions were embedded in larger cultural practices and in the logic of a larger economic system, and in my view these deserve more attention than they receive in Connors's history. Indeed, the innovative intentions of some composition teachers were thwarted by the fact that modern composition developed at a time when U.S. education and society were in the grips of an obsession with *efficiency*— in the midst, in other words, of the incorporation of America and its schools.

Consider, for instance, that the cost-efficiency movement was in full swing by the time *EJ* appeared in 1912. In the very first article to appear in *EJ*, Edwin Hopkins (who would later become president of NCTE) wonders, "Can Good Composition Teaching Be Done under Present Conditions?" Answering his titular question in the negative, Hopkins complains that composition teaching in secondary and postsecondary institutions is "abnormally inefficient" (1). What to do? His answer is telling:

> If in business affairs an investment fails to bring desired results, the common practice is to ascertain whether those results will justify an increase of an investment sufficient to insure obtaining them, or whether the business shall be discontinued. This is precisely the nature of the English situation. (6)

The real question facing English, urged Hopkins, was this: "is or is not training in English expression necessary to a successful industrial and business future?" (6). Thus arose a movement in English to apply cost analysis to determine whether this upstart—composition—was "worth it." Just as administrative progressives were applying business practices to the operation of schools, so were they applying them specifically to composition instruction. And just as the value of the schools was measured by their service to business, so was the value of composition tabulated.

For the next decade, Hopkins would sit on the Committee on the Labor and Cost of the Teaching of English in Colleges and Secondary Schools with Especial Reference to English Composition (hereafter, for obvious reasons, referred to as the Hopkins committee). This committee began in 1909 under the aegis of the Modern Language Association, and NCTE began sponsoring it in 1911. NCTE occasionally published reports from the committee in *EJ*, as well as its final report (in its sixteenth edition) in 1923 (Hopkins, *Labor*). The work of the Hopkins committee is significant because it shows us what administrative progressivism looked like when applied to composition. In my reading of the report, however, the committee in fact appropriated the language and ideology of administrative progressivism in an effort to subvert the mania for bottom-line "efficiency" and to support the pedagogical work of composition.

As Hopkins's 1912 *EJ* essay suggests, the committee began with the assumption that composition was woefully inefficient. For administrative progressives, "inefficient" was code for "not cost-effective." That is, economy was *equated* with efficiency. Therefore, the task would be to reduce the costs of composition in the high schools and universities. The Hopkins committee, however, found that the "inefficiency" of composition was owing to inadequate resources and support for teachers. In its report, for instance, the committee declared that theme-reading work for composition teachers at both educational levels was "two and a half times the limit of physical endurance without undue strain" (Hopkins, *Labor* 6). The average high school teacher had more than 125 students, though "maximum efficiency" would demand that they be responsible for no more than

50. Similarly, teachers of first-year composition were typically assigned 105 or more students, while maximum efficiency would require no more than 35. While composition teachers typically received less pay and lower status than teachers of other subjects, their workload relative to their colleagues in other disciplines was 1.75 to 1 (28).

The committee used the language of economy and efficiency to couch its findings and recommendations, but it refused to equate economy with efficiency. For instance, it determined that when tabulated per pupil, English cost less than any other subject. The average *total* cost was higher, but only because it served a greater percentage of students. Of course, reducing the number of students to efficiency levels would raise cost, but the average "unit cost" would remain 10 percent below the average for scientific and vocational subjects (Hopkins, *Labor* 7). Therefore, the committee recommended fewer students per instructor, fewer sections of composition per instructor, smaller classes, and increased pay for composition teachers. In so doing, it appropriated the language of efficiency and economy to protect responsible teaching and labor practices.

While the Hopkins report may point to a constructive response to the fervor for efficiency, it is also true, as Hopkins himself noted in 1917 ("Wanted"), that composition's association with the cult of efficiency was pulling English apart, with particularly negative results for composition. Because the fortunes of literature-oriented English had never been tied to its practical consequences (at least according to its defenders) but rather to its humanizing function, a great debate emerged between those who advocated "culture" and those who advocated "efficiency." Although *EJ* printed numerous articles throughout the 1910s refusing the easy distinction between efficiency and culture (Hill; Lewis; Palmer; F. N. Scott, "Poetry"; Webster; Williams), English began to split between humanist elitists on the one hand and "reformers" who "share the ideals of the efficiency expert [and whose] thoughts run to standardization and quantity production" (Bode 387) on the other. The defenders of "liberal culture" insisted that the primary responsibility of English was to preserve and pass on the great classical and Christian traditions

(Babbitt 69). Meanwhile, composition was becoming a "vast industry for the manufacture of good English in school and college, [with] stupendous machinery and ingenious tools, . . . processes and paraphernalia of all sorts" (Osgood, "No Set" 160).

Responses to this latter development varied. No sooner was first-year composition established than it came under attack by critics (Duncan; Osgood, "No Set"; Manchester; Thurber; see also Connors, "Abolition," on the "first wave" of abolitionists in the 1890s and the second after 1911; and Russell). Conversely, because composition was deemed more amenable than literary study to objective measurement, it was more often thought to be an important part of the effort to make English more efficient by nailing down, once and for all, its "minimum essentials." "Minimum essentials" referred to "standards of knowledge" (Reynolds 349), and the ultimate goal was to have English teachers reach consensus on what and how they wanted their students to learn. In 1926, Sophia Camenisch reported that the most drastic change in English during the 1920s was an increased demand for widely shared "standards and objectives" (181). But long before then, in 1912, *EJ* found "occasion for rejoicing in the prospect of a national syllabus of the high-school course in English" (Hosic, "Signs" 439; see also Hosic, "Nationalization"). Both *EJ* and NCTE were active in the movement to ground English more firmly in "scientific" facts and conclusions, rather than "personal opinion." In her 1924 NCTE president's address, for instance, Essie Chamberlain claimed that "English suffers from a lack of organization and the precise marking of its limits" (6). She encouraged her colleagues to shore up the discipline: "Scientific facts painstakingly gathered must justify the superiority of the chosen material, and methods as well, over those which have been rejected" (7). An astounding number of articles reporting on such experiments appeared in *EJ* in the following several years.

And composition, it was thought, could lead the way. At the University of Illinois, for instance, efficiency was sought through the systematization of the evaluation of writing. The grading procedures were draconian in their unstinting emphasis on mechanical correctness. Students received an E for any of the following: three or more misspelled words; two sentences with violent changes of construction; two unclear sentences; two straggling sentences; one comma fault; one incomplete sentence; two grammatical errors; a noticeable number of improprieties or barbarisms; a marked lack of unity; a marked lack of coherence (Tieje et al. 593). This was in the first semester of first-year composition; in the second, the standards were raised.

At the high school level, too, there was hope that "inefficient" composition could be turned around through standardizing curriculum and measurement. This was understood as part of a larger effort of administrative progressivism, as we see clearly in this passage from a high school English teacher:

> Now just as the study of methods of business has produced the new application of science to industry known as scientific management, so the demand of the age for the measurement of results is bringing forth a new science of education based upon exact measurement and judgment ascertained by the facts. (Noyes 532)

Moreover, composition measurements, especially the Hillegas scale, devised by Milo Burdette Hillegas of Columbia, portended the day when "all teachers may feel that their gradings are just and uniform because based on a definite, fixed standard" (Noyes 536; see also Hudelson; Fulwider; the 1915 report of the NCTE Committee on the Scientific Study of the Teaching of English). In fact, the influence of administrative progressives here was direct: in 1913 arch-administrative progressive Edward Thorndike published an article in *EJ* urging the use of the Hillegas scale in composition. If *EJ* is any indication, this call was answered by English teachers and administrators at all levels of education (see Courtis; Gunther; Henderson). Although enthusiasm for fixed, objective measurements for composition was never entirely untempered (see Parker; F. N. Scott, "Our"), one *EJ* writer was able to report by 1928 that nearly two hundred standardized tests were in use in English programs across the country, most of them for composition (LaBrant; see also Certain). Thus was composition conscripted into the service of what Callahan calls the "cult of efficiency."

Not coincidentally, this orientation served the labor market particularly well. At the high school and college level, many teachers were experimenting with what was called "Business English," "Industrial English," or, later, "Commercial English" (Clapp; Cody, "Organizing"; Cook; Cooke; Duddy; Lyons; Opdycke; Struble). These courses typically taught students how to write business letters and other workplace genres; they always emphasized "clean, clear" prose (see especially Cody, "Ideal"). Their primary purpose was to prepare students for what the functionalist 1926 "Report of the Committee on the Place and Function of English in American Life" called "practical affairs"[13] (NCTE Committee on the Place).

*EJ* itself seemed to be lukewarm on the vocationalization of composition (see "Business English"; "Efficiency Wave"; Hatfield, "Clapp"), but it did see fit to publish a 1913 article titled "The Demands of the Business World for Good English." Written by W. R. Heath, vice president of a mail-order house, this essay alerts English teachers to what they "must teach" in order to please the corporate world. This article is very much in line with the prevailing conception that businesses ought to provide the blueprints for composition work. In Chicago, for instance, Sherwin Cody reported on a joint venture of the Chicago Association of Commerce and the Chicago Board of Education. The first step was to "get a concrete expression of just what business men did want" ("Organizing" 412). Then, tests would be designed to test those skills, and the tests would be implemented "under the auspices" of local businessmen's organizations. Finally—and this was evidently the program's crowning achievement—an "efficiency employment list" would be created so that businesses could see which students were most "efficient." In the process, the Board of Education would also learn which teachers were most efficient; indeed, it would offer "efficiency certificates" to teachers with high-performing students.

On the college level, the vocationalization of composition was even more pronounced, perhaps because college teachers were not accustomed to teaching for such practical ends. As one University of Illinois teacher wrote in 1912:

> In the good old days when composition courses were unnecessary, going to college meant one thing; today it means another—a dozen others. The type of student now chiefly represented in

our thousand theme-writers was then sticking to his farm or shop or office. Now he demands special training from the state, in agriculture, engineering, or commerce. He is a Philistine. (Guild 412)

If not to destroy the temple altogether, the philistines had come to make it their training facility (see also Frank Scott).

Defenders of liberal culture and public rhetoric never completely died out at either the high school or college level. Still, the spirit of the times supported projects like that described by Cody— and for the reason he states: "It appeals to the imagination of every American to get a business measurement, to be able to meet a business standard" ("Organizing" 418). The secondary and postsecondary composition classroom could be a place where such a standard became visible—where, in fact, that standard could become the driving force of instruction.

Composition's utilitarian, vocational emphasis was ideologically consonant with administrative progressivism and the corporatized U.S. university, with their focus on efficient (that is, cost-effective) bureaucracy. As Gerald Graff suggests, in the changing academy of the early twentieth century, "bureaucratic administration took the place of traditional ideology as the bond holding the institution together" (*Professing* 60). While the old U.S. college was designed to provide wealthy young men with high culture, the new U.S. university was organized toward the same end that Joel Spring identifies for the schools: the development of human capital for the purpose of economic growth. It both participated in the broader corporate economy and developed a corporate, pyramidal economy of its own. And as Stephen North has shown, first-year composition fit the corporate bill nicely (*Refiguring*). Almost everyone in the (mostly elective) U.S. university was required to take at least one first-year writing course, but those who taught it were not well compensated (to put it mildly). As the Hopkins committee report shows, for cost-effective delivery of credits for cash, no course could touch first-year composition *(Labor)*.

But the new U.S. university was a product of more than home-grown U.S. corporatism. As has been widely noted, it was also influenced by the model of the German research university (Graff,

*Professing;* North, *Refiguring;* Scholes, *Rise;* Shumway). The German tradition emphasized dispassionate research, the production of (scientifically derived) knowledge rather than the teaching of it, and the specialization of knowledge into discrete institutional and disciplinary units. It was concerned primarily with "producing" researchers: those who would contribute to disciplinary knowledge.

Although composition was thought to be useful in standardizing teaching practice and developing a body of knowledge about "what works" in the classroom—contributing to making the corporate university more efficient—it fit decidedly less well into the *disciplinary* orientation of the new U.S. university. First of all, as John Brereton suggests, casting its lot with NCTE—"an organization with distinctly pedagogical aims that fostered a Midwestern, egalitarian attitude toward education rather than the Eastern elitist approach"—had "serious consequences" for college composition (24). In effect—with exceptions such as Fred Newton Scott aside—allying oneself with teachers in the schools meant giving up the privileges of disciplinary and institutional authority. Schoolteachers, it was thought, did not *produce* knowledge; they disseminated or applied it. The German tradition demanded that researchers commit themselves to the dispassionate pursuit of knowledge, not to these lower activities. Also, composition's vocational emphasis did not serve it well on this front: German professors and researchers-in-training hardly concerned themselves with the "philistines." Published research on literature may have fit the disciplinary bill, ensuring national "progress" through the maintenance of "our" cultural capital (see Hutcheon; Shumway), but training undergraduates (first-year students, no less) for the workforce would not advance knowledge.

And then there was the matter of *who* taught composition. Soon after its inception, first-year composition came to be staffed primarily by teaching assistants and instructors, a disproportionate number of them women. Professors, most often male, avoided the course, for reasons the Hopkins committee's research makes clear: overwork, poor pay, low status. Young, often female, instructors were recruited to do the dirty work of remediation, thus freeing up the more established (male) members of English departments to pursue the "real" work of the discipline: the analysis of literary texts. Whatever hopes early compositionists may have harbored for composition as a "masculine," scientific pursuit, composition soon became "the distaff partner in a socially important 'masculine' enterprise, the cultural maintenance of linguistic dispositions of power and enfranchisement" (S. Miller, "Feminization" 40).[14] The yoking of modern composition to first-year writing, then, gave rise to two related developments: (1) authorization of exploitative, specifically sexist, labor practices, and (2) ratification of the idea that the proper purview of English was the study of literary texts, understood as the reception and interpretation of a narrowly defined "type" of discourse (literature), and not the production of multiple discourses. This drove a wedge between literary study and composition, authorizing the former as the official "content" of the discipline and relegating the latter to the seemingly paradoxical status of permanent remedial work, evacuated of content and therefore of true (that is, extra-practical) value. These assumptions in turn authorized the continuation of the corrupt labor practices that kept underpaid and overworked pre- and nonprofessionals hard at work but discouraged them from making the teaching of writing or their students' writing objects of theoretical or scholarly study. Of all positions in the academy, perhaps the instructor of first-year composition most closely approximated the factory worker (or the composition teacher in the public school): he or (more commonly) she was considered little more than a theme-correcting machine, an executor of training in basic decoding and encoding skills.

## "Progressive Composition"

Placing the formation and development of modern composition within the complex context of educational progressivism yields no simple, neat lessons. Perhaps the most important service this historical material can offer, in fact, is to complicate our sense of the field's history. Neither of the common versions of "progressive" that I outlined in the introduction—the grand march toward the enlightened present or the traditional retreat to naive, liberal politics—can capture the complexity of where we have been, and so neither is likely to serve us well in understanding where we are or where we're going. It is tempting to tell history as a story of winners and losers. We might read this material to suggest that administrative progressives "won" and pedagogical progressives "lost." (See Cohen and Mohl for one such reading.) Then we could cast ourselves as contemporary heroes, *true* progressives: finally enlightened, fighting the good fight not only against our ideological enemies but also against "tradition." But while administrative progressives clearly were able to consolidate their power during the Progressive Era, and while pedagogical progressives never did create a formidable alliance, administrative progressives' power was never total. As William Reese makes clear in his case studies of grassroots reform efforts during the Progressive Era, important local efforts were underway throughout this period to resist the incorporation of the schools. Reese's work on socialists, trade unionists, women's groups, parents' groups, and other agitators for school reform provides an important supplement to the more traditional focus on business elites. And it reminds us that there are always voices other than those that speak loudest. In this chapter, I have spent more time on the influence of administrative progressives on composition than on that of pedagogical progressives because it is important to understand the perspective and practices that were dominant during this period. At the same time, it is equally important not to lose sight of pedagogical progressivism—precisely because its alternative visions and versions of "progressive" work in English may point us toward a more useful and humane model for such work today.

# On Assessing Corporate Culture

*I cannot tell what I want to tell about my work at the private assessment firm. They made me sign papers promising I wouldn't tell.*

*But then, this story is not "about" a particular firm, or a certain project, or anyone specific. It is about assessing corporate culture.*

---

I am moving to the middle class.

I am well into my long academic apprenticeship to this class, having earned my master's degree and begun teaching writing at local colleges. And yet the money and the summer work—factories, construction, landscaping—hardly seem middle-class fare.

But now a friend knows of a summer job—"in education, sort of." Holistic assessment. It sounds New Age-y, but I apply and am hired to score reading and writing.

---

The firm has two buildings: a modern brick-and-glass office space on the fringes of the northeastern town and an old mill building downtown. I'm to report to the mill.

When I do, I find the surroundings strangely familiar: a large, open space interrupted only by the occasional support beam. High windows. I think of the tractor factory, where I assembled fenders. At first I don't even notice the people, but in a moment I see hundreds of them, already busily at work. Unlike the tractor factory, this place has few machines—but you'd never know it by the constant hum of the room.

---

Training time:

"I could train a monkey to do this."

"Your job isn't to know writing; it's to know scoring."

"The goal is for everyone in this room to score *as one person.*"

That last one frightens us—not because we believe it's not possible, but because we know, somehow, that it is.

"You don't have to believe a paper *deserves* the score you give it; you simply have to see it as we would have you see it. *Then* you can trust yourself."

One sign reads: "Always let the guide be your conscience."

One of us jokes: "When you start thinking, you're in trouble."

I think: *Remove fender from rack, place fender carefully on table, taped side up, insert two #34 screws. . . .*

---

Aspirin. Bengay. Heating pads. Hot water bottles. Ice packs. They litter the tables here, as they did at the tractor factory.

Complaints. Whines. Moans. Groans. Sighs. They litter the air here, as they did at the tractor factory.

---

"They" are the same, too—They sneak; They skulk; They appear when you least expect Them ("Here They come!").

The Roamers.

They breathe down our necks (literally), checking our tally

sheets. Are we on task? How many booklets? How many did we do yesterday?

(*"You assembled 110 fenders yesterday; you can do 120 today. I don't CARE if your last cart came in at 4:50. . . ."*)

---

I didn't plan to return for a second summer, but here I am, compelled by a promised pay increase and an enduring fear of returning to the kind of jobs where it is definitely *not* a good thing to be a 130-pound "college boy." (Or worse: a 130-pound college *teacher*, which is what I really am.) Besides, I know now that I have been accepted into a Ph.D. program a few states over—I'll be a "college boy" again—and so this will definitely be my last year here.

---

Midsummer, midprojects, and the firm is shorthanded. A familiar call goes out: "Anyone with a pulse." The requirements for the job have dwindled from college degree to two years of college. There is talk of changing the minimum requirement to *enrollment* in college. The practicing and retired teachers are being replaced by college students, mainly from the state university.

"Anyone with a pulse." I think of the contract on which we fell behind at the tractor factory. At 10 o'clock break, we would hit the streets for warm bodies. ("I'm docking your pay if you're not back by 11:00 with a carful of men.") Most days, the illegal immigrants and recently arrived Puerto Ricans who hung around the parking lots hoping for a day's work would suffice; other days, we'd head downtown, picking up the men—and occasionally the women—who stood idly on streetcorners, often not physically fit enough to walk the two miles to join the others in the factory parking lot.

"They have to have full use of their hands," we were told, "and if they're illegal, we don't want to know about it. They get paid—cash—at the end of the day, but only if they stay all day."

Only the demographics are different. While the factory be-came far more diverse during a labor crisis, the assessment firm gets even whiter, even younger, even more middle class, even more suburban. But like the factory, this place does not care *who* does the work—not now, in the middle of a crisis. What matters is *that* the work gets done.

---

The project leader tells us to watch for "the halo effect of a well-turned phrase."

"Don't be taken in by smooth but empty prose. We're after higher-order skills. These people want to be teachers, remember. They want to get into a *teachers college*, for Chrissakes. Higher-goddamn-order skills."

We nod, waiting for him to look down at his notes so we can exchange the slight shakes of the head and the furrowing of eye-brows that say, *Ignore that.*

We run through a practice scoring session, and as usual, those who rate according to the number of surface-level errors they find best match the prescores. The others—the new ones—will learn soon enough. "Standard, edited written American English" is what we're looking for—"command of the language." This seems fair, some of us reason; everyone is held to the same stan-dard.

And so the would-be teacher who writes (in "standard" prose) that the problem with this country is that too many "uppity" women go to school and take men's jobs enters an education program, while the would-be teacher who argues that good teach-ers should have "adaquate knowledge," "empathy," and, most important, "a belief in the possbility of education to change people and their worlds for the better," sits at home, presumably work-ing on her spelling (or is it typing?) and waiting for the next humiliating test . . . or, more likely, looking for another career. And we who score these essays are happy: we have suppressed our reader biases, assuring an "objective" score.

I am back—unbelievably—for year three.

My wife lives two hundred miles away in our new state, and I have dragged our toddler daughter back home to stay with my parents while I work as table leader at the assessment firm. I vow this will be my last summer here—even if I don't make it onto the short list for grad student summer teaching appointments again. Self-pitying or not, I am sick of paying dues to the middle class.

I have, at any rate, an ulterior motive this summer: research. My graduate advisor tells me that assessment is "hot"; maybe I can write my dissertation about this place. Maybe, someday, a book. A tell-all, maybe. *Assessing Corporate Culture* has a ring.

I work on a multilevel, multidiscipline statewide assessment project: our largest contract. Table leaders are to "norm" the scorers at our tables, "read behind" scorers once the project is underway (two each morning, two each afternoon), resolve arbitrations on the occasional double-scored papers, and ensure that the table is scoring consistently—and silently. We are told that table discussion during training must keep to the language of the scoring materials, and that we ought at all costs to avoid "philosophical" discussion and all talk that might serve to heighten "reader biases."

Our project leader tells us that this is a high-stakes project: writing scores will be included on students' high school transcripts; money is involved for teachers and schools; schools whose students perform poorly on overall assessments will, in severe cases, be declared "in crisis" and put under the control of an educational expert who will in effect run the school as a receivership until test scores are raised. All of this, we are assured, is in the interest of "equity" and "fairness" to the students. All students in the state deserve schools that place high test scores at the top of their priority list.

Qualifying round. Scorers must meet a minimum "agreement rate": their scores must match with relative frequency the scores given to the sample tests by the scoring committee back in the home state. The scoring committee, we are told, consists of test developers, representatives from the state Department of Education, and a handful of "carefully chosen teachers."

We begin. Soon enough it becomes clear that four of the eight scorers at my table will not meet the minimum agreement rate. I am mortified; they're not sufficiently normed.

But then the project leader—a state Department of Education representative who was not on the scoring committee for the writing portion of the test—announces that, lo and behold, *her* scores don't match, either, and by God, she's going to throw out this qualifying round. She leaps up, runs for the phone, and returns a few minutes later, the room still abuzz with confusion.

"*Teachers!*" she sighs, shaking her head in mock exasperation. "Who let them on the committee anyway?" With a wink, she announces that we'll use the training set most of us "aced." Almost all scorers qualify for the project.

Each day, sometimes twice a day, we "recalibrate" with a brief norming round.

"Look," I tell my scorers, "you need to see it as a three. You think it's a four; I think it's a four—it doesn't matter. It's a three because They tell us it's a three."

That was no "three." That was a kid who didn't understand the prompt.

Like that "two" who would have had something great if he could have revised.

Or that "one" who was obviously an ESL student and needed some assistance.

Or that "off task" who understood, probably better than

any "four" ever would, the politics of "THESE ENDLESS FUCKING TESTS."

———————

Out of another labor crisis comes good news: extended hours, overtime (at overtime pay!), new hires, free lunch on Saturdays. But I'm worried: I remember what inevitably happened after the factory picnics.

———————

Crunch time, of course.

Someone realizes that the extended hours, overtime (at overtime pay!), new hires, and free lunches cost too much. At this rate, cost will exceed revenue on this project. Regular hours are resumed; overtime is no longer offered; scorers need to document how many booklets they score each day (as table leader, I monitor this closely, regularly reporting to the Roamers); timed readings are introduced (scorers whose rates are a certain percentage below the average will be reprimanded, even let go); long-time scorers are declared "dead weight" and released (very few new workers, who earn the company minimum, are so declared). We work on contracts with fixed dollar amounts, we are reminded, so all cost overruns come out of "our" pockets. We're not running a charity here. Balance speed and accuracy. Don't agonize over each booklet. (The reluctant are reminded—again—that our "first impression" is usually most accurate.)

———————

*"Do it for the kids,"* urge the project leaders.

*"Do it for the American farmer,"* urged the factory supervisors.

— 38 —

At least the factory supervisors knew a good joke when they told one. ("Think of that poor farmer out there on his old, busted-up tractor, waiting for his new machine so he can finish his work and put food on his table for his poor, starving rugrats. Do it for them. Do it for the farmer's children, college boy.")

*Week one on the flagship assessment project*: "This is about providing equal opportunity for all of America's children. You are fighting the good fight, ensuring that poor schools are punished, and good schools are rewarded. All kids deserve excellence, and you are part of making that a reality."

*Week six on the flagship assessment project*: "Do it for the kids . . . but do it quickly."

No one at the factory had any illusions about the realities of corporate need/greed. No one pretended not to know that when crunch time comes, the numbers will be crunched in ways that secure the company's profit margins first.

---

I am moving more deeply into the middle class. I am assured by the graduate program that, as an advanced teaching assistant, I will get a teaching appointment next summer.

*I'm in*, I think. *Out of corporate culture; into the academy. I'm in.*

(Coda: I *was* in; I'm still in. But I was not out; I am not out. Another story.)

*I have kept my promise; I have not told what I promised not to tell. But sometimes the devil is **not** in the details.*

# CHAPTER TWO

# The Conservative Restoration as Administrative Progressivism

To an administrative progressive from the Progressive Era, many features of the present educational scene would make perfect sense. The teaching of basic skills is being "contracted out" to private corporations; schools are being placed under the control of businesses; corporations generate prepackaged instructional procedures, curricula, and standardized tests; universities are coming to rely more and more on corporate support and to function as corporate entities themselves. In short, "[t]reating schools as if they were open-market institutions and teachers as if they were employees in competitive organizations" has become educational common sense (Tyack and Cuban 127). An administrative progressive might take heart that efficiency and bottom-line economy are again the order of the day.

Indeed, historian Joel Spring observes that the great legacy of twentieth-century education in the United States has been the retooling of schooling to serve "the development of human capital as a means of solving problems in the labor market" (153). Education, in other words, has been put in the service of capitalist "progress"—the march toward a more efficient, more economically productive society. To be sure, our computer-driven, transnational-corporate-controlled Information Age economy lays down different specifications for student-products than did the nascent industrial economy of the Progressive Era, but what Russell Jacoby calls a "mercantile ethos" remains the driving force behind school reform (5).

Of the two chief visions/versions of progress offered by "progressives" during the Progressive Era, then, only one has become central to educational reform. John Dewey's notion of schooling—a means of expanding democratic possibilities by engaging students in meaningful, student-centered pedagogy aimed at helping them live well with others—has been largely overshadowed by administrative progressives' idea that schools ought to serve as an arm of capitalism, ensuring the values of cost efficiency and scientific management. In fact, despite considerable interest in democratic education in the 1930s, Dewey and his followers were widely criticized in the 1940s for purveying "soft" pedagogies. The intensification of cold war nationalism—i.e., international economic competition—further exacerbated this negative perception of Deweyan "permissive" pedagogy, and by 1955, with the demise of the Progressive Education Association—its journal, *Progressive Education,* followed suit in 1957—Deweyan progressivism had faded, seemingly permanently, into the educational background.

Such, at least, is the commonsense historical narrative offered by mainstream historians (Cremin; Ravitch). But again, I am not interested in telling a simple story of winners and losers. The truth is, neither pedagogical nor administrative progressivism has ever fully died out; we saw a revival of Deweyan progressivism in the 1960s, for instance, and then again in more recent years in response to the back-to-basics movement. What I offer in this chapter is not a postmortem on the victory of administrative progressivism over pedagogical progressivism. While the dire trends I note above have demonstrably taken root in U.S. education, it is also true, as I show in later chapters, that what I call here the "reincorporation of schooling" is *not* total. Innovative teachers and learners at many sites are finding and creating spaces to act, working for institutional and cultural change that may well lay the groundwork for a reinvigorated pedagogical progressivism.

Still, while we must remember that the story I offer here—the story of efficiency revisited—is not the only story to tell, it is at this cultural moment the most powerful of the competing scripts for educational (and social) reform. The story needs to be told this way—as *the* story—because it presents itself, as all hegemonic stories do, in this fashion.

In choosing to tell this story, I choose not to offer an exhaustive, continuous history of pedagogical and administrative progressivism in composition or U.S. education from 1930 to 2000, however useful such a history might prove to be. Rather, I turn now to the present in order to show that a form of latter-day progressivism—the phenomenon many observers have termed the "conservative restoration" (Apple, *Official;* Aronowitz and Giroux; Ohmann, "Introduction"; Shor, *Culture*)—has indeed become the dominant script of educational reform today. I read the conservative restoration as a form of administrative progressivism in an effort to show that the struggles that educators, including compositionists, continue to face have deep roots in U.S. education, and specifically in conflicted traditions of "progressivism."

In making these claims, I presume no exact correlation: that *we* are precisely where *they* once were, or that administrative progressivism at the turn of this century is exactly what it was at the turn of the last. And yet, this is not the first time that the media and politicians have attacked teachers and the public schools as "inefficient" and in need of more stringent accountability. It is not the first time that the public seems to have lost faith in the public schools (a questionable, but common, perception). It is not the first time that "experts" remote from the scene of learning—test developers, businesspeople, "nonpartisan think tanks"—have been handed the reins of U.S. education. It is not the first time that students' allegedly poor literacy skills have been used as an indicator of a broader failure of U.S. schools to "measure up." In other words, U.S. education in general and composition in particular have been shaped, and continue to be shaped, by the ideology and the practices of administrative progressivism.

## The Reincorporation of Schooling

In revis(it)ing the conservative restoration, I begin with the educational/literacy crisis that began after the launching of *Sputnik* and blossomed in the 1970s. For like the incorporation of schooling at the turn of the twentieth century, the more recent reincorporation of schooling has emerged amid widespread insistence that Johnny (and now Jane) cannot read, write, or learn. Since approximately the mid-1970s, the popular press—especially periodicals such as *Newsweek*, which ran a 1975 cover story on "Why Johnny Can't Write"—has been trumpeting the "news" that our educational system is a "sick" institution, woefully inefficient and ineffective. In 1975 the U.S. Office of Education sponsored and issued the Adult Performance Study, which found that over 20 percent of U.S. adults were functionally ill-equipped to handle even the most rudimentary of "life skills" such as reading a job ad or a label on a medicine bottle. In 1977, an advisory panel headed by former Secretary of Labor William Wirtz issued a report chronicling a recent decline in SAT scores (cited in Flesch, *Still*). In 1981, Rudolf Flesch, author of the 1955 phonics-first tract *Why Johnny Can't Read*, claimed that Johnny *still* couldn't read *(Why Johnny Still)*.

These cries of crisis have hardly abated in the twenty-five years that have elapsed since that first Office of Education study. Indeed, we continue to hear attacks on the public schools by those whom David Tyack and Larry Cuban dub "prophets of regress." Each morning, Americans read of the sorry state of our educational system in editorials written by a slew of conservative syndicated columnists. Bestsellers continually remind us that *Sputnik*'s shadow is remarkably long: the United States, once again, is "falling behind." Students are culturally illiterate (Hirsch) and illiberally educated (A. Bloom; D'Souza; Sykes, *Profscam*). Worse yet, they continue to be denied training in "the basics" (Sowell; Sykes, *Dumbing*). Thomas Sowell sums up the current education scene with a familiar analogy:

> The general decline in educational performance that began in the 1960s encompassed elementary and secondary education, as well as education at the college level. The evidence of this decline include not only results on a variety of objective tests, but also first-hand observations by teachers and professors, and dismaying experiences by employers who have found the end-product seriously lacking. (1)

This familiar language is no accident; in fact, the current reincorporation of the schools shares four notable features with the incorporation of the schools during the Progressive Era: it places a premium on standards and standardized tests; it is couched as a "progressive," democratic reform; it is top-down and antiteacher; and it features literacy as a central concern. I treat each of these features in turn.

## Standards and Standardized Tests

To date, forty-nine states have adopted statewide standards, and forty-eight have adopted statewide standardized tests.[1] While standardization of education has never been uncontroversial or gone unchallenged, it clearly makes good political sense today among educational "experts," as it did during the Progressive Era (Brannon). Indeed, at the same time that we have seen a groundswell of scholarly and public resistance to high-stakes standardized testing as unreliable and inequitable,[2] we have also seen a renewed commitment to this educational reform among pundits and policymakers (Archbald and Newman; Darling-Hammond, Ancess, and Falk; Haney and Madaus; Henriques and Steinberg, "Right Answer," "When a Test"; Johnston, *Constructive, Knowing;* Medina and Neill; D. W. Miller; National Council of Teachers of English, "English Teachers"; Michael Powell; Rothstein; Sacks; Schrag; Sheldon and Biddle; Smith; Wiggins).

In fact, we have seen an explosion in the use of standardized tests in recent years. Granted a virtually unfettered marketplace, the testing industry has become big business. Walter Haney, George Madaus, and Robert Lyons estimate that in the early 1990s, state and local governments invested upwards of $20 billion annually in direct and indirect costs for standardized testing programs (95). Surely that number is much higher today—Fairtest claims that 100 million standardized tests are now administered each year in U.S. public schools ("Fact Sheet")—and it will grow yet further if President George W. Bush's ambitious testing plan, discussed below, is enacted.

State-mandated standards and assessments have even expanded to include postsecondary education, which has traditionally enjoyed autonomy from such strictures. In the last decade, more than forty states have issued assessment mandates for postsecondary institutions. And such mandates are not restricted to public institutions, for they are also emerging from regional accrediting agencies, which, under the Higher Education Act, must accredit institutions—public *and* private—in order for those institutions to participate in federal student aid programs.[3] While postsecondary institutions continue to enjoy far less public pressure for accountability than do P–12 schools, there is little doubt that such pressures are making inroads into the academy.

Standardized testing has such staying power in educational reform not only because the industry that supports it is powerful, but also because it generates an easily recognized, self-perpetuating logic.[4] Standardized testing is a numbers game in which the objective is to generate a set of numbers that validates what the testing industry has done. The story the numbers are always made to tell is that we need more testing. They maintain the educational and literacy crisis by ensuring that their results validate and precipitate more of the same. To testing apologists, low test scores do more than identify deficiencies and measure skills: they confirm the existence of a crisis ("Just as we thought . . ."); they confirm the wisdom of having tested ("We never would have known how *bad* the problem was . . ."); and they confirm the need for more tests ("We must stay on top of this. . . .").[5]

## Leave No Child Behind

Like administrative progressives at the turn of the twentieth century, proponents of the reincorporation of the schools couch their proposals in "progressive," democratic rhetoric. In the 2000 presidential election, Republican hopeful George W. Bush declared high-stakes standardized tests the "cornerstone" of an educational agenda that aimed to "leave no child behind." Democrat Al Gore countered by raising the ante: he proposed that not only children, but also their teachers, be subjected to regular standardized tests. In the name of fairness to *all* children, both candidates reminded voters that "underperforming" schools should be shut down or, failing that, put into receivership by outside educational "experts." Neither campaign acknowledged the intensifying grassroots challenges to these "democratic" reforms.

As this book goes to press, President Bush and Congress continue to work toward legislation mandating standardized testing in every state for children in grades 3 through 8. Commitment to standards and assessment is a more or less bipartisan initiative in this highly partisan age because it is driven by a rhetoric of inclusion. In fact, these reforms constitute a response to the radical demographic diversification of education, particularly at the secondary and postsecondary levels. A higher and more diverse percentage of our population than ever is attending high school. For the first time, partly as a result of open-admission programs at major public universities in the 1970s, more than half of our college-age population is attending college (Spellmeyer, "Response"). As did the waves of immigration during the Progressive Era, this more recent diversification stokes fear—articulated clearly in the 1983 National Commission for Excellence in Education tract *A Nation at Risk*—that the United States will not be able to keep up with its foreign competitors or measure up to its "progressive" national promise. In raising the specter of a "rising tide of mediocrity" and in seeking to "seal the fate of the Industrial Revolution," in fact, *A Nation at Risk* established a vision of U.S. "progress" that has informed public discourse around education for two decades.

The same irony we saw in administrative progressivism of the early twentieth century is at play in the present conservative restoration: many reformers seek to level the playing field by applying corporate models of competition to the schools. In other words, as Michael Apple suggests, educational reformists tend to define "equality" not as a democratic value, but as a commercial one (*Official* 31). This is true even of many moderate or liberal reform efforts. Consider, for instance, Ernest Boyer's centrist Carnegie report *High School,* released the same year as *A Nation at Risk*. Although the report makes many unobjectionable recommendations (e.g., "improvement of conditions in the classroom, better recruitment and preparation, better continuing education, and better teacher recognition and rewards" [7]), it is also premised on a corporate model of education that places schools in the service of business by treating them as sites for the inculcation of market values. For instance, the report proposes that "needy" children role-play as executives of Sunkist or Dr. Pepper. The idea, of course, is to teach *all* children that they can be successes in the corporate world. But this program effaces a fundamental economic reality: a competitive marketplace is structured to ensure that most will *not* succeed, will *not* rise to positions such as those Boyer's program asks students to role-play. This service model does a disservice to students—while servicing corporations by providing free (internship and volunteer) labor. It is the reincorporation of the schools in action. Boyer even suggests, in an eerie echo of Progressive Era administrative progressives, that "[b]usiness and industry also can be administrators, particularly in aiding the principals in their capacity as both manager and leader" (277).

More recently, we have seen a spate of reforms aimed at treating schools as competitive, corporate entities, including school vouchers, charter schools, and the Channel One program. And again, each of them is proposed as a democratic initiative that will provide equality for all schoolchildren, including the "disadvantaged," who, we are told, do not thrive under present conditions. Channel One, for instance, brings television advertising into the classroom in return for often badly needed technology for participating schools. It is vigorously marketed to poorly funded schools with the promise of increased resources and increased cultural literacy for students who might otherwise have little access to technology of any kind. While some of us worry about "the *officially sponsored* opening up of school content to commercial sponsorship and organization" (Apple, *Official* 94), such features of the latter-day incorporation of the schools continue to be accorded legitimacy in the public imagination both because they seem fair and egalitarian, and because they satisfy the corporate logic that has come to stand (in) for American common sense: what's good for General Motors (or Microsoft) . . .

### Writing Teachers Out of the Script

Also familiar from the Age of Efficiency is the practice of writing teachers out of the script of educational reform. Behind the accountability movement is an insidious but clear message: teachers cannot be trusted. Educational reform, therefore, must be top-down and controlled by external authority.

Indeed, as becomes clear in John Jennings's *Why National Standards and Tests?*—a useful (though largely uncritical) history of the debates and legislation surrounding national standards and testing—teachers have rarely been given voice in this educational reform movement. George Bush, in consultation with governors and corporate leaders, pushed hard for national standards and tests.[6] But it was perhaps President Clinton who best articulated the spirit of the national standards movement in 1997: "[W]e can no longer hide behind our love of local control of the schools and use that as an excuse not to hold ourselves to high standards. It has nothing to do with local control" (qtd. in Jennings 176). Although Jennings himself does not dwell on this point, his history of the national standards and tests movement demonstrates clearly that politicians, corporate leaders, and educational "experts" have conspired to wrest control of education from those who actually participate in it.

Another "nonpartisan" report—this one from the Kettering Foundation—shows just how successful this antiteacher campaign has been. In 1996, David Mathews reported on the findings of a decade of Kettering studies on the relationship between public education and the public at large. Those findings are disturbing: public schools and the public are moving apart; citizens are concerned for their own children's welfare but seem unmoved by the plight of underserved children elsewhere; the schools today have been given a vote of "no confidence" by the citizenry (even, interestingly, as most continue to be pleased with the education offered by *their* local schools); schools have not been successful in communicating with the public about their work. But Mathews' book, *Is There a Public for Public Schools?,* is—in the tradition of Boyer's *High School*—more than a report; it is also a call for reform. It begins with the premise that engaging the public is not enough precisely because there is no public waiting to be engaged (3). Therefore, according to Mathews, change must begin in communities and move into schools rather than the other way around. On this point, Mathews is clear: he calls for what he terms a "public first" strategy, which places community purposes before "professional criteria" (7). Communities, he suggests, must build mandates for schools.

The Kettering report seems reasonable enough on its surface: because public schools are public trusts, communities must collaboratively arrive at educational mandates. Strangely, though, Mathews makes no mention of the role of educators in the process by which "the public" would develop these mandates (naming problems, framing issues, engaging in deliberative dialogue, making decisions, taking action, and judging results). If not precisely top-down, this process is outside-in: that is, those *outside* the educational institutions set the agenda for what happens *inside* of them. The effect of this move is to deprofessionalize teachers (imagine a community deciding to change the plumbing system without relying on the expertise of its resident plumbers, or deciding to change its skyline without looking to their local architects for guidance). This is precisely what administrative progressivism has always done: built educational reform for and around teachers, never with them. While the movements for national standards and public-first strategies might be posed as democratic, "progressive" reforms aimed at bringing all U.S. schoolchildren into the twenty-first century, their intellectual heritage—whether or not their architects are aware of this—dates back to the turn of the twentieth century and the ascendancy of the antiteacher administrative progressives.

## Literacy in Crisis

Finally, the reincorporation of the schools today echoes earlier administrative progressivism in its emphasis on literacy as the primary measure of the failure of the schools to function efficiently. Just as the results of Harvard's 1874 entrance exams pushed literacy into the public imagination as the measure of our failure to educate U.S. children, so the furor over why Johnny (and Jane) can't read and write (again? still?) has raised the stakes of the present education crisis.

Consider, for instance, Paul Copperman's popular book *The Literacy Hoax* (1978). Copperman, founder and president of a private institute for the teaching of reading skills, tells a familiar story: from the turn of the century to the mid-1950s, students in U.S. schools show steady achievement gains; after the launching of *Sputnik*, this trend accelerates until the mid-1960s, when basic academic skills—and, not coincidentally, standards—fall at an alarming rate. Although Copperman indicts the entire public school system, he names the problem "the literacy hoax." This hoax has been engineered, Copperman tells us, by educational liberals and their "soft" pedagogies, which have created lazy, underachieving students who lack respect for authority (62).[7]

Copperman's rhetoric, of course, is very much of a piece with the conservative restoration. He makes it clear that at stake here are *functional* reading and writing skills: "I believe that the primary function of our schools is to teach students a body of skill and knowledge that will enable them to function in modern society. Far and away the most important of these skills are the primary academic skills: reading, writing, and computing" (22). How is functional literacy defined? Copperman explains:

> A recent study indicates that it takes approximately a seventh-grade reading level to hold a job as a cook, an eighth-grade level to hold a job as a mechanic, and a ninth- or tenth-grade level to hold a job as a supply clerk. I believe it is a reasonable inference that a job as a teacher, nurse, accountant, or engineer would demand a higher minimum level of reading ability. (23)

It is not entirely clear here whether Copperman is proposing that skill level determine occupation, or that occupation determine skill level, but in either case the mercantile ethos is clear enough: education serves the marketplace. Reading and writing skills are mere tools for efficient participation in the workforce.

Functional literacy—an important feature of the reincorporation of the schools—is a contemporary version of "minimum essentials." It echoes administrative progressives' approach to literacy in that it aims at the efficient production of workers by purveying a form of literacy that severs performance from reflection.[8] That is, functional literacy asks us to imagine literacy as a neutral tool, a set of isolated encoding and decoding skills and subskills to be mastered. To view literacy as strictly functional, as Knoblauch and Brannon protest, "sustains conformity to existing power arrangements, the status quo, with little regard for the literacy of critique and dissent" (*Critical Teaching* 80). In severing writing and reading from critical reflection (or what I have termed "reflexive inquiry"), and in claiming an objectivist position "above politics," the functionalist view of literacy insulates what *is* from critique, thus deflecting attention from what *could be.* In functionalist views of literacy, schools train students simply to take their places in society; schools are much what the administrative progressives of the Age of Efficiency imagined them to be: factories, which manufacture student-products to the specifications of the business world.[9]

## Composition and Rhetoric and the Literacy Crisis

If the reinvigorated literacy crisis has proven amenable—and profitable—for purveyors of standardized tests (and conservative pundits), it has also benefited Composition and Rhetoric, now an institutional fixture of higher education. Harkin and Schilb, in their introduction to *Contending with Words,* explain how the literacy crisis of the 1970s provided the impetus for the expansion of Composition and Rhetoric:

> The term *literacy crisis* in the seventies named students who used minority dialects, nonnative speakers of English, white middle-class students whose SAT scores were lower than those of their parents, people who lacked experience with the conventions of academic discourse, unemployed adults who could not read the instructions for filling out their welfare applications, and soldiers who failed to comprehend the instructions for making and deploying nuclear weapons. The term functioned as an umbrella to cover and isolate those persons who, for whatever reason, did not have "normal" standards for discourse. (2–3)

The institutional response from higher education was predictable: it began to "manage" the crisis, and even (since it profited from this new role) to maintain it "by creating new books, journals, PhD programs, and conferences to deal with smaller and narrower aspects of 'literacy'" (3).[10]

While Composition and Rhetoric was not born out of this crisis management—its principal journal had been founded more than two decades earlier, in 1949—it was certainly a beneficiary of it. Insistence that Johnny and Jane (still) couldn't write provided the rationale for an entrenchment and expansion of first-year composition programs in the college curriculum. Parents, community members, administrators, and business leaders agreed that students "needed" first-year composition or, alternatively, basic writing. In the wake of crisis, "[n]ew positions for writing specialists were created and new resources of funding became available" (Horner and Lu 61; see also Faigley). These responses are not surprising when we recall that first-year composition itself originated in the last quarter of the nineteenth century as a program aimed at "reforming" the nonstandard language habits of college-bound young men.

But while Composition and Rhetoric has surely benefited from the literacy crisis, so too has it been harmed by its association with this deeply conservative cultural project. The general conviction that all college students should be required to take at least one course in composition is a mixed blessing. Consider, for instance, the widely remarked exploitation of college writing teachers (Crowley, *Composition;* R. Miller, "Let's Do"; S. Miller, "Feminization"; Schell, "Costs," *Gypsy;* Trainor and Godley). The exploitation of undervalued, overworked, and underpaid labor in writing programs is a function both of the administrative exigencies of universally required courses and of the belief— purveyed by functionalist reformers—that writing is merely a set of "user skills" that virtually anyone can teach. I treat this issue in greater depth in Chapter 4; here, I'm suggesting that writing teachers at all levels of education are still subject to the demands and expectations of administrative progressivism. To be sure, college writing teachers don't (yet?) face quite the same pressure from the accountability hawks as do teachers in the schools, but neither should we underestimate how similar the working conditions are for these two groups of teachers. Recall the findings of the Hopkins report early in the twentieth century: that the labor of writing teachers in the schools *and* in the universities was "two and a half times the limit of physical endurance without undue strain" (*Labor* 6); that the workload for both sets of teachers relative to those in other disciplines was 1.75 to 1; and that both sets of teachers received lower pay and lower status than their colleagues in other disciplines. Surely, with the increasing use of part-time and non-tenure-track faculty in writing programs across the country, the struggles faced by writing teachers in the academy are similar in kind, if not precisely in degree, to those faced by writing teachers in the schools.

Moreover, administrators of first-year writing programs, who often (but not always) hold tenure-track positions, typically have limited control over their programs, which are perceived to be institutional and communal property (Crowley, *Composition*). Again, I have more to say about this later; here, I note that first-year writing programs typically adhere to a central tenet of administrative progressivism: that primary control of the educational enterprise ought to be in the hands of those removed from the scene of instruction. While teachers in first-year programs *may* have some autonomy in their classrooms, and administrators in such programs *may* have some decision-making authority, the larger truth of universally required "service" courses is that they are fundamentally institutionalized—that is, regulated and controlled by the institution at large rather than by the individuals who participate in them—in a way and to an extent that courses without such a designation are not. This is not to diminish the innovations that have taken place within first-year writing classrooms. Rather, it is to suggest that *despite* these changes, first-year composition nonetheless typically continues to function as it did during the Progressive Era: as a mass production machine organized (by virtue of its sheer size and its institutional/cultural status) around the values of economy and efficiency. In this way, among others, even the work of tenure-track and tenured compositionists continues to be shaped by the forces of administrative progressivism.

## Two Examples

Two examples will illustrate the continuing influence of administrative progressivism on composition/Composition and Rhetoric. First, we have Linda Brodkey's "Troubles at Texas." The story of Brodkey's proposed first-year writing course, English 306: Writing about Difference, is well known; broad outlines will suffice here. In the summer of 1990, Brodkey and a committee of graduate students and faculty met to design a shared syllabus for the University of Texas at Austin's first-year composition course, which was required for over half of each entering class. Late in the summer, however, under pressure from local media and a conservative faculty group, a dean decided to "postpone" implementation of the syllabus. What followed was a "local frenzy" about the politics of the course, which resulted in the scrapping of the syllabus designed by this group and the ultimate adoption of an alternative syllabus.

Why was the syllabus so offensive? As Brodkey makes clear, the syllabus was not the issue; no one outside the committee had read or even requested to read it ("Troubles"). The fear, instead, was more ambiguous and more pervasive. William Cunningham, president of the university, perhaps said it best: "Multiculturalism has become a code word for some people, signaling efforts to politicize the curriculum by promoting a particular ideology. We must not, and we will not promote such developments" (qtd. in Brodkey, "Troubles" 183). Earlier that year (1991), the *Houston Chronicle* had run a "news story" with the headline "Effort to Include Bias in UT Class Aborted" and then an editorial with the title "Good Riddance" (183). The syllabus, which had never been read outside of the planning committee, was nonetheless dismissed as a "PC" effort to push a left-wing political agenda. The call was to teach "just writing"—an evidently neutral technology. English 306 was scuttled because it did not reduce writing to a discrete set of mechanical "user skills," but instead conceived it as a mode of learning and a means to public participation.

The administrative politics of these events are all too familiar. One of the goals of those who opposed the "politicization" of English 306, according to Brodkey, was to "colonize" the department by suggesting that it was "incapable of self-governance" ("Troubles" 188). A leading opponent offered a plan that called for placing the English department under receivership. University administration undermined departmental decision-making processes. As Brodkey explains, "Whenever an administration gratuitously contravenes decisions, it colonizes the department's intellectual life along with its administrative autonomy" (189). The story of English 306 is the story of pedagogical innovation sacrificed to the vagaries of administrative expediency. Nothing could make this clearer than the fact that the syllabus for Writing about Difference was ignored outside of the committee. The syllabus was firmly grounded in rhetorical theory; it was premised on the analytical study of U.S. court cases; and it encouraged students to develop their own argument vis-à-vis the issues raised in these "hard cases" (see Penticoff and Brodkey). But none of this is germane here because the syllabus never entered the debate. There came a point for the administration at which political pressures made it expedient to dismiss *whatever* the syllabus represented—and that is precisely what it did.

My second example shows clearly that Texas has hardly cornered the market on administrative progressivism. On the other side of the country, and somewhat more recently, we have seen the dismantling of open admissions and remedial education at the City University of New York. I begin with a brief reconstruction of recent events surrounding this development.[11]

In 1970, CUNY became an open admissions university, despite claims by those on the right (then–Vice President Spiro Agnew, for instance) that the system was pampering the "new barbarians" who had come to storm civilization's gates (Horner and Lu 8, 14, 34). (Compare this sentiment with the fear of philistinization in the Progressive Era.) But CUNY pushed ahead and has been an open admissions institution and a leader in the democratization of higher education for the past thirty years. In May 1998, however, and again in January 1999, the fear of the philistines reemerged, and the Board of Trustees of the City University voted to deny admission to CUNY's senior colleges to students who failed to pass proficiency exams in writing, reading, and math. (This despite the fact that almost one-half of the 13,000 students entering CUNY's senior colleges each year fail at least one proficiency exam.) The board also voted to do away with most remedial courses at the senior colleges, thus forcing students who need remedial help to turn to one of the system's two-year colleges—or, as Mayor Giuliani evidently hoped, to privatized remedial programs.

Giuliani has played a crucial role in the dismantling of open admissions at CUNY. In November 1997, citing the need for "higher standards," the mayor threatened to cut off the city's $111 million allocation to CUNY unless the colleges cut remedial courses (Healy). In January 1998, he stepped up his attack by calling simultaneously for privatized remediation for writing, reading, and math skills and for an end to open admissions to CUNY. As Richard Stone, a Giuliani-appointed CUNY trustee, pointed out, Giuliani is not doing away with remediation, but rather relocating it "to either the community colleges or to a private provider" (Healy A26). In an effort to determine how best to shift the burden of remediation, Giuliani appointed a task force headed by Benno Schmidt Jr., director of the Edison Project, a program which is working to establish a national network of for-profit schools (Healy and Schmidt; Arenson). We could ask for no clearer indication of Giuliani's insistence that education should operate on the principles of "free market" than his appointment of this nationally known advocate for privatizing public schooling.

As I write, a New York judge has placed a temporary injunction on moving forward with the board's plans; by the time readers come across this account, it will, no doubt, be dated. But whatever the ultimate outcome of these events, it is clear that Mayor Giuliani, Governor Pataki, and the board appointees have tapped into administrative progressive values to buttress their challenge to open admissions and remedial education at CUNY. Their rallying cry, of course, is "higher standards," though some observers have claimed that administrative expediency—or, worse, the deliberate banning of the philistines, those lower-income whites and ethnic minorities who do not meet CUNY's arguably white-middle-class-biased entrance requirements—is what is really at stake. Like the "apolitical" businessmen and local officials who came in to take over the "inefficient" public schools of the Progressive Era, the businesspeople and local officials in New York are applying "sound business practice" to this public institution, treating it as a competitive business venture rather than a public trust. And they do so in the name of efficiency, economy, standards, and "good common sense."

Some of Composition and Rhetoric's most thoughtful and visible scholar-teachers work in the CUNY system, including Barbara Gleason, Karen Greenberg, Ira Shor, and Mary Soliday. While there are some fundamental disagreements among them (see Shor's "Our Apartheid" and Greenberg's response), perhaps the most important point to make here is that, despite their valiant efforts, their work is often trumped by the outside "experts" who make policy decisions. Indeed, I have come across only one citation by one of these "experts" of the ideas of people who actually work in these programs: in May 1998, a conservative CUNY trustee used Shor's thoughtful critique of basic writing in support of his position that remedial education ought to be removed from the senior colleges. (See Collins's warning about just this possibility in the *Journal of Basic Writing*.) By contrast, unsupported assumptions by those who are not educators at all are hardly in short supply: *Of course* standards should be higher. *Of course* standards and access are in conflict. *Of course* remediation has no place in four-year colleges. *Of course* basic writing is failing. *Of course* CUNY needs to be made more efficient. *Of course* the best way to do that is to downsize and outsource.

The tragedy of the CUNY situation is that important pedagogical and political work is being erased by those who control the enterprise. For instance, Gleason and Soliday conducted a three-year pilot project in which "remedial" students were mainstreamed into "regular" (and, significantly, credit-bearing) college composition courses. That is, students who had been placed by the CUNY Writing Assessment Test (CWAT) into basic writing courses were enrolled in a course alongside those who had placed into the regular (nonremedial) first-year course. This rigorously designed empirical study generated some interesting conclusions, the most important of which is that the CWAT—a single, impromptu writing exam—is not a good indicator of pass rates for either the first-year writing course or related humanities courses. That is, Gleason and Soliday found no statistically significant differences in pass rates between the students who had been coded "basic" and those who had not (Gleason, "Evaluating").

Considering that students who wish to enter one of CUNY's senior colleges must pass a battery of tests that includes the CWAT, this study should prove sobering for those who support this policy. According to Gleason, however, such has not been the response to the study:

> One influential professor was heard to say many times that such a finding could only mean that students did very little writing in those courses. A more serious concern was voiced by our college's provost, who expressed the view that journalists and other CUNY critics (including, for example, some of CUNY's own trustees)

would use the results of this study to argue that City College "lacks standards." (579)

The real conclusion to be drawn here—and this is, heartbreakingly, the conclusion of Gleason's article—is that the "empirically verifiable account that we were striving for in this evaluation was fatally compromised by the socio-political forces that had gathered around the issue of remediation" ("Evaluating" 582).

Like Brodkey's first-year writing course, basic writing at CUNY's senior colleges is being phased out not because its pedagogy is seen as bankrupt, but because it has become a political and administrative nuisance. The troubles in New York, like the troubles in Texas, signal that pedagogy itself has become collateral damage in the war over student "illiteracy." Moreover, they show us that those who teach, administer, and take required composition courses often have little control over how the courses function.

## Composition and Rhetoric Contained?

On the other hand, even in bleak stories such as Gleason's, there is reason to be hopeful. Gleason does point out that the study "has placed on the record a fact that is there to be seen by those who wish to see it" ("Evaluating" 582). While this must seem cold comfort for those whose work tends to be scrutinized only by those who seem committed to *not* seeing, it is also true that our field as a whole has produced an impressive body of work that resists the reincorporation of the schools and the functionalism that attends it.

To take a single but apt example, consider the work the field has done on assessment. As the role of the CWAT in the struggles over remediation at CUNY and the role of standardized tests in the reincorporation of the schools suggest, assessment is often the conservative linchpin of administrative progressivism. While this is not the place for a full survey of the enormous body of work that Composition and Rhetoric has produced in response, it is worth tracing its contours, if only to show that despite our demonstrable marginalization in public debates over literacy, compositionists continue to develop responsible, pedagogy-oriented alternatives to standardized testing and the administrative progressive values it represents.

Recently we have seen a spate of collections on assessment by highly visible scholars in the field (Belanoff and Dickson; Black, Daiker, Sommers, and Stygall; Cooper and Odell; Graves and Sunstein; White, Lutz, and Kamusikiri; and Yancey and Weiser). We've also seen the appearance of a new journal devoted exclusively to writing assessment (*Assessing Writing*), as well as a Conference on College Composition and Communication (CCCC) position statement on assessment (CCCC Committee on Assessment). Although it would be too reductive to say that the field has developed a single theory or framework for assessment, it is true that much of this work is informed by what we might call a *constructivist* orientation to teaching and learning.

As Murphy and Grant suggest, the term "constructivism" connotes a theory that treats knowledge-making as a process of interaction between and among teachers and learners, rather than (as in functionalism) the transmission of skills and bits of information. Within the constructivist framework, assessment is part of the process of constructing knowledge, not a disinterested subsequent measurement of what has been learned (or memorized). It guides teachers and students in making choices about their teaching and learning by offering them a portrait of where they are as knowledge-makers. Murphy and Grant explain:

> In the constructivist perspective, assessment procedures are inevitably a part of the dialectic of teaching and learning, part of the process that defines what is learned and what knowledge is. Thus a constructivist perspective acknowledges the role of assessment in defining the curriculum. Placed at the service of instruction, writing assessment helps teachers hear individual students' voices, discover the strategies students are using, and discover the knowledge students have already constructed. Assessment becomes an opportunity for planning the next move in the conversation. Further, assessment provides a means for engaging students in self-reflection and for acknowledging their role as collaborators in the learning process. (288)

Clearly, constructive assessment shares John Dewey's fundamental pedagogical principle: teachers and students must collectively determine the purposes, forms, and functions of their work to-gether through reflective action. Indeed, the fundamental insight of constructivist assessment is that teachers and learners must themselves develop and apply assessment as part of the reflective activity (or, as I have termed it, *reflexive inquiry*) of pedagogy. Assessment becomes a means of producing "reflexive knowledge": knowledge about how and why knowledge is made. Outside "ex-perts" cannot do this work for teachers and learners.

The most important device for constructivist assessment in writing has been the portfolio, about which the field has pro-duced an enormous amount of scholarship (e.g., Belanoff and Dickson; Belanoff and Elbow; Camp and Levine; Daiker, Sommers, and Stygall; Elbow and Belanoff; Graves and Sunstein). In fact, for the past twenty years, compositionists have tirelessly explored the virtues of portfolios, arguing that they help teachers to consider students' writing development over time; offer a "por-trait" (to use a familiar term) of students' "multiple literacies" across genre and purpose; involve students in the assessment pro-cess; align assessment with process-based classroom instruction; give students "ownership" over their own writing; and so on. While some compositionists have warned against the unreflec-tive use of portfolios (Belanoff; Condon and Hamp-Lyons; El-bow, "Will"; Forbes; Hamilton; Hamp-Lyons and Condon; Huot; Reither and Hunt), this assessment tool represents a powerful intellectual response to the simple-minded devotion to standard-ized testing at all levels of education.

In fact, portfolios are used widely in writing classrooms across the grade levels, in large part owing to the efforts of compo-sitionists. At the same time, as the examples discussed earlier show, despite compositionists' status as writing experts in the academy, latter-day administrative progressivism continues to shape the national mandates for literacy and literacy education, and functionalist approaches to literacy continue to hold sway in the public imagination. Although we have grown impressively as an academic specialization (with all the familiar trappings: jour-nals, book series, conferences, programs, hires, etc.), we—like our colleagues in the schools—are typically not given central roles in the script for educational reform. In fact, as we ponder events such as those in Texas and New York, we might begin to suspect that our position in the academy allows for a kind of containment that would be difficult to achieve otherwise.

Does this mean that administrative progressivism has finally won out over pedagogical progressivism, and that Composition and Rhetoric is doomed to languish in academic impotence? On the contrary, as I make clear in the second half of this book, I believe that it is possible to reframe and reclaim pedagogical progressivism for the twenty-first century. I also believe that compositionists and writing teachers can be at the forefront of this reform effort, making more effective use of the hard thinking we have done on assessment and on teaching and writing more generally. But we will need to think carefully about how to "progress" as a discipline and as an institutional, social, and pedagogical enterprise. This is why I turn in Chapter 3 to a vision of "progress"—critical pedagogy—that commits itself to rewriting the grand narrative of the reincorporation of the schools, but which I argue finally limits our "progress" toward pedagogical progressivism.

# On Institutional Literacy

*Fall 1993*. The snow swirls as I rush across the campus of the two-year women's college near Boston where I have taken my first adjunct position as a writing instructor. Headed for the warmth of the student center and morning coffee, I notice that the display window maintained by the fashion design department is frosted over. As I pass, a professor from that department steps out, motions for me to stop.

She seems agitated; she exhales long streams of vapor. "Why is it," she asks without introduction (too cold for pleasantries), "these students can't write?"

My head spins. These students can't write? None of them? Are they illiterate? Bad spellers? Can't use commas? And I'm responsible for this? And I can "fix" this?

Before I can formulate a response, she adds, "You have to keep on top of them. You're not doing them any favors by being lax on grammar. These kids need to be able to function in their jobs. Just give them what they need."

I don't know what to say. I stammer, I stutter, and all I am able to say is "Thanks for the advice." And I rush off, even more quickly now, through the snow.

---

*Fall 1993*. I am just out of my master's program: lots of ideas about *the* classroom, little experience in classroom*s*. But here— at *this* college—*this* classroom is located in a specific set of institutional and cultural contexts. And it is populated by a specific, complicated group of students. Many, though not all, are lower- and lower-middle-income women from Boston and surrounding communities; many, though not all, are first-generation college students whose families at one time worked, and sometimes still work, in the all-but-defunct mill towns of eastern Massachusetts; many, though not all, are students of color; many, though not all, have come here to learn writing "skills" that will serve them well in the workplace.

But the point is this: As I stand before this diverse group of students in this strange place for the first time, I am not thinking these things. Because I have worked all summer to envision a "critical classroom," I don't realize that I should be thinking these things. I don't suspect that it matters who shows up here.

I have organized my Writing about Literature course around "identity and representation" in African American literature. Although I have been told by my program director that at the end of my course I must document students' ability to apply a clearly delineated set of writing "skills" (utilize strategies for getting started, document sources, use grammatical sentences, generate thesis statements), I think my (subversive) choice of topic has ensured that I will do more than purvey a merely functional literacy. Students will "connect" with the material; they will "relate"; they will be empowered.

But they don't; they won't; they aren't.

––––––––––––

*Fall 1993.* What do I know, really, about them? How can I "start where they are" if I don't *know* where they are? How could I know what they will find relevant? These are not, after all, the eighteen-year-old New Hampshire-ites I taught last year.

The social debates between Booker T. Washington and W. E. B. Du Bois have been met with "that's ancient history"; Zora Neale Hurston's stories have been met with "the language is too hard to read"; Toni Morrison's *The Bluest Eye* has been met with "I guess we just don't go in for all that political stuff." Students will not talk to me about anything but grammar, citations, thesis statements, and the like. And how can I be surprised? Why *would*, how *could* they trust me?

As I stand before this diverse group of students in this strange place for the last time, I am thinking these things.

I ask students what has gone wrong. Perhaps hoping to win some sympathy, or even—can I admit this?—some gratitude, I remind them that I could have chosen more traditional texts.

"You might as well have," they tell me.

"But why?" I ask, thoroughly confused.

"Because," comes the reply, "in here, we made them just another set of texts."

A critical teacher, my Freire books teach me, makes the invisible visible. But my students are teaching me how blind *I* am, how much they can see that I cannot. A critical teacher demystifies, but I am learning how mystified *I* am, and how much they can see *through* that I cannot.

------

*Spring 1994.* The Writing I course. I am to teach, students are to learn, and we are to document "basic writing skills": correct usage, grammar, citation format—the familiar pieties. Last semester, I taught Writing about Literature, a disaster by all accounts.

I bring in a syllabus but only a skeleton schedule. I prepare a few readings; we can decide collaboratively on the rest. On the first day, I read from the syllabus:

> Individually and collaboratively, you will design writing projects intended for "real" readers, not the General Reader or Generic Teacher. I don't want you to think of yourselves as *student-writers* in here, but as *writers*: people who use language to pursue a variety of goals, and who view writing as worthy of careful reflection. We will be learning both *by* writing and *about* writing in the company of other writers and readers. We will "go public" with our writing by entering conversations that are personally meaningful and engaging to others.

Most of the students look at me as if I have called them a bad name. But I continue: "We will begin the course by forming focus groups and choosing topics to research and write about together.

Each group will be responsible for contextualizing the topic, the readings, and the writing of the group members."

Then I stop. It is all I have. I feel guilty, unprepared, unrigorous. I wonder if the students will drop the course—or worse, tell my program director that I hadn't prepared.

But they don't drop and they don't run to my program director. I will learn later that many are confused (why is he doing this to us?), some excited (this should be *easy*), some curious (maybe he's *crazy*), some intrigued (this *could be* interesting), some indifferent (what*ever*). These are the makings of the most difficult, the most challenging, the most frustrating, the most exciting course I have taught.

---

*Spring 1994.* Nicole, Joan, and Mary have formed a focus group on multicultural education. Nicole has written about her Asian American heritage and specifically about Japanese internment during World War II; Joan has written about the need for white women such as herself to connect with women of other cultures under the banner of feminism; Mary, who is from Greece, has written about how the battles over multicultural education mirror struggles over immigration.

In our workshop, their classmates are clearly hesitant to engage their ideas; instead they focus solely on grammar and mechanics. When the women patiently return the conversation to their notions about multiculturalism, the response is this: "How about letting us up with all this PC shit?"

I want to defuse this but also make it more concrete. "How about my Writing about Literature class?" I ask the focus group, describing it to them. "Is this what you have in mind when you say 'multicultural education'?"

"What did you do with the material?" Nicole asks.

"Did you just treat them like any other texts?" Mary wants to know.

"That's not multicultural," Joan points out.

How could students know so easily what I work so hard to begin to appreciate?

The class discussion continues well into the next class period. We talk about my assumptions, about the limits of the pedagogy I had imagined for Writing about Literature. Many others are interested now. This isn't just "PC shit" anymore; we're talking about education—their education. And mine: They ask and I tell about the town in which I was raised. I tell them of the conservative New Hampshire community; the fear and loathing of the "apartment people" who lived—literally—on the other side of the tracks; the one African American family that moved to my town when I was in high school and the complaints of "reverse discrimination" by white boys who didn't make the basketball team when the oldest black boy did. We talk about what "culture" means and who "has" it. We talk about home and about school, about the politics of reading multicultural texts, the politics of *not* reading them. We talk about what constitutes multicultural texts and courses. And, most important, we talk about the texts that Nicole, Mary, and Joan have written, not as editors searching for mechanical errors, but as writers and readers engaged in meaningful conversation with other writers and readers.

Two hours later, few positions have changed, and several white women continue to insist that they have no culture at all. But maybe—maybe—some students leave our discussion, as I do, asking new sets of questions.

---

*Summer 1994.* Nicole, Joan, and Mary approach me. "We want you to be staff advisor for the school newspaper," they tell me. "Why me?" I ask.

"Because," they answer, "you're the Man and we need you to get what we want."

I laugh. As a part-time adjunct, I am surely not "the Man" in quite the way they suspect. But then, they recognize in me, this white man with a ring on his finger, a potential ally who "has" the authority to help them implement their projects. They understand that while I exercise power *over* them by virtue of my role as instructor, I can also exercise power *with* them by using my institutional privilege, limited though it is, to further their project. They also realize the power that *they* might exercise if they can write their way into the community. I am not "one of them," but with me, they can "work together across differences" (Ellsworth 106) to perform the campus interventions they have in mind. They have what I largely lack: institutional literacy.

———————

*Fall 1994.* Nicole is editor of the newspaper. Mary and Joan are staff writers and editors. Several other students, all from my current Writing I course, are working with us as well. (The newspaper is one option among many for participation in a writing project outside of class.) On this campus where functional literacy is the order of the day, the program director of the fashion department has responded in print to our work:

> [I]t is refreshing to find a group of students willing to stand up and express their opinions and beliefs no matter how they may be received by society. I feel you have struck a positive blow for diversity and at the same time a slap in the face of prejudice and ignorance.

In the past few months, we have run articles and editorials on a lesbian support group on campus, AIDS awareness, multiculturalism, the Homes for the Hills project (which built homes for poor people in rural West Virginia), religious diversity, women of color in the workplace, safety for women on campus, and inner-city poverty. The once entertainment-oriented newspaper is now the center of a vital learning community.

Nicole, Mary, and Angela are in my office. Angela, an African American student in my Writing I class, reads the end of an editorial she has written: "College is to prepare us for life in the great expanse of the world and the one thing that does not come out of the texts or notes is how to be a strong woman."

Nicole, remembering something, picks up a copy of the paper and reads from her own editorial: "Multicultural studies opens the door for all people of every race, creed and color, and reminds us that we can only live with one another if we can first understand each other. Knowledge sets the foundation to understanding, and without education we will remain socially blind to those around us."

"I guess," she says to Angela, "I have more faith in education than you do."

"But," I wonder aloud, "does knowledge always lead to understanding? And does understanding always lead to justice, or even to living well together?"

Mary wonders, too: "Besides, is this what we're getting here, at school? Are you learning about other cultures? Is studying making you a strong woman?"

"I was already a strong woman," says Nicole. "But yes, some of it has made me stronger. The paper has. Having people come up to me and tell me that I made them think, that they changed their minds or their actions because of what we wrote about abortion or poverty or homosexuality or whatever—that makes me stronger."

"But that's the paper," says Angela, "not school."

"It's both," says Nicole.

*This*, I am thinking, *is how it sounds when writers talk.*

---

*Spring 1995.* I am stopped in the hallway by a full-time literature professor.

"Looks like you're making liberals out of the whole bunch of them," he says.

"I'm not making anything of them," I say.

"Then they must be remaking themselves in your presence."

A condescending joke. But maybe he is not entirely wrong. I have remade myself in their presences as well; their presences—their differences—have made a difference. This is what writers do: continually remake themselves in the presence of others. They use language to construct themselves and their relations to the world and others in that world. They use language to envision and revision their selves-in-relation (Lee).

But the only "commonsense" explanation that institutional arrangements offer for the students' campus interventions is that a (white, male, heterosexual) instructor must be making liberals of them. Institutional discourses don't position students as knowledge-makers, as interventionists. Cultural discourses don't position young women (particularly women of color and lesbians) as knowledge-makers, as interventionists. These subjectivities must be forged; they cannot be given, or received, or imposed.

The script of critical pedagogy, which I am still learning, has taught me that my job is to enlist students in my critical projects, but here they have enlisted me in *their* critical projects. I am not naive enough to think that my participation in those projects doesn't change them, that my authority over them doesn't matter, but I also understand that that authority matters *differently* because they have written themselves into the script of institutional reform as knowledge-makers, as interventionists.

And yet this work is not easy, and sometimes our differences are not conducive, or generative, or even particularly interesting. Sometimes we tire of each other, of the self-important mantle we have taken on, of the endless work and the meager rewards. It is difficult to work, always, within and against. Sometimes we wonder if it wouldn't just be simpler, safer, and more fun if I were The Teacher and they were The Students. And we know by now that most of us will move on next year (I, for one, am leaving this adjunct position and returning for my Ph.D.); we will not return to the newspaper or to the school. Maybe the work will continue without us—we have promising replacements—but we do not know. Our interventions might be short-lived indeed.

But then we remember what we're doing: we are working hard not to be "socially blind," as Nicole writes, "to those around us." And this work, we know, never ends.

# CHAPTER THREE

# Critical Pedagogy:
# Another Progressivism

I began this book by recalling my sense in graduate school that Composition and Rhetoric and critical pedagogy were virtually inseparable. The collections to which we were introduced—*Composition and Resistance, Contending with Words, Left Margins, The Politics of Writing Instruction: Postsecondary,* to name a few—were clearly informed by the tenets of critical pedagogy. Moreover, the work of many of the Big Names in the field—Berlin; Bizzell; Brodkey; Faigley; Gilyard; Knoblauch and Brannon; Shor; Smitherman; Trimbur; Villanueva—was clearly in accord with, and often drew on, the critical pedagogy texts (Freire; Giroux; McLaren) that I had read before returning for my Ph.D. As a doctoral student in Composition and Rhetoric, I would have found it difficult *not* to take up critical pedagogy given the foothold it had developed in the field.

But what is the source of critical pedagogy's power? Why does it hold such allure for compositionists? How has this alliance shaped the work of Composition and Rhetoric? And what are the connections between critical pedagogy and the two "progressivisms" I have delineated? These are the questions that drive this chapter. They are important questions because while this alliance marks the field's most significant attempt to confront the latter-day administrative progressivism described in Chapter 2, many compositionists have come to question the wisdom of this rapprochement. In fact, I build on these critiques here to argue that our relationship with critical pedagogy has, ironically, drawn us *away* from pedagogical progressivism.

This chapter also marks a shift in this book. For the most part, I have confined myself thus far to discursive analysis—of *English Journal* during the early decades of this century (Chapter 1) and of more recent public discourse on educational and literacy reform (Chapter 2). I continue this analytical work throughout the rest of the book, but beginning with this chapter, I also write toward new ways of thinking about our work as compositionists. That is, I start here to draw out implications of our history and our current scene for reimagining our work as a discipline of teachers and scholars.

## Another Progressivism

I use the term "critical pedagogy" to name a discursive field whose boundaries are fluid but nonetheless marked by certain broadly conceived commitments. Drawing on the critical theory of the Frankfurt School, on Gramscian concepts of hegemony and resistance, and on Freirean notions of "conscientization," critical pedagogy opposes functionalist views of schooling, whether these views emerge from the corporate right or the economic and cultural reproduction theories of the left (see Apple, *Education;* Aronowitz and Giroux; Freire, *Education;* Giroux, *Theory;* Luke). Advocates of critical pedagogy, motivated by a democratic, often (neo-)Marxist political imperative, view education as a vehicle for individual empowerment and social reconstruction (see Giroux, *Border;* Giroux and McLaren; Giroux and Simon; Shor and Freire; Simon).

To name critical pedagogy as a set of discourses is to emphasize statements, concepts, constructions, assumptions, relationships, and strategies of/in language. It is also to call attention to how critical pedagogy functions: how it positions its writers, its readers, and its objects of study; how it is produced, disseminated, regulated, and received; how it affects the material realm. Moreover, to foreground discourses is to emphasize relations of power—between writers and readers of the discourses; between writers and their objects of study; between readers and objects of study; and so on. Jennifer Gore suggests that it is useful to apply Foucault's notion of "regime of truth" to discourses (Foucault's analysis of regimes of truth focuses on "society," not on discourses per se). Gore claims that discourses can be viewed as producing "normalizing technologies of the self," by which she means ways in which individuals come to internalize relations of power, thus "disciplining" themselves as a result of being subjected to certain discursive representations of themselves (*Struggle* 52–53).

An example may help to demonstrate this understanding of discourse. In response to Elizabeth Ellsworth's widely read critique of critical pedagogy as insufficiently attendant to material context and cultural/institutional positions of power, Henry Giroux and Peter McLaren, two of the most visible proponents of critical pedagogy, interrupt their theoretical arguments in the same issue of the *Journal of Education* to make an *ad hominem* strike at Ellsworth. They charge "Liz" with self-righteousness, bad faith, and "the type of careerism that has become all too characteristic of many left academics" (Giroux, "Border" 178). They also claim that Ellsworth's "self-professed lack of pedagogical success can hardly be blamed on a failed critical tradition but is rather attributable, at least in part, to her inability to move beyond her own self-doubt" (McLaren 72). Notice the discursive positioning accomplished here: the male *theorists*, who are buttressed by "tradition," strike out at a female *practitioner* (who is not understood as a theorist in her own right). Essentially, the argument here is that if critical pedagogy does not seem to live up to its far-reaching promises (as Ellsworth claims), the difficulty must reside in the "translation" to practice—in other words, in some personal failing of the practitioner. Thus, the male theorists and their "tradition" stand above and beyond critique; *they* can "hardly be blamed" for the female practitioner's failings. The tradition itself is construed as a stable and unified body of knowledge, a theoretical field on which practitioners can draw but to which they may not contribute. In this way, the discourse of critical pedagogy teaches practitioners to discipline themselves, to attribute classroom dissonance not to a gap or inconsistency in critical pedagogy, but to their own flawed execution of it.

This example is particularly apt because this chapter is about how critical pedagogy discursively positions students, teachers, and theorists. Gore's concept of the localized "regime of truth" is useful because it allows us to identify what we might call the "mainstream" discourse of critical pedagogy. It is possible to take up the term "critical pedagogy" without functioning within its regime of truth, just as it is possible to *not* take up the term but to function within its regime of truth nonetheless. When I refer to critical pedagogy, I have in mind what Giroux and McLaren refer to as the "critical tradition," or what poststructuralist feminists have insisted is the "male-authored" discourse of North American critical pedagogy. In what follows, I argue that this discourse, though named as a pedagogy, in fact positions students and teachers in *dis*empowering ways, and in doing so displaces pedagogy as I have defined it in this book (as reflexive inquiry) from the center of its project. Thus, critical pedagogy is a form of neither administrative nor pedagogical progressivism. Rather, it is a new strand of progressivism which is driven by a progressive politics and a belief in the possibility of social change through education, but which is not at heart a *pedagogical* project.

## "The Student," "the Teacher," and "the Theorist"

It is not difficult to see why compositionists would be attracted to critical pedagogy. The very term "critical pedagogy," after all, signals commitments that have been central to the history of our field. The first word in the term suggests a willingness to critique the status quo in the name of a more democratic social order; this is attractive to our "radicalized" field (Crowley, "Reimagining"; Faigley). The second word echoes progressive faith in the power of pedagogy to effect/affect social change; this, too, resonates with many compositionists' sense of—or, at any rate, hopes for—their work. Moreover, at the heart of critical pedagogy is the concept of critical literacy. Critical literacy is the means by which people intervene in the status quo by rereading and rewriting what has come to seem natural or common sense (see Lankshear and McLaren; Freire and Macedo). Although there is no one model for critical literacy either within Composition and Rhetoric or outside of it, this general notion has infused the work of the field, aiding a group of traditionally marginalized teacher-scholars in the development of intellectual and political frameworks for the teaching of writing. This has been important for many writing teachers during the reincorporation of the schools, when writing and teaching are devalued as mere functional skills. Placing one's labor in service of a more democratic social order strikes many writing teachers as far nobler than allowing it to serve its more traditional function of equipping students with skills that will serve them within existing social relations.

I count myself among this group of writing teachers. As Intralude 3 suggests, I was initially drawn to the intellectual and political frame that critical pedagogy offered for my work. I was drawn to the image of the transformative teacher:

> As teachers and scholars, we are bearers of critical knowledge that should empower others to make sense of their position in the world, become alert to the ideological workings of the cultural process, discover the neglected or suppressed aspects of the tradition, and seize the initiative to disrupt the hegemonic order. (Kecht 7)

When my first semester at the college turned out so disastrously, then, my conclusion was that I simply didn't "have" enough "critical knowledge" to "give" to others.

But I soon began to wonder: if critical pedagogy is a matter of giving critical knowledge to others, how is it different from the traditional, transmission pedagogies that Freire denounced in *Pedagogy of the Oppressed*? And where, I wondered, does this leave students? Janet Zandy claims that her students— "Reagan's kids"—are "emotionally flat" and, in their zeal for jobs, resistant to critical knowledge (37), but I knew that these students' resistance was more complicated than that. They may have wanted good jobs (so, frankly, did I), but I couldn't see how that disqualified them from wanting—or perhaps even already having—"critical knowledge." It seemed to me then, and it seems to me now, that the students at the colleges in which I was teaching (not unlike students I have subsequently taught in state universities) stubbornly refused to conform to the construction of "the student" offered by critical pedagogy.

This construction emerges clearly in the "critical" Composition and Rhetoric text *Left Margins*. The editors open the collection by identifying the impetus for their project as "the general invisibility to students of the work of culture" (ix). As Fitts and France tell the story, their initial proposal emerged out of conversations that turned on cultivating that moment of (sometimes profound) rhetorical conflict between the teacher's articulation of an oppositional stance—an agenda that moves against the political grain—and the student's resistance to it: how teachers prepare for contention, generate it, receive it, and use it as a further teaching occasion; how students respond to the teacher, each other, the texts, and activities when asked to read culture critically. (x)

The actions ascribed to each group are telling: teachers cultivate, articulate, prepare, generate, receive, and use—while students *respond*. "The teacher" runs against "the political grain," while "the students" run *with* it (for they will resist an "oppositional stance"). Students are not imagined as living, breathing, material bodies with various and varying interests, investments, motivations, faiths, and beliefs, but rather as purely reactive (and reactionary) mechanisms. And those reactions are predictable, accessible before they walk into the classroom.

Numerous contributors to *Left Margins* follow their editors' lead in assuming that culture is invisible to students and that their job is to make it visible: Bodziock and Ferry ask students to inspect their previously unacknowledged "big stories" (42); Paul Gutjahr seeks to "give form to the invisible" (69); Kathleen Dixon helps her students "to see what is ordinarily invisible" (112); Christopher Wise seeks "to alert students to their own ideological subjectivity" (129); Donald Lazere hopes to "remediat[e] many students' near-vacuum of knowledge about political terminology and ideology" (193)—and the list goes on. The notion that students are culturally blind, and that critical teachers can bring them sight, is ubiquitous in this volume.

This is not to suggest that the contributors to *Left Margins* are somehow corrupt; in fact, I suspect they are dedicated teachers who care deeply about students. Nor is it to deny that *all* teachers walk into classrooms with "prior texts"—ideas about students, goals for the course, pedagogical and political commitments, and so on. It does seem, however, that the discourse of critical pedagogy often functions to cast teachers and students in oppositional and seemingly immutable roles that are extremely difficult to rewrite from within that discourse, that regime of truth. Critical pedagogy defines and predetermines the pedagogical script, with uncritical students and critical teachers dutifully playing their prescribed roles. Although every teacher and student knows that classroom interactions almost never follow predetermined scripts, these discourses exert pressure on the narrating teacher to "read" (and later to write) classroom interactions through this unchanging, inflexible prior text.

Consider, for instance, how Ira Shor—perhaps the critical pedagogue who has done the most to represent classroom practice in his scholarship—poses the relationship between "the teacher" and "the student." According to Shor, critical pedagogy uses dialogue to "bridge" the "grand cultural canyon" between teacher and student culture (*When* 24). In *Empowering Education,* he calls for the creation of a "border culture," a "learning area between students' speech and understandings and those of the teacher" (203). The teacher poses problems within this borderland to create a "third idiom" (255). This dialectic presumes a strict binary between "teacher culture" and "student culture." In this way, the "dialogic" model deployed by critical pedagogy can elide differences among students and teachers even as it calls for interrogation of the differences between "the teacher" and "the student."

On the other side of the "grand cultural canyon" from students, we find critical teachers, bearers of "critical knowledge," who dedicate their days not only to student change but to broad social change as well. "Transformative intellectuals" seek to transform not only their students, schools, or communities, but indeed "the larger society" (Aronowitz and Giroux 46). James Berlin explains:

> Transformative teachers must also work outside the school to make possible the conditions of the critical classroom. They must join with other transformative teachers as well as with established teacher associations. . . . Teachers must become involved in school board elections, in local school councils, and in parent-teacher groups, articulating their democratic and liberating notions of schooling. They must also support alone and collectively political candidates, as well as form alliances with other groups working for emancipation—with ecologists, feminists, peace groups, trade unions, and neighborhood groups. ("Teacher" 13; see also Shor, "Educating")

Although I support political action by teachers and work with teachers in my home state on a number of political initiatives, I worry that this construction of the transformative intellectual ignores the temporal and administrative constraints that teachers face daily. Consider a typical day for a high school English teacher: she teaches writing and reading to 150 to180 students (six classes of twenty-five to thirty students each). She runs an after-school writing club or reading circle, coaches a sports team, or organizes a drama club or debating team. Because she has a late meeting in which she is "debriefed" on the standardized test she must administer next week (this on top of the curriculum meeting her principal wanted her to "sit in on"), she heads home late to her own family, carrying with her the fifty student papers she didn't get to during her free period because she was returning phone calls to parents and the printer who had misplaced the student anthology disk. In the discourse of critical pedagogy, all this work is only a minor aspect of the transformative project. Now she "must" focus her attention on transforming the larger society, even though she knows that when she goes public with her politics, she'll be called in again to her district office for another stern lecture about the need to be more discreet.

The point I want to make here is not that we (researchers, scholars, theorists) should not involve teachers in political projects, but that when we do, we must be sensitive to what is at stake for whom in such an endeavor (indeed, this question seems to me a fundamentally critical gesture). What risks are we asking teachers to take? What sacrifices are we asking them to make? And, significantly, what risks will *we* take? What sacrifices will *we* make? If we don't account for the risks and sacrifices of others, and if we don't theorize our own participation in such projects, we risk disempowering teachers through posing a limited and limiting expert/teacher or theorist/practitioner hierarchy.

In other words, we perpetuate what Peter Vandenberg calls "institutional clientism." In the institutional and disciplinary economy that privileges the production of scholarly text over what Vandenberg calls "local values" (chiefly teaching), teachers are too often "clientized," made mere consumers of the authorized knowledge of researchers. In the case of critical pedagogy, this explicitly pedagogical discourse aimed at teacher and student empowerment often reinscribes a class system in which researchers (the managers) hand down knowledge and projects to teachers (the workers), who are expected merely to absorb that knowledge and execute those projects. The relationship between the critical theorist and the critical teacher thus reenacts the relationship between critical teachers and unenlightened students. Both students and teachers are imagined as objects of their more critical betters. Despite Freire's insistence on "beginning with where [students] are," pedagogy is too often theorized not with teachers and students, but for and around them. In fact, under the conception of pedagogy I have posed in this book—the process of reflexive, shared inquiry—much of critical pedagogy does not represent pedagogy at all, even sometimes when it *is* focused on teaching.

## Transforming the Transformative Intellectual: Toward Institutional Literacy

Of course, I am not the first to be troubled by the relationships posed in critical pedagogy between teachers and students and between theorists and teachers. We've seen a number of important feminist critiques of critical pedagogy's inattention to the en-gendered, em-bodied relationships that attend teaching (Ellsworth; Lather; Lee; McWilliam; Orner; Todd) as well as the theorist/teacher hierarchy (Gore, *Struggle,* "What"; Luke and Gore, Introduction, "Women"; Luke; Walkerdine). Several critiques emerging from Composition and Rhetoric have focused on the unrealistic, unattractive, and even disempowering discursive positions that critical pedagogy offers to teachers and students (Elbow, "Pedagogy"; Goodburn; Janangelo; Lee; R. Miller, *As If;* North, "Rhetoric"). All of these critiques—some emerging from decidedly left positions—have put pressure on the teacher/student and theorist/teacher hierarchies in critical pedagogy.

In addition to—or as part of—reimagining these relationships, I believe that we need to rethink the relationship between "the transformative intellectual" and "the institution." In the discourses of critical pedagogy, the transformative intellectual is often posed as a universally oppositional force to institutional arrangements and structures that conspire against her or him. In C. Mark Hurlbert and Michael Blitz's "The Institution('s) Lives!," for instance, the academic institution is understood as a soulless, intrinsically conservative, self-perpetuating mechanism designed to appropriate all activities performed under its auspices. The institution insulates itself from effective critique by making itself inscrutable, extending "beyond the boundaries of the language needed to describe it" (67). Because academics are scripted by the institution itself, the only option open to transformative intellectuals[1] is to "create counter scenarios, staging places for improvisational actions designed to throw spotlights (perhaps search-lights) on the university and to inspire other, more perturbing scenarios" (69).

Although I find Hurlbert and Blitz's reading of the politics of institutionality instructive, their revised script poses the transformative intellectual as "the academy's moral conscience—the lone voice of the dreamer who is fundamentally opposed to the senseless but indomitable forces" of the institution (R. Miller, *As If* 201).[2] In claiming for the transformative teacher a uniformly oppositional role, this script limits the extent to which such a teacher might work both within and against the constraints endemic in any institutional context.[3] Instead of positioning the transformative intellectual as one who "reforms" students, faculty, the institution—indeed, all of society—by uniformly opposing all institutional constraints, we might more profitably rethink the variety of subject positions available to teachers, students, and administrators working within and against institutional constraints and possibilities. This means developing what I call *institutional literacy*—a notion and a practice that I believe is central to reframing and reclaiming pedagogical progressivism, as I show in the second half of this book. To be institutionally literate is to be able to read institutional discourses (and their resultant arrangements and structures) so as to speak and write back to them, thereby participating in their revision.

Crucial here, of course, is the notion that institutions are in fact revisable. While it is undeniable that institutions change slowly and incrementally, it is also true that they do change. In fact, we might say that institutions are in constant states of change and flux. It's just that this change isn't typically visible on any given day. Porter, Sullivan, Blythe, Grabill, and Miles define institutions as "rhetorical systems of decision making that exercise power through the design of space (both material and discursive)" (621). And while individuals are rarely in positions to change those rhetorical systems with sweeping gestures, the systems themselves are constituted (and reconstituted) by and through the daily interaction of human participants. According to Porter et al.'s understanding of institutions, a reorganized Web site, a new teaching or research center, a curricular revision, a revitalized writing center, a new use of old technology—all of these, however local and seemingly minor, constitute institutional change. Indeed, critical attention to the local is fundamental to the methodology Porter et al. call "institutional critique": "[L]ocal institutions (and local manifestations of national or international ones) are important locations for written activity, and furthermore, we believe that constructing institutions as local and discursive spaces makes them more visible and dynamic and therefore more changeable" (621). I share these beliefs, and this is why throughout this book I write about local attempts to develop institutional literacy for institutional change. In Intralude 3, for instance, the women I was working with practiced institutional literacy and enacted institutional change. Intraludes 4, 5, and 6 all represent moments of collective efforts toward institutional change as well.[4]

Institutional literacy is not metaphorical; institutions are in fact sets of discourses that must be read and written by their participants. These discourses may take obvious, tangible forms such as bylaws, handbooks, codes of conduct, contracts, reappointment guidelines and merit reviews, memos, syllabi, and the like, but they are also made up of what David Tyack and Larry Cuban call the "grammar" of an institution—that is, the institutional habits and beliefs that guide its everyday work. Teachers do not teach "inappropriate" materials; students do not leave their seats until given permission to do so; teachers and students do not get "too friendly"—although these strictures may not be literally on the books, they are understood to govern institutional conduct nonetheless.

Once we understand institutional literacy as a *form* of literacy and not a metaphor for it, we begin to think in more complex ways about how transformative intellectuals might function in a variety of institutions. First, we would recognize that institutional literacy is an ongoing process. Literacy researchers have long argued that literacy is not learned and practiced in isolated, discrete steps, and so we should not expect institutional literacy to make itself visible in isolated and dramatic moments. We should also not expect institutional literacy to develop in a linear fashion; like all forms of literacy, it is recursive and often uneven. We are better positioned (and, frankly, more willing) at certain moments to intervene in institutional scripts than we are at other moments. Finally, if literacy is an ongoing intellectual process, it is also an ongoing social process. As literacy theorists have shown, literacy necessarily involves interaction and engagement with others (see, e.g., Baynham; Brandt; S. B. Heath). Although we tend to think of institutions as mechanisms that function beyond the control of human efforts, they function through administrative, curricular, and pedagogical practices and the people who practice (and resist) them. Institutional literacy is no less a matter of social engagement, of collective action, than other forms of literacy.

What does all this mean for our rethinking of the transformative intellectual? It means giving up the notion that transformative intellectuals rewrite institutional scripts only or primarily in dramatic moments that bring about drastic and immediate institutional change. It means letting go of the idea that the transformative intellectual is like Emerson's Romantic Poet—the inspired Genius who possesses caste knowledge that would set ordinary people free, if only they were open to it. It means that instead of thinking of the transformative mandate as transmitting "critical" knowledge in isolated moments, we might think of it as developing the collective ability—with our colleagues *and* our students—to read and write, and *re-vision*, institutional discourses.

It is particularly important to think with more complexity about students' potential roles in challenging repressive institutional and cultural forces and arrangements. In fact, I suspect that the most effective way to mobilize wide-scale institutional literacy for transformative ends would be to open up the category of transformative intellectual to students—or, more accurately, to recognize that students often do function as transformative intellectuals and to nurture that function. At the least, we need to acknowledge that students, like us, are positioned in various relations of institutional power, and that they also have much to gain by becoming familiar with the institutional constraints and possibilities in the context in which they work and live. Without institutional literacy, they, like us, run the risk of becoming institutionalized, mystified by what appear to be inscrutable institutional relations.

## From Critical Tradition to Critical Practice

When I think of why it is important to involve teachers and students in educational reform, to listen to their voices and their experiences, I think of projects I have learned about in the Nebraska Writing Project:

- ◆ A fourth-grade teacher and her students collaborate every year to write kid-friendly assessment rubrics—complete with drawings by the kids—so that everyone has a hand both in setting learning goals and working toward them.

- ◆ A middle school teacher and her students share their writing portfolios with peers, other adults in their school, parents, and community members. These portfolios become part of the conversation—part of the very identity, she tells us—of the school by giving students' words a prominent place in the institution.

- ◆ A high school teacher ("the pastor's wife," she says with a wry smile) teaches a unit on the Holocaust at her Lutheran school by having her students study other annihilation programs: Stalin's killing of Ukrainians; Pol Pot and the Khmer Rouge's slaughter of Cambodians; ethnic cleansing in Bosnia and Kosovo. She and her students then study incidents in U.S. history when "disposable peoples"—African American slaves, Native Americans, Japanese Americans during World War II—were systematically attacked and abused. Students perform their projects at a public reading.

Are these examples of critical pedagogy? Certainly, these teachers—who had never heard of critical pedagogy—didn't identify them as such. But these are just the kind of projects, in my view, that are the stuff of a sustained and sustaining grassroots school reform movement. In sharing these projects with us, participants in a state writing project, these teachers helped us think critically (again, asking *What's at stake for whom?*) about the politics of institutional literacy by talking reflectively about how far they and their students could and were willing to push the envelope at their schools and in their communities. Perhaps most important, they all understood themselves and their students as potential change-agents in those schools and communities.

I argue in Chapter 6 that compositionists can use their institutional and cultural leverage to support teachers and students like these who practice subtle and critical forms of institutional literacy every day. This is not a new concept, of course: compositionists around the country are already doing this work and have been for some time. Still, in our zeal for critical pedagogy, we risk devoting ourselves to discourse that effectively removes itself from this arena by idealizing the transformative intellectual and by not paying attention to specific institutional contexts.

Consider, for instance, the role—or lack thereof—of assessment in critical pedagogy. As I suggested in the previous chapter, Composition and Rhetoric has devoted a great deal of its energy to developing responsible alternatives to standardized testing. But critical pedagogy does not offer a theory or practice of assessment; indeed, its proponents rarely take up the issue at all. One searches in vain through texts such as the interdisciplinary *Critical Literacy* (Lankshear and McLaren) and the Composition and Rhetoric text *Left Margins* for talk of assessment. When it does show up in "critical composition," assessment is most often posed as anathema to the aims of critical pedagogy: "If we can do anything as writing teachers and as writers, it should be to stop teaching students to underwrite the university, to stop demanding written material which can be easily *gathered* and *assessed*" (Hurlbert and Blitz, "Resisting" 7).

Given the political significance of assessment, it is strange that assessment is not a systematic part of critical pedagogy's critique of educational politics. Typically, standardized testing is bundled with a number of other "regressive reforms"—school choice, reprivatization, vocationalism, watered-down multiculturalism, funding cuts, standardized curriculum, and the like—but critical pedagogues rarely go beyond simply mentioning the dangers of "teaching to the test." In *Education Still under Siege,* for instance, Aronowitz and Giroux promote the idea that teachers should control their own work, but they offer no program for wresting power over teachers' professional lives back from the remote "educational experts" who now hold it. Just ignore them, the writers seem to be saying, and become "transformative intellectuals" in spite of them. But as Aronowitz and Giroux's own treatment of the politics of educational reform would suggest, just ignoring *them* is hardly enough when *they* hold sway over educational common sense.

Ira Shor offers an exception to the rule that critical pedagogues do not concern themselves much with assessment. In his latest effort, *When Students Have Power,* Shor does write about assessment by focusing on how he grades students. But as constructivist assessment insists, grading is only a very small part of the larger intellectual practice of assessment (though it is perhaps what most critical pedagogues have in mind when they scoff at the word *assessment*). Shor's more substantial contribution to thinking on assessment comes in *Empowering Education*:

> [T]eachers and students need freedom from standardized tests, commercial textbooks, basal readers, and required syllabi. These traditional practices restrict student-centered, dialogic, and participatory education. There should be frequent and rigorous assessment of student learning. There need to be high standards for student development. But the instruments used to test and measure students should be based in a student-centered, cooperative curriculum. This means emphasizing narrative grading, portfolio assessments, group projects and performances, individual exhibitions, and essay examinations that promote critical thinking instead of standardized or short-answer tests. (144)

This will not be easy, Shor admits, because educational common sense supports those traditional practices. This is why it is imperative that critical pedagogy draw on and develop alternative assessment theories and practices. To date, though, few critical pedagogues have followed Shor's lead in exploring assessment. This is a crucial gap in critical pedagogy because assessment is the primary tool through which remote "experts" control the work of teachers and students. In eschewing assessment, critical pedagogy effectively cedes this powerful ideological ground to administrative progressives, who have used it to control not only classroom practices, but also teachers' willingness to get involved in educational reform. In this way, too, critical pedagogy draws Composition and Rhetoric further away from its radical roots in pedagogical progressivism.

Indeed, as I have suggested, instead of involving itself in the messy site of pedagogy, critical pedagogy has become another academic regime of truth. The *ad hominem* response of the most prominent advocates of critical pedagogy to thoughtful, if challenging, feminist critiques bears this out. In fact, in Giroux's and McLaren's responses to Ellsworth (recounted earlier), critical pedagogy functions much like Hurlbert and Blitz's institution: it insulates itself from effective critique by seeming to expand beyond the intelligibility of those who would critique it. This response not only disempowers practitioners, but also severely limits the purview of critical pedagogy. Again, it understands critical pedagogy as a body of knowledge, a theoretical tradition.

Interestingly, Bruce Horner turns the tables on Ellsworth, claiming that *she* is the one who treats critical pedagogy as a "commodity" (82). "Like an angry consumer," Horner writes, "she rejects critical pedagogy as repressive rather than liberatory, as a commodity that does not 'work' as advertised" (83). In support of this argument, Horner points to Ellsworth's response to students who questioned the meaning of the term "critical" in her syllabi: "I referred them to answers provided in the literature" (Ellsworth 92). Horner reads this as evidence that Ellsworth treats critical pedagogy as a fixed, stable product, a pedagogy that may be enacted in the same way irrespective of context. But Ellsworth's very point is that mainstream critical pedagogy offers very few representations of "actual, historically specific struggles" (92), and thus *presents itself* as a transportable commodity. While Horner faults Ellsworth for misreading "the pedagogy alone" (83), Ellsworth's point in the first place is that she had nothing other than the obviously unsatisfactory "answers in the literature" to which to refer students.

More important, the effect of this Ellsworth-Giroux-McLaren-Horner dialogue is that critical pedagogy remains uninspected, free from the kind of critique Ellsworth was attempting to initiate in the first place. Instead of inspecting how critical pedagogy works as a discourse and as a classroom practice, the conversation instead revolves around the supposed failures of a particular teacher/reader. In my view, critical pedagogy itself is put in peril by such a move. As John Dewey writes in *Experience and Education,* "any theory and set of practices is dogmatic which is not based upon critical examination of its own underlying principles" (22). If theorists of critical pedagogy do not enact this kind of self-scrutiny, critical pedagogy risks becoming a moribund set of social visions and prescriptions. As Purpel and Shapiro suggest, as theorists we "have the responsibility to avow and celebrate our convictions, but as educators we have further responsibility to look for other reasons than stupidity, denial, or false consciousness to explain the failure of some to accept our ideas" (116–17). The danger here is that critical pedagogy reenacts the top-down programs for reform proposed by administrative progressives. Teachers aren't written out of the script, but they are written into it in such problematic ways that it is difficult to imagine critical pedagogy garnering much support among what should be its power base: teachers—and students.

Moreover, while the chief virtue of critical pedagogy is its insistence that the status quo can be opposed and altered, its functioning at a remove from the lived experiences of teachers and students ironically reinforces the grand narrative of the reincorporation of the schools. It is true that theorists of critical pedagogy subscribe to what Aronowitz and Giroux call "resistance theories" and insist on a "discourse of hope" (Giroux, *Border;* see also Apple, *Education;* Giroux, *Theory*). But while critical pedagogy clears a theoretical space for meaningful agency for teachers and students, that space is constructed in such a way that most would-be transformative intellectuals will find it extremely difficult to see themselves in it. In fact, constructing the transformative intellectual as the "lone voice" who reforms his or her institution and society in a grand gesture effectively covers over important daily acts of resistance.

Mainstream critical pedagogy's vision of progress, then, is predicated on effecting sweeping social changes. Acts of resistance that do not effect such changes are labeled "reformist" and discarded as merely cosmetic.[5] Thus, critical pedagogy discounts visions and versions of progress that involve what Tyack and Cuban call "tinkering." On the other hand, I have begun to suggest that this kind of tinkering, which is the stuff of teachers' and students' lived experiences, is crucial to any meaningful, lasting program for educational and social reform. In the unpredictable and messy terrain of pedagogy, we are not likely to find many grand moments of social transformation, but we are likely to find important (though small, fleeting, and decidedly local) moments in which teachers and learners work together to assert their agency in the face of institutional and cultural scripts that do not assign them active or crucial roles.

Ellen Cushman has suggested that the notion of false consciousness, a central component of mainstream critical pedagogy, often leads theorists to ignore the important fact that in "the minute interactions taking place in contexts of highly asymmetrical power relations, individuals will both accommodate and resist, both reproduce and undermine, both enact and challenge" (*Struggle* 8–9). False consciousness is the notion that through the invisible workings of prevailing ideology, people—especially oppressed people—come to view their living conditions as a result of a natural order that they cannot control, and as a result they become passively or actively complicit in supporting the status quo. But Cushman argues that this argument doesn't account for the complexity of these lives and essentially blames the victim. She attempts to rewrite the notion of false consciousness by turning it on its head: "We must assume, instead, that individuals cultivate counterhegemonic ideologies in and from their everyday lives. Working from this assumption, we can better distinguish the nuances of strategic actions individuals employ in their daily strivings to gain resources and respect" (9).

Cushman's rewriting of agency is helpful because it refocuses our attention from critical literacy as a grand gesture of social transformation toward critical literacy as a strategic employment of institutional literacy in daily interactions. It also helps us counter the grand narrative of the conservative restoration and maintain some measure of real hope that we are not—as the "prophets of regress" teach us—inexorably falling ever deeper into a slough of despond. That narrative of regress—which critical pedagogy plays into when it raises the bar of "meaningful change" to impossible heights—is simply the flip side of that triumphalist story of progress which teaches us that every day, in every way, we are getting better, and one step closer to that finally enlightened future.

Although I believe that critical pedagogy has indeed reinforced the grand narrative of the reincorporation of the schools, once again I do not believe that this signals the ultimate victory of the forces of administrative progressivism over pedagogical progressivism. We cannot judge the effectivity of pedagogical progressivism until we see an educational and social movement which places pedagogy at its center; which functions from the bottom up (or the inside out) rather than the top down; which views the work that teachers and students do together as the sine qua non of reform; which harnesses the important work that teachers, students, and literacy workers in our communities are doing every day. For Cushman is right: "counterhegemonic" work *is* going on, all the time. The task, for those of us in positions of institutional privilege, is to recognize, push forward, and get a hearing for this work among various publics, including other teachers, community members, and policymakers.

As someone drawn to Composition and Rhetoric precisely because it has historically invested a great deal of time and resources in such efforts, I have written this chapter with some anxiety that the rapprochement between our field and critical pedagogy signals a "disciplining" that will make this historical commitment more difficult to sustain. That the "critical" teachers I work with in the public schools often feel alienated from—and sometimes silenced by—critical pedagogy worries me. That some doctoral students in Composition and Rhetoric graduate with an intimate knowledge of the corpus of critical pedagogy but without having developed (and without being particularly interested in) sophisticated pedagogies of writing worries me as well. I fear that like critical pedagogy, Composition and Rhetoric risks "clientizing" teachers and becoming another "critical tradition" perpetuated by and for researchers alone.

At the same time, as I have suggested throughout this book, I believe compositionists are well suited by temperament and well positioned by history to reframe and reclaim pedagogical progressivism. Whether we will do so depends on what version(s) of disciplinarity we pursue in the coming years. Can we forge a disciplinary identity that preserves our commitment to working with teachers and students? Can we develop a disciplinarity that places pedagogy as reflexive inquiry at its center? Can we practice disciplinarity in ways that enable, rather than constrain, ties with literacy workers beyond the academy? These questions are at the heart of the second half of this book.

## II

# Reframing and Reclaiming Pedagogical Progressivism

# On Becoming a Compositionist

## Phase 1: The Master

I am a Master. Of twentieth-century American literature.

"What," I ask my graduate advisor, "can I *do* now that I am a Master?"

"You *could* go on for the Ph.D., son, but I don't recommend it. Too much post-this and post-that. Everything's *problematic* or *hegemonic*. I can't stand the way doctoral students talk these days."

"So . . . "

"So teach. Find a small school—maybe a community college—and teach your heart out. There are lots of schools near Boston looking for good M.A.s."

## Phase 2: The Adjunct

So I teach. But not, for the most part, American literature, of which I am a Master. I teach writing—lots of writing. Five sections a semester at three different colleges. $1,250–$1,500 per course. Ten courses annually puts me at somewhere between $12,500 and $15,000 a year. In Boston. No health insurance, no job security.

I am an adjunct.

---

These kids can't write. (Even the adults I teach in a continuing education program at a four-year school can't write. No wonder these kids can't write.) I spend hours each night at the kitchen table correcting their countless mistakes and listening for baby noises through the monitor that sits next to the damn stack of papers. My wife sleeps, having worked all day and taken care of the baby all evening. I barely know the baby, and I resent my stubbornly flawed students for it.

---

First-year course evaluations are not good. Nice guy, bad teacher. At the two-year women's college, after a disastrous fall semester, the spring semester was merely bad. I think I've begun to connect with some of the students; at the least, we're talking—really talking. But there's so much work yet to do, so much to learn.

Maybe, after all, it's not that they can't write; maybe it's that I can't teach. Maybe I'm not just unlucky in drawing the weakest writers in all three colleges; maybe they're unlucky in drawing *me*. Maybe teaching writing is more complicated than I had thought. Maybe mastery of a set of literary texts doesn't qualify me to teach writing. Maybe I need to *learn* about teaching writing.

I hit the library stacks. Composition and Rhetoric. The unfamiliar names—Berlin, Bishop, Bizzell, Brodkey—overwhelm me (and that's just the B's). This is more complicated than I had thought. No simple tips here. Post-this and post-that. Everything's *problematic* or *hegemonic*. Interesting, though. I begin to formulate plans to return to graduate school (can one study this in doctoral programs?).

---

I carry the B's with me from class to class, school to school. I skim them in stolen moments, half understanding. They seem to ask a lot of me, these people I've never met. They want me to think differently about students, about myself, about education, about society. Can I? Should I? Is this masterable? I'm not sure, but I'm still interested. I am desperate to know what I am doing and why I am doing it, and I am thrilled by the idea that there are people "out there" writing about this.

I ask the English professors at one of my schools to recommend programs in Composition and Rhetoric. They do.

"You know what else?" they ask. "We have an Introduction to Composition Studies course here. How about teaching it next semester?"

Terrified, I agree.

------

Nicole, Mary, and Joan are still in my office, debating multicultural education, at 4:30. I gently steer them toward the door; they know that the newspaper office becomes my office again at 4:30.

I have a half hour before I begin my journey to my six o'clock class in another college thirty miles north. I reach into my bag, pull out a sandwich and my application to the doctoral program in Composition and Rhetoric. I work as I eat (as usual). I fill out the information, fill in the blanks. I make some notes toward the personal statement:

- ◆ ~~I am a master.~~ I am a teacher.

- ◆ Multicultural education—learning *from* students.

- ◆ Maybe it's not them; maybe it's me.

- ◆ Hitting the stacks. More complicated than I thought—so much to learn.

------

I am a teacher. Of Composition Studies. This is complicated.

But the students—continuing education students in a four-year college who, like me, are simply curious about this thing called writing—are patient with me. They know this is new to me, too (who knew we could *study* writing and teaching writing?).

We struggle, together, to keep the ideas (and even the names) straight: expressivism, cognitivism, current-traditional *(current-traditional?)*, social construction, cultural studies, critical pedagogy. Our heads swim, but our guiding question helps: What assumptions or claims do they make about writing and its teaching? We do a lot of mapping of ideas, a lot of simple juxtaposition: How are these two different? What is Bruffee saying that Elbow isn't? How does Berlin's (or Faigley's or Knoblauch's) taxonomy help us keep these ideas straight?

We know no one will become a Master. We muddle through, together. We find this frustrating but empowering—we will not Know, but we might learn. A few students, too, wish they had a teacher who knew what he was talking about. I sympathize.

And so I am relieved when the package arrives from the graduate school, and I am accepted into the program in Composition and Rhetoric. I will Know; I will master this strange and exciting discourse. I will be a compositionist (my new favorite word).

---

Late spring, I am called into a tiny seminar room (I didn't know we had seminar rooms) at the two-year women's college. I am glad to meet the other writing teachers (I didn't know there were so many of us) and to have been invited to something. Adjuncts don't get many invitations from administrators.

Food would have been nice. This meeting will take me right to 5 P.M. No time for dinner—again—before heading north.

Still, I will be moving on next year; the acceptance letter from the graduate program sits on my kitchen table next to the resignation letters I've begun to draft. I've already decided that if we're here to hear again how *these kids can't write* (we get that a lot), I'm walking out. A year ago I'd have carried that flag to the end of the earth; today, I'm ready to burn it. These kids can write. If we let them, and if we help them.

At 4 P.M. sharp, we are informed by a cold-looking associate something-or-other that this is a "debriefing" on the new administrative portfolio assessment. This is not a penalty (she knows we are doing the best we can with *these students*). It will not be used as the *sole* measure of our teaching (she knows this *sounds* like surveillance, but it *isn't*). It is the *next thing* (she knows we want to be cutting edge). It is in everyone's best interest (she knows we are team players).

But we know that if this new assessment weren't all the things she insists it isn't, this wouldn't be the first time we "writing experts" were hearing about it. I look at the administrator, thinking that this is not a monster, or a mean or bad person, but rather a perfectly reasonable technocrat who believes in efficiency, in performance, in excellence, in skills training—all the familiar pieties. As she speaks eloquently of "outcomes," "competencies," "rubrics," and "administrative checks," I look at my newfound colleagues for what I know is the last time. This is the final indignity I will have to endure. But what about the others? What will this mean for them?

I get no hint when the administrator finally stops talking some time later to ask if there are any questions. We all stare at her dumbly, wondering what there is to say.

When I get home at 10 P.M., I finish my resignation letters, knowing how privileged I have become in taking on a job that pays $8,000 a year and comes with a tuition waiver.

## Phase 3: The Professional-in-Process

So I study.

> The Doctor of Philosophy in English with emphases on writing, teaching and criticism is a professional degree designed primarily for those planning on or already engaged in careers as teachers and writers in four-year colleges and universities. Focusing attention less on bodies of knowledge than on the making of knowledge and on the questions that arise out of the movement between theory and practice, this program prepares individuals for positions in which particularly strong credentials in rhetoric, poetics, pedagogy, and theory are desirable. ("Doctor of Philosophy")

And I teach.

> The Writing Sequence is a series of courses, mostly workshops,
> for English majors who wish to place writing at the center of
> their undergraduate program. It seeks to provide study and prac-
> tice of rhetoric and poetics, exploring the relationship between
> these, and emphasizing the functions of writing in culture and
> society. Maybe most important, the Sequence carves out a space
> in the curriculum where students and teachers can meet together
> as writers. ("Writing Sequence")

---

The coffeehouse is nearly empty this week; we take one of the
large tables in the back. We have been meeting all year long,
talking about our courses and developing the still-new Writing
Sequence over coffee and bagels. We—there are usually six or
seven of us—are full, associate, and assistant professors and graduate students.

I am facilitating discussion today. I have a handout, with
questions:

> Do the workshops need shared objectives? Shared standards?
> Shared pedagogical and assessment practices? If yes, what might
> these be? If no, how do we ensure some measure of coherence, of
> *sequence? How much* and *what kind* of coherence do we need?
> Should the later courses be more difficult than the earlier ones?
> More complex? More rigorous? Simply *more*—more writing,
> reading, workshopping, etc.?

I ask them to choose the questions that are most important to
them and to write on them for ten minutes or so.

And they do. Full professors on down. In earnest.

I watch them scribbling away, and I think, *Don't they know
I'm just a graduate student?* They treat me as a professional-in-
process. Much like themselves.

---

I read in "the field." I take the courses. Composition Theory. Research in Composition. Composition and Pedagogy. Composition Theory again. History of Rhetoric. Seminar in Composition and Critical Pedagogy. A conversation, a history, a tradition. More than one, really: I couldn't possibly read it all. Much less master it.

But I can position myself in the conversations, the histories, the traditions. And I can speak back to them from my classrooms, my experiences as a teacher and a writer.

So I write. And write. And write.

And they read. And respond.

Full professors on down. In earnest.

I am a professional-in-process.

---

The graduate curriculum in which I learn places my projects, my writing, at the center of my program. The undergraduate curriculum in which I teach places students' projects, their writing, at the center of their program.

And this makes all the difference.

---

My Introduction to Rhetoric and Poetics class is gathered in the writing center working on a local high school newsletter, trying to finish before the student reading tonight. Some sit at computers, some in the chairs scattered about the room, a few on the couch. The Writing Sequence's literary anthology is just out. They leaf through it. They're excited by the diversity and quality of the writing: poems, personal essays, literary criticism, fiction, creative nonfiction. One of them reads aloud from the introduction: "This anthology . . . creates a forum for young writers' expression and experimentation. . . . It is a representation of the purpose of the Writing Sequence—to become familiar with a range of voices through the *study* of writing, and to become more aware of the micro-workings of texts and the processes of writing" ("Moving").

As Sarah reads, I recall a scene from a campus interview a few months back:

*Sipping coffee, we chat, and she is affable, interested. But then her eyes go cold, and she leans in, looking now very deanly.*

*"If you were hired here," she begins, "you would be one of only a handful of people paid expressly to teach students how to write."*

*She pauses, allowing me, I suppose, to absorb the impact of that statement. Then she leans back, hands folded on her enormous desk, and continues, slipping into hushed, almost conspiratorial tones: "Every day, professors come into this office and tell me the same thing: these . . . kids . . . can't . . . write. Now, as one of only a handful of people paid expressly to teach students how to write, how do you respond to this?"*

Sarah reads from the introduction: "For writers everywhere, the importance of a 'writerly' community cannot be underestimated because it is an integral part of fostering the pens of fledgling writers. We hope that our anthology will be a catalyst for others to rejoice in the spirit of writing."

"These . . . kids . . . can't . . . write," the dean had said.

"I'm going to submit something next year," says Sarah. The others nod, reading.


## Phase 4: The Professor

A manageable workload and a decent paycheck. Relative autonomy. (Everything's relative.) I am a professor, a compositionist. One of several at this university.

We are the best and the worst of what's typical of a large research university: Innovative, complex program and effective enthusiastic teachers—but many underpaid, overworked "adjuncts" and graduate students. Solid administrative and departmental support from people who understand and value the teaching of writing, rhetoric, and literacy—but the usual local culture problems.

*New faculty orientation:* "Oh, it would take me forever to fix their grammar."

*An English department meeting:* "Oh, we've hired another Composition person, eh? So now they'll be writing even *more* personal essays?"

*That same meeting:* "Oh, you lucky dog—teaching freshman comp in your first semester. We all wanted it, but thought we'd let the new guy teach his passion."

And then, in my students' informal responses to the first five weeks of the course:

> I figured [the course] would include basic grammar, spelling, and thesis-writing activities.

> I had not expected this course to be so thought-provoking.

> I thought we'd do the usual—read and analyze books and write out analysis on them. . . . [This course has gone] beyond my expectations in terms of letting me be the author.

> I expected the professor to blindly assume all the students had no previous writing experience. . . . [But] the professor assumes we have actually had some writing experience. (Unlike my [first semester of writing], in which the teacher assumed we had the knowledge of a slug.)

---

Once I worked with writers; now I work with students. Or so they insist.

"I am not a writer," they say. "It's been ten years since I used writing for purposes that were important to *me*. And now you're telling me to write as if I meant it. Good luck."

Or: "Just tell us what to do; we'll do it. We're good students." Which they are.

The institutional imagination lives in them.

---

I "graduate" to Advanced Composition. (I am a professor.)

"What's going on?" I ask them. "*Why* don't you want to write self-assessments? Or workshop? Or revise?"

"Why start now?" they ask. (One of the better students adds, "I expected a writing class, not an intellectual development class.")

"What about your first-year writing courses? Didn't you do these things there?"

"Freshman Comp? No, not there."

So they say: however innovative and complex our program is on paper, students report that their class was either pure "self-discovery" (journal, journal, maybe a short story or poem, journal, journal) or traditional grammar and form (endless formulaic thesis-driven expository essays). So they say.

The institutional imagination lives in them.

------

I dwell on the negative, the *problematic*. But they also do great work:

- ◆ Sarah develops a workshop curriculum for young evangelists, complete with music, activities, minilectures, and reflective writing.

- ◆ Laura explores the rhetorical work of picketers who protest at a local church that supports the right of one of its elders to perform abortions.

- ◆ Jill designs a pamphlet for a local children's advocacy center.

- ◆ Beth writes a letter to her hometown about racism in a Homecoming ceremony in which white students perform Native rituals.

I know, too, that my colleagues and their students are doing interesting, often rhetorically based work in their first-year writing classrooms. Why, then, the focus on the negative, the *problematic*?

The institutional imagination lives in me.

End of semester, and their portfolios are full of conversion narratives: I once was audienceless, but now I am audienceful. I once was purposeless, but now I'm purposeful. I once was undisciplined, but now I'm disciplined. I once was lost, but now I'm found. But then I wonder: Are conversion narratives easier to come by when expectations begin so low? When the course has ended and this curricular anomaly is behind them?

As they pick up their portfolios: "I will try to keep taking risks, to be self-reflective about my writing, to keep seeking readers' responses to my work, to keep reading as a writer and writing as a reader, to keep writing into my communities, . . . but I don't think I'll have much time, with all the work I have to do for my major."

The institutional imagination lives in them.

Our committee is charged with reducing enrollment i[n] composition by 20 percent. It appears that we can no [af]ford our traditional, land-grant-inspired commitment t[o] first-year writing to almost all incoming students. This [is a bud]get problem, but it is also a staffing problem: we want t[o] the professional nature of teaching writing at our instituti[on] yet, for us compositionists, this feels a bit like cutting o[ff a] switch.

Or, as one of us proposes, like they're putting the gun in our hand, aiming it at our heads, and making us pull the trigger. Later they will say, "But this is what they wanted; *they* pulled the trigger." (Imagine, another of us adds, doing this to lit people.)

What to do? No option seems good. Use AP or ACT scores to exempt students from the requirement? Develop an assessment program to place incoming students? Create a midsemester assessment utilizing the advice of first-semester comp teachers? Combine the two first-year writing courses and reduce the total number of credits?

We pick our way through the none-too-good possibilities. We struggle. We are frustrated with the task and, in time, with ourselves. We talk of placing students *into*, not *out of*, courses, but we revert again and again to the language of needs and deficiency: the "good" ones don't "need" us; the "bad" ones do. We talk of complex assessment practices, but we revert again and again to administrative quick fixes that trivialize the complicated nature of this work. We talk of the *problematic*, the *hegemonic* demands made on composition by others in the university, but we revert again and again to the view that institutional requirements for our courses are "givens."

And there's this: we talk *about* "adjuncts," and we talk *for* "adjuncts," but we don't talk *to* them. They are invisible, as I was once invisible. We reason that it's too much to ask that they participate. They often teach 4-4 and would get nothing in return for their service on this committee. We're right, of course, but that's where the conversation should start, not end.

Being a compositionist is more complicated than I had thought.

The institutional imagination lives in us.

---

We may not control the destiny of our program, we decide, but we are not powerless either. Our committee report offers a set of principles and two proposals.

The principles:

◆ The program is not remedial; it is a site of inquiry into and through writing.

◆ The program recognizes the complexity of writing as intellectual inquiry and encourages writing for various audiences in multiple contexts.

◆ The program recognizes the disciplinary expertise of both Composition and Rhetoric and other academic disciplines.

◆ The program recognizes the professional expertise of writing instructors and is committed to staffing its courses with well-trained writing teachers.

And the proposals:

1. Invite students to apply, during their first semester, to fulfill their remaining three credits (many programs require six) by completing an upper-level writing intensive course.

2. Ask other colleges and programs to reduce the number of required hours of first-year composition for their students. The committee lists the number of hours required by each program or college and encourages the department to pursue discussion with the appropriate administrators.

But the proposals are not the point. This budget crisis offers us a stage for making public what we do, why we do it, and what it means. We are not thrilled by our own proposals, and we have effected no revolution, but we have refused administrative quick fixes in favor of protecting—and we hope enhancing—the good intellectual work that students and teachers do together in our program. We have not allowed those outside the program to set the agenda for it by shortchanging the university's, the department's, or the program's commitment to student literacy and teacher professionalism. And while we are more aware now of how we are complicit in the institutional problems we're trying to address, someone else will need to pull the trigger.

But not before we begin to speak back to the institutional imagination.

# CHAPTER FOUR

# Toward Pedagogy-Centered
# Disciplinarity

In Chapter 3, I suggested that Composition and Rhetoric's recent alliance with critical pedagogy has had the ironic effect of deflecting our disciplinary attention away from pedagogy as shared, reflexive inquiry. It has encouraged notions of teaching as the application of a preexisting "critical tradition," to use Peter McLaren's term, and not as a knowledge-producing process engaged by teachers and learners alike, as pedagogical progressivism would have it. This alliance with a critical tradition may have helped Composition and Rhetoric garner legitimacy in the academy (thereby beginning, at least, to establish *itself* as a critical tradition), but it marks a radical departure from our historical roots in pedagogical progressivism.

In this chapter, I extend this line of inquiry by taking a closer look at the concept of disciplinarity. Specifically, I ask: What visions and versions of "progress" are represented by Composition and Rhetoric's quest for disciplinary status? I also explore how our continuing commitment to that "temporary stopgap" of the Progressive Era, first-year composition, has informed our struggles with and for disciplinarity. My analysis begins with the claim that our historical relationship to the universal requirement has forced us into a disciplinary identity crisis. On the one hand, if we stake our academic value on our instrumental service to the university as administrators and teachers of first-year composition, we fear that we will never gain the kind or measure of academic legitimacy that other disciplines receive, and that we will merely support the dominant corporate logic of the university, which places a premium on the administrative progressive values of economy and efficiency. On the other hand, we are wary of traditional disciplinarity, and we don't want to become "just another discipline": a body of knowledge, a critical tradition that supports the modernist knowledge project of the academy. Along with James Slevin, I suggest that Composition and Rhetoric can and should refuse both of these institutional/disciplinary identities. Although institutional common sense teaches otherwise, we do not need to make a choice between discipline-as-instrumental-service and discipline-as-critical-tradition. Although whatever we do under its auspices is likely to support the academy's institutional agendas (including those of self-reproduction), there is much more to the story. I suggest that Composition and Rhetoric's present institutional position, though hardly ideal, points to possibilities for being at once within and against, inside and outside, academic disciplinarity. In fact, our conflicted institutional identity might prove useful in pushing the academy to rethink and reconfigure the relationship between disciplinarity and pedagogy—and perhaps even to launch a reclamation project for pedagogical progressivism.

## The Trappings and the Trap of Disciplinarity

David Shumway proposes that under the auspices of the German-influenced U.S. university, "the discipline of English was organized in order both to limit what might be said and to ensure that it might be said over and over again" (100). While this Foucauldian pronouncement might sound excessively cynical, it does serve to focus our attention on disciplinarity as an essentially conservative institutional and discursive practice. A discipline is a self-reproducing set of procedures, rules, practices, assumptions, and discursive strategies. Perpetuated by and through institutional sites such as journals, conferences, and publishers, it is designed to regulate and sanction what can and cannot be said and who can and cannot speak. But what I suggested about discourses and institutions in Chapter 3 holds for disciplines as well: while they function beyond the power or authority of any particular individual, they are also perpetuated by individuals. This means that while grand, sweeping disciplinary changes are unlikely, it is also true that disciplines are changing all the time—though in ways that are not always immediately visible. New journals appear; established ones change their policies; conferences refocus their attention on previously marginal concerns; publishers put new ways of making knowledge into circulation, or find new ways to circulate knowledge. All of these constitute change in how disciplinarity is practiced and in its consequences. Later in this chapter, I argue that changes in knowledge-making procedures and in what counts as knowledge have been particularly pronounced recently in Composition and Rhetoric.

But as Shumway suggests—and as a number of compositionists have likewise noted—the model of disciplinarity adopted (or adapted) by the U.S. research university is one that privileges the production and maintenance of a more or less stable, unified body of knowledge. Where, then, does this leave Composition and Rhetoric?

In *Under Construction*, Christine Farris and Chris Anson claim that Composition and Rhetoric has long searched for a disciplinary Holy Grail—a "coherence made possible by a unifying theory" (2). We have searched for this coherence in models of the writing process designed from empirical studies of what writers do, for instance, in critical theory (including, I have argued, critical pedagogy), or in some curricular vision, such as cultural studies. But Farris and Anson see this practice changing: "Compositionists' knowledge-making activity is increasingly bound up in context and self-reflexivity rather than in a quest for models that will tell us the best way to produce 'good writing' or the most effective teachers of writing" (3). They claim that our "expertise" is "increasingly interdisciplinary if not post-disciplinary" (5).

It is not difficult to find support for the claim that many compositionists eschew traditional disciplinarity. We have read our Foucault well enough to know that institutions and disciplines limit what is "sayable" and subjugate "counter-knowledges." And we have read our own history inside English studies well enough to know that disciplinarity in the academy sanctions specialized knowledge and expertise of/for the few at the expense of the knowledge and labor of the many (see Bizzell, "Thomas Kuhn"; Connors, "Composition History"; Ferry; Harkin; Spellmeyer, "After," *Common;* Trimbur, "Writing Instruction"; Vandenberg). And yet, however uneasy many compositionists seem to be about the prospect of academic disciplinarity, and however sanguine some of us might be about the prospect of postdisciplinarity (see Harkin), we cannot deny the lure of disciplinarity. It's as though compositionists don't really want to go to the disciplinary ball—we would have to dress up and take ourselves far more seriously than we are willing to do—but we do want to be invited. Or, perhaps more tellingly, we want the trappings of disciplinarity—the tenure-track lines, the journals and conferences, the book series, the endowed chairs, the undergraduate and graduate programs, the sense of belonging to an academic community—without the trap of disciplinarity: the containment and normalization of intellectual work and knowledge.

In fact, some contributors to the Farris and Anson collection *Under Construction* compellingly argue that Composition and Rhetoric, for all its ambivalence about the academy, is increasingly becoming a traditional, modernist, disciplinary enterprise. Christopher Ferry, for instance, claims that we continue to strive for "scientific" knowledge "at the expense of seeing composition as an intellectual endeavor located in classrooms with students" (12). A professional class of researchers, Ferry suggests, pursues an overarching theory on the backs of a teaching working class (14). Similarly, while Farris and Anson seem to find hope in the "disciplinary boundary crossing" of compositionists who make forays into deconstruction, feminism, multiculturalism, and cultural studies (4), Peter Vandenberg worries about class rift within the field:

> To "work in rhetoric and composition" means either to publish or to teach; well aware that those who publish typically teach as well, my argument is that the "disciplining" of rhetoric and composition insures that those who do much of one do comparatively little of the other. This bifurcation constitutes an economy that serves those who are at its head; publishing scholars, whose work is defined by acquiring and advancing the specialized literacy of heavily theorized professional discourse, assume a professional-client relationship with those whose work is defined predominantly by teaching a more basic literacy—first-year English. (20)[1]

Long the undervalued stepchild of English studies, Composition and Rhetoric has begun, it seems, to appropriate the very disci-

plinary assumptions, practices, and structures that have historically disenfranchised it.

Of course, it is not difficult to see why this is so: in the American academy, institutional resources—tenure-track hires, endowed
chairs, programs, research centers, and so on—are accorded to
those who demonstrate themselves to be "legitimate" holders of
identifiable disciplinary knowledge. And yet Composition and
Rhetoric has not, for the most part, staked its claims to academic
legitimacy as other disciplines have. Rather, institutional resources
are typically allocated to compositionists as a result of an unspo-
ken but mutually understood bargain: the institution agrees to
hire a compositionist on a tenure-track line as it does for professors in "real" disciplines (including English, through which
compositionists are most likely to land jobs), and compositionists
agree—in addition to teaching and publishing—to run the
institution's first-year composition program (including, typically,
instituting and maintaining assessment programs; staffing and
administering many sections of first-year composition; staffing
and supervising the work of writing centers; overseeing the work
of a corps of part-time and full-time non-tenure-track instructors; working with others in the institution on undergraduate
writing; and training/teaching TAs). Our curricular anomaly—
first-year writing is typically the only universally required course
in the elective-oriented university—makes us a disciplinary
anomaly: housed in English, we are the "service specialists," and
even if we don't make many disciplinary claims directly on the
basis of this work (few of us make the claim that we are researchers *because* we administer and teach first-year writing), we know
that our disciplinary status is largely the indirect result of these
deals. In other words, whether or not publishing compositionists
do research in or on first-year composition, our institutional positions are most often secured as a result of an institutional
economy that demands the administration and teaching of first-
year composition programs. In this way, as Vandenberg observes,
those who secure tenure-track positions at research universities
and then pursue careers as compositionists do so on the backs of
those who teach the bulk of first-year writing courses at most
institutions: poorly paid and often overworked TAs and instructors.

But there are further complications. In return for maintaining first-year writing programs, we maintain our position—again, at most institutions—within English. As Shumway reminds us, and as I described in Chapter 1, English evolved around the principles of the nascent, German-influenced U.S. university: that professors are responsible primarily for producing knowledge, not teaching it; that researchers are specialists, not generalists; that knowledge produced by the university must be organized into discrete specializations, expressed institutionally as "departments," each responsible only for its own body of knowledge; and that knowledge is ratified by disciplinary researchers through scientific inquiry. Though these ideas are hardly compatible with the commitments of most interdisciplinary-minded and teaching-oriented compositionists, we have nonetheless acceded to them as part of the bargain we have struck with the academy.

## Disciplinarity as Progress

How did we get here? How did this odd arrangement develop? And why? The answers to these questions have everything to do with the "progressive" status of composition/Composition and Rhetoric throughout the twentieth century and into the twenty-first.

In his rendering of how composition became Composition, Stephen North, following Arthur Applebee, cites the mid-1950s reform movement in secondary education as the driving force behind the shift from "English the school subject" to "English the discipline." In Applebee's terms, this movement marked a repudiation of "progressive" commitments to "the immediate needs and the characteristics of the student," and an embrace of the "long-term goals and the nature of the subject" (qtd. in North, *Making* 9). The reports of the Basic Issues conference of 1958— where English professors gathered to define the nature of their work—ratified the idea that English should be a static body of knowledge to be transmitted to students.

Following on the heels of the Basic Issues reports was NCTE's 1961 *The National Interest and the Teaching of English*. This document represented NCTE's response to the lack of provisions for English in the watershed 1958 National Defense Education Act (NDEA), which provided funds for wide-scale educational research and reform. This document argued in no uncertain terms that English could not be excluded from the national(istic) effort to equip students with citizenship skills necessary to lead the free world to victory in the cold war (see North, *Making* 11). As both North and Applebee note, *The National Interest* had a powerful influence on policymakers. It led both to the eventual inclusion of English in the NDEA (in 1964) and to other forms of federal support for research in English, including the long-lived Project English. For our purposes, however, what is most important about this document and the larger reform effort of which it was a part is that it provided the impetus for the emergence of big-C Composition. After all, while composition and language (linguistics) were able to garner big federal research dollars, literature was not, for it was, in North's words, "less easily amenable to the 'scientific' modes of inquiry favored for government support than either language or composition" (12). This meant that at the postsecondary level, English departments would need to gather expertise in literature, linguistics, *and* composition.

This left Composition in a kind of crisis of leadership. There were some folks who could make a claim to expertise in the nascent field of Composition: most of the studies that would be published in Braddock, Lloyd-Jones, and Schoer's 1963 *Research in Written Composition*, after all, had been conducted by this time, and of course curriculum designers and textbook writers were everywhere. "But," North explains, "the expertise they claimed was of the wrong—i.e., 'progressive education'—sort, inappropriate in that it was not disciplinary in the sense of deriving, by whatever means, from the body of knowledge that was English" (*Making* 13). It was then up to the most unlikely group of people to shepherd this emerging field: the lowly teachers and administrators of first-year composition. But their claim to expertise was limited precisely because their "lore," to use North's (in)famous term, was deemed unrigorous and therefore insufficiently "disciplined."

Interestingly, North marks the birth of Composition as a field at precisely the point that institutional forces conspired to make necessary the supplanting of "Practitioner knowledge" with the supposedly tougher stuff of scientifically derived "disciplinary" knowledge (*Making* 16). This was also the point at which Composition became a largely top-down affair in which college faculty and educational experts took the lead in nailing down the standard components—or what administrative progressives of an earlier era had called the "minimum essentials"—of English. This move was necessary, according to J. N. Hook, the first director of Project English, because "in English teaching we have relied too long on our best guesses" (qtd. in North 16). Hook's sentiment is echoed by Braddock, Lloyd Jones, and Schoer's *Research in Written Composition,* with its well-known analogy between research in Composition and alchemy. According to Braddock and colleagues, Composition—much like chemistry as it emerged from alchemy—was just beginning to define its terms and methods. The field, however, was still riddled with the "dreams, prejudices, and makeshift operations" of uninformed, often careerist so-called "researchers" (qtd. in North 16–17). North treats *Research in Written Composition* as the "charter" for the field of Composition, the call to push Composition out of the darkness of haphazard practice and into the light of scientific inquiry.

Again drawing on Applebee, North *(Making)* views the reform movement of the 1950s as a turning away from progressive education with its emphasis on students rather than on the static content of an already-worked-out discipline. While this is no doubt true in one sense, it is also possible to read the events of the 1950s and 1960s as the consummation, rather than the repudiation, of progressive composition. After all, the parallels between North's narrative of the midcentury reform movement and my own narrative in Chapter 1 of early-century administrative progressivism are unmistakable. The quest for scientific knowledge, the sneering disregard for teachers' "best guesses" (that is, professional judgment), the top-down nature of reform, the ambivalent status of composition as "useful"—all of these were familiar in the Progressive Era. Indeed, it seems no exaggeration to suggest that the political and rhetorical work accomplished by NCTE's 1961 *The National Interest* represents the culmination of NCTE's self-proclaimed "progressive" charter fifty years earlier: to lift English, with composition at the lead, from the ever-shifting terrain of "mere opinion" to the terra firma of scientific, disciplinary knowledge.

Of course, a great deal has changed in this "emerging field," even (or especially) since the publication of North's 1987 book. Composition and Rhetoric has been claimed not only as a field, but also as a discipline in its own right. As I have suggested, some have argued that Composition and Rhetoric is fundamentally interdisciplinary or even postdisciplinary. But what hasn't changed is the frank ambivalence that North admits to in *The Making of Knowledge in Composition*. Should Composition and Rhetoric strive for academic legitimacy at all? Should this legitimacy be based on a coherent body of knowledge, on service to the academy, or on practitioner "lore"? Should postsecondary composition be separate from composition in the schools or in communities? Should it take the form of a field, or a discipline, or something else altogether? Should it focus on first-year composition, or should it move beyond this curricular space? Should it be housed in English, or should it break its ties with literary studies, linguistics, and creative writing? These are the questions North posed to the field some fifteen years ago; they remain very much with us today.

And so we compositionists find ourselves in a vexed position; we are unsure how or whether we want to participate in the institutional and disciplinary structures that have exploited for so long our labor and alienated us (and our students) from our work. The pedagogical progressive values we have nurtured—respect for teacher and student inquiry and knowledge; bottom-up or inside-out rather than top-down educational reform; literacy as democratic social action—are not shared by the institutional and disciplinary economy of the academy, in which "progress" still means nailing down what we (researchers, professors) know through disinterested, dispassionate inquiry, and then disseminating it (preferably in cost-effective ways) to those who don't know (students, teachers, community members). And yet, if we refuse to participate in that economy, we risk losing not only the institutional resources we have amassed, but also our standing to fight unjust labor practices and the general devaluing of composition that are still (or should be) the great scandal of the university.

Indeed, many compositionists—those who have secured tenure-leading lines in colleges and universities—have used their institutional authority to respond to this troubling dilemma in various ways. In the following section, I focus on what Roemer, Schultz, and Durst call our "Great Debate": the ongoing struggle over the universal requirement for first-year writing. I do so not because this is the only way compositionists have responded to the ambivalence surrounding the status of college composition, but because our love-hate relationship with the universal requirement provides a useful lens through which to view our struggles with disciplinarity. A product of the Progressive Era, the required course is also our closest link to administrative progressivism, as I suggested in Chapter 1. In recent years, however, "progressives" of various stripes have positioned themselves in various ways vis-à-vis the universal requirement. Our Great Debate, then, is the most obvious place today where (often conflicting) ideas about "progress" and "disciplinarity" meet.

## First-Year Comp as Progressive

The Great Debate is of course not new. As I showed in Chapter 1, the debate over the value of the first-year course is as old as the course itself. What is new is that many of the voices advocating abolition of the universal requirement now come from compositionists in positions of institutional and disciplinary authority rather than from the three more traditional groups of malcontents: mistreated composition teachers; foes of composition; and those who do not believe that writing can be taught (Connors, "Abolition Debate"; Russell; Crowley, *Composition*). Indeed, some "progressive" compositionists—including Sharon Crowley, Robert Connors, and Susan Miller—have launched their critique of the requirement precisely on the grounds that it necessitates the exploitation of teachers and students; that it tends to standardize or "water down" composition pedagogy and curricula; and that it devalues the disciplinary and professional authority of the study and teaching of writing (Crowley, *Composition* 241–43). Although these writers don't use this language, a

significant feature of this argument is that the requirement is inexorably linked to the legacy of administrative progressivism: its
sheer size in most institutions precludes responsible pedagogical
and administrative practice, as it places a premium on the effi-
ciency-equals-economy equation of the administrative progressivism tradition. In order for Composition and Rhetoric to
"progress" as a discipline and to achieve its pedagogical and
political aspirations, the argument goes, it must refuse to allow
the required course to remain at the center of its institutional
identity.

On the other hand, we have "reformists" (as Connors dubs
them), some of whom claim that the first-year composition requirement does offer a platform for progressive, democratic work.
Typically, these claims are posed as part of a critical pedagogy
agenda. Consider the following:

> Whatever its ideology, a freshman writing program introduces
> students to the institutional world they have just entered. And
> conceivably the program can offer a *critical* introduction to that
> world, while at the same time encouraging critique of the world
> beyond it. Keep in mind, too, that thousands of students now
> take freshman composition. Why abandon the chance to get such
> a large audience thinking about the art, ethics, and politics of
> discourse? (Schilb 67)

> If our disciplinary desire is to intervene strategically and effec-
> tively in the struggle over literacy in this country, it would be
> very strange to throw away the term and institutional space that
> lets us practice our discipline and effect [sic] the literacy of large
> numbers of students. Rather than imagining a sphere outside in-
> stitutions where writing is pure (purer, purest), our efforts were
> put into conceiving a strong composition, an emancipatory and
> reflexive composition. (Sullivan, Lyon, Lebofsky, Wells, and
> Goldblatt 380)

> We argue for the value of the course as a pedagogical site with
> the potential to influence very large numbers of students, and for
> its importance as a site of struggle and change within the institu-
> tional hierarchy of academia. (Roemer, Schultz, and Durst 378)

The common denominator here, obviously, is the idea that giving up the universal requirement would mean giving up access to

"thousands"/"large numbers"/"very large numbers" of students. Put crudely, the argument goes like this: if the mass production machine worked for *them* (our *re*gressive predecessors), we can make it work for *us* (their *pro*gressive successors).

While I am not interested in merely weighing in on the Great Debate, it seems to me undeniable that the universal requirement establishes a historical link between composition and administrative progressivism. Although many reformists have done important work in ensuring better working conditions for the teachers and students who participate in their programs (see, for instance, Sullivan et al.), the universal requirement, even at most fair-sized universities, continues to place an enormous amount of administrative pressure on the teaching of first-year writing. However "democratic" we might wish it to be, the requirement is of an ideological piece with the bureaucratization and corporatization of the university, as well as the cultural and institutional logic that tells us that "these kids can't write." As I showed in Chapter 1, first-year composition in its early days was quickly swept up into the "cult of efficiency," and it was ratified as a crucial component of the new U.S. university on that basis. And, by dint of their structure and size, required first-year programs tend to be organized in a top-down fashion, are beholden to efficiency-as-economy to an extent that smaller programs are not, and hold teachers and students responsible to remote "experts" (increasingly so with the rise of standardized tests for college writers; see Chapter 2). Put simply, they have not been able to cast off their legacy as an Age of Efficiency effort to corporatize college writing.

Richard Miller, no friend of the abolitionist position, (unwittingly) offers evidence to this effect. In a *Profession* essay provocatively titled "Let's Do the Numbers," Miller, associate coordinator of Composition at Rutgers University, tries to imagine how his university could enact MLA President Phyllis Franklin's proposal that first-year writing courses be staffed with a minimum of 55 percent tenure-track and full-time faculty. To achieve this goal, Miller claims that his administration would need to hire, at a minimum, twenty-two new full-time instructors, or forty-four additional tenure-track professors, or some combination of these (100). Simply put, Miller tells us, this "is never going to happen at my institution" (101). Thus, he suggests that those who critique the academy's labor practices are not proposing practicable solutions.

Surely Miller is right: no financially strapped institution (and how many of us work in institutions that aren't financially strapped?) is likely to sink these kinds of resources into this kind of program. But while Miller reads this as evidence that people in his field are making impracticable proposals, I read it as evidence that Rutgers runs too many sections of required first-year writing. Miller tells us that his university runs five hundred sections of first-year writing a year, only two of which are staffed by tenure-track faculty. But though his critique of Crowley's ideas shows that he is aware of arguments against the universal requirement, he seems to take those five hundred sections for granted.

Interestingly, though, Miller poses his analysis against what he views as Crowley's regressive version of disciplinarity: "I think it is a mistake to abandon the ethic of service that defines the field in the hope that doing so will bring about a broader respect for the intellectual work done in the discipline" ("Let's" 103). Severed from its service function, Miller fears, Composition and Rhetoric would, at best, be put "on a par with all those other departments where a handful of committed scholars pursue research projects unlikely to have material consequences either inside or outside the university" (103). Like other reformists (e.g., Roemer, Schultz, and Durst), Miller charges abolitionists with pursuing a kind of ivory tower version of disciplinarity that will serve the professional and intellectual needs of professors while abandoning the needs of students.

On the other hand, Crowley and other abolitionists have charged that the universal requirement is tied to "an oppressive institutional history and a repressive intellectual tradition" that serves neither students nor teachers well (*Composition* 235). In effect, she turns charges such as Miller's on their head: "the requirement has nothing to do with what students need and everything to do with the academy's image of itself as a place where a specialized language is in use" (357). Moreover, Crowley is careful to suggest that what she desires is a discipline that is more, not less, student oriented. That is, she advocates a discipline that is in service not to the entire university, as Miller imagines it, but rather to students who choose the study and practice of composition in the university.

If the Great Debate has made anything clear, it is that compositionists continue to struggle over what it means to be a "progressive discipline." But I confess that the debate, as it has been posed thus far, seems something of an intellectual dead end, as it tends to produce what I see as a false dilemma: the choice between disciplinarity-as-instrumental-service and disciplinarity-as-ivory-towerism. This is a choice that I do not believe the field needs to make. Rather, we need to rethink disciplinarity altogether. We need a kind of disciplinarity that values diverse visions and versions of writing pedagogy both inside and outside university walls. And we need a kind of disciplinarity that puts pedagogy—reflexive, shared inquiry—at the center of the knowledge-making project. In other words, we need a kind of disciplinarity that neither reduces Composition and Rhetoric to a single curricular vision or structure nor poses it as yet another academic "critical tradition."

## Toward Pedagogy-Centered Disciplinarity

What might this kind of disciplinarity look like? How might we organize our disciplinary pursuits around the knowledge that we produce with students? In short, how might we enact a discipline that is responsive to and encourages pedagogical progressivism? I begin my thinking about these questions in the work of John Dewey.

It may come as a surprise to some readers that Dewey, that great defender of science, worried deeply about the formation of the disciplines (or "the studies," as he called them) in the late nineteenth century. Dewey did believe that science had an important role to play in education, but he also feared that science was being conceived and applied far too narrowly. Although to a (post)modern reader, Dewey might seem to place inordinate faith in science, we should take care to understand what he meant by "science." Specifically, we should understand what science meant to Dewey in the context of education:

> [In] education, we must employ the word "science" modestly
> and humbly; there is no subject in which the claim to be strictly
> scientific is more likely to suffer from pretence, and none in which
> it is more dangerous to set up a rigid orthodoxy, a standardized
> set of beliefs to be accepted by all. Since there is no one *thing*
> which is beyond question . . . and since there is no likelihood that
> there will be until society and hence schools have reached a dead
> monotonous uniformity of practice and aim, there cannot be one
> single science. ("Science" 172)

Dewey was also careful to distinguish between science as a static
body of knowledge and science as a method and an attitude.
Science's value, according to Dewey, lay in the model of inquiry
it offered. In fact, Dewey often wrote of science as a (critical)
habit of mind, an unwillingness to take things for granted (see,
for instance, "Logical"). His interest always lay less in the results
of inquiry than in the inquiry itself. And so his was a philosophical—and, we might say, a rhetorical—concern: "The real question is not whether science aims at statements which take the
form of universals, or formulae of connection of conditions, but
*how* it comes to do so, and *what it does with* the universal statements" ("Logical" 29). Indeed, Dewey saw science as a *construction*: "The entire science considered as a body of formulae having
coherent relations to one another is just a system of possible predi-
cates—that is, of possible standpoints or methods to be employed
in qualifying some particular experience whose nature is not clear
to us" (33).

Dewey held in contempt any attempt to organize education
around the transmission of static bodies of knowledge to passive
students. And science, because it is often presented as already
worked out, runs the risk of perpetuating this traditional educational arrangement (*Democracy* 189–90). Another danger of
defining science and scientific knowledge narrowly is that it leads
to the increasing fragmentation of the curriculum into distinct
branches of learning, from each of which students are asked to
cull just a bit of information (*Democracy* 187). This fragmentation of the curriculum not only places the branches of knowledge
at a remove from each other, but it also places knowledge at a
remove from the students: "The studies as classified are the prod-

uct, in a word, of the science of the ages, not the experiences of the child" (*Child* 341).

Although Dewey's "child-centered" educational philosophy is often characterized/caricatured as pandering to students, he in fact sought educational methods and built educational programs that would bring curriculum and child into useful relation. In *Experience and Education,* he even chided progressive educators for abdicating responsibility for organizing students' learning (see also Fishman and McCarthy, *John Dewey;* Dewey, "Science"). Specifically, Dewey advised that teachers pose "problems" for students to work on, rather than simply present them with information. Dewey proposed two criteria for useful problems: "First, that the problem grows out of the conditions of the experience being had in the present, and that it is within the range of the capacity of the students; and, secondly, that it is such that it arouses in the learner an active quest for information and for the production of new ideas" (*Experience* 79). This last part is important: the learner must see him- or herself as an active producer of knowledge and ideas. While Dewey deemed it important that educators organize material "progressively," with an awareness of how students develop, he was adamant that teachers "cannot start with knowledge already organized and proceed to ladle it out in doses" (82).

It is clear, then, why Dewey viewed the formation of the disciplines in the new U.S. university with suspicion. If the goal of education is to engage teachers and students in inquiries that will both examine what is known and produce new knowledge, then "the studies" cannot be presented as once-and-for-all bodies of knowledge. But with the scientific stamp of approval, Dewey knew, that is just what they were becoming. Students were not viewed as participants in the formation and development of scientifically derived disciplines; they were merely subject to these bodies of knowledge.

Dewey's critique of "the studies" points to a very different vision of disciplinarity than does the scientistic model we have inherited from the German research university. And yet Dewey's ideas *are* commensurate with another, much older version of disciplinarity, as James Slevin explains:

> In its original form, "discipline" derives from the Latin word *discipulus*, "learner," which itself derived from *discere*, "to learn." The first and primary meaning of discipline involved "instruction imparted to disciples or scholars; teaching; learning; education, schooling," a meaning the *Oxford English Dictionary* now declares "obsolete." In contrast to the knowledge imparted (called "doctrine," which comes from *docere*, which also gives us, among other words, "doctor"), discipline entailed the activities of imparting and learning. . . . [I]n Latin, *discipulus* meant simply a pupil or student or learner. And a discipline involved learning, studying, and the process and structure of imparting knowledge; it included centrally the work of teachers and students together. The body of knowledge that was passed on, and debates about that body of knowledge, fell under the category of doctrine. At the heart of the real work in a discipline was not the scholar (or doctor, concerned with doctrine) but the learner and the teacher who helped that learning. (156–57)

This model of disciplinarity was all but lost as the U.S. college was transformed, through the influence of the German university, into the new U.S. university. However radically we have departed from it, though, it has had a much longer run in the history of education, and we may yet be able to reclaim these radical roots.

In fact, Slevin claims that in the context of an academic economy that privileges and trades on static bodies of knowledge and (typically agonistic) conversations about these bodies of knowledge, Composition and Rhetoric is well-suited—by conviction and standing—to lead the way toward disciplinary reform. Indeed, Slevin argues that Composition and Rhetoric is already a discipline in that older sense of the word:

> Our discipline is about the encounter of ordinary people with different ways of reading and writing; our discipline exists in acts of instruction and discussion, not as a bounded field of knowledge expanded by research. . . . Our discipline arises from the need and the desirability of promoting and enriching a dialogue already underway. (159)

Slevin admits that institutions—research universities, funding agencies, and university presses, most obviously—are not organized to recognize and reward this kind of disciplinary work.

And yet he insists that institutional and disciplinary change can happen, and that Composition and Rhetoric can lead this way toward reform. Provocatively, Slevin contends that our goal ought to be to "make the discipline of composition not just a model but *the* model for other academic disciplines" (162).

As a compositionist, I am certainly drawn to this version of my discipline; after all, it places my colleagues and me at the vanguard of institutional and disciplinary reform. But I suppose I have already tipped my hand: I am not quite convinced that Composition and Rhetoric has "progressed" as far (or as far *back*, in this case) as Slevin suggests. I do not think that the reading and writing of "ordinary people," including students and those outside of our institutions, "*is* the work of the discipline of composition" (162). Also, I am not altogether comfortable with the notion that the work of this field should be considered a model for all academic disciplines; at any rate, it seems to me that we have some work to do to get our own house in order.

On the other hand, Composition and Rhetoric certainly has much to recommend it as an academic enterprise. Most important, in my view, it remains connected to teaching on a number of levels. Perhaps my own teaching life as a compositionist can serve as illustration. I teach at a large, Research I university—making me a big-C Compositionist if ever there was one. And yet I teach writing to everyone from first-year students to last-year graduate students. I also teach prospective public school teachers and graduate student teachers who teach at my own and other postsecondary institutions. In addition, I work with teachers in other venues: in the public schools and in the community (the latter through a local literacy program). Finally, I write and give (local and national) conference presentations about teaching. Mine is a teaching life to an extent that is unusual among my colleagues in other disciplines, and it is sponsored by my membership in the field of Composition and Rhetoric.

Now, as is typical, only some of my work "counts" as disciplinary knowledge-making in my university and department (though I am more fortunate than many in this regard). And it's worth noting that none of it would likely count for much if I didn't write—or, more to the point, publish—about it. It's also worth noting that as a pretenure faculty member, I have not been asked to administer the writing program at my university, as many of my colleagues across the country have been, often to their detriment. This is an issue that many in Composition and Rhetoric face daily and at key administrative moments (such as reappointment and tenure or promotion decisions). We hear too often of cases in which compositionists are in effect punished for doing the work—running a writing center, administering a writing program, working with teachers in the schools, sitting on graduate students' advisory committees—for which they were ostensibly hired. Many university gatekeepers do not know how to read—and frankly do not value—the kind of work that Slevin insists "*is* the work of the discipline.*"*

What to do? Can compositionists escape this unhappy circumstance and make their own work, as well as the work of other literacy workers, visible and fairly rewarded? Can they interrupt the process of what North calls "discounting," whereby the teaching of writing is devalued, outsourced, and/or offered at cut-rate *(Refiguring)*? Can they use their institutional positions and the institution itself to enable literacy projects that serve "ordinary people" inside and outside the academy? The analysis I've offered thus far suggests that we ought not hold out hope for some grand, immediate change that will cure all our ills. I hope, however, that my analysis has been just as insistent that it *is* possible to effect institutional and disciplinary change from within—through the development and use of institutional literacy. Although I have pointed throughout this book to what I see as negative trends in Composition and Rhetoric, in fact I see at least two reasons for hope.

First, while I can't agree with Slevin that Composition and Rhetoric in its present form offers an alternative disciplinarity that other disciplines should emulate, its vexed position in the academy does put it in unique relation to dominant disciplinary and institutional procedures and rules. Composition and Rhetoric is not by any means wholly outside the traditional disciplinary economy, but neither is it a full-fledged discipline, with all the trappings and traps. As a number of compositionists have suggested, teaching not only disseminates but also produces knowledge (see, for instance, Berthoff; Daiker and Morenberg;

Donahue and Quandahl; Goswami and Stillman; Harkin; Harris, *Teaching;* Knoblauch and Brannon, *Rhetorical;* North, *Making;* Salvatori; Schilb). Composition and Rhetoric's understanding of pedagogy as knowledge production does make it unique in disciplinary terms since any body of knowledge it produces could not, by definition, be complete or static.

In fact, Harkin has gone so far as to suggest that our teaching "lore" is in fact aggressively "postdisciplinary": "it is actually defined by its inattention to disciplinary procedures" (125). With Mina Shaughnessy's work serving as example, Harkin argues that the best explanations for what is going on in students' writing often are not "disciplinary" ones, which "assume that they are visible to everyone regardless of situation and agenda and that they are valid in all circumstances," but rather ones that emerge from "situated knowledge" (131). But Harkin doesn't have in mind either a strictly practical or a strictly idiosyncratic enterprise. Rather, she sees lore as (potentially) a site of praxis that produces knowledge that "travels," and that (unlike disciplinary knowledge, which is deemed to be replicable only under conditions identical to those in which it was first produced) "adapts" across experiential sites. This is not, in other words, "atheoretical pluralism," but a critical and judicious use of practice-as-inquiry. Nor is it pie-in-the-sky idealism; Harkin is well aware that we must use lore in ways that have "a reasonable chance of earning the academy's institutionalized respect" (135). Indeed, the challenge of valorizing lore as inquiry involves nothing less than "getting the academy to change its understanding of knowledge production" (135).

This leads to my second reason for hope: while I have argued that we have sometimes engaged in a problematic scrambling after traditional disciplinarity, we have also been producing a range of intellectual work, typically (though not always) centered on teaching, that pushes against what traditionally counts as knowledge-making in the field—and therefore in the academy. In other words, compositionists have been using their scholarship to put pressure on the academy to recognize the kind of "postdisciplinary lore" that Harkin lauds. In addition to empirical accounts of "what writing is" or "what writers do," we have opened up disciplinary knowledge-making to alternative forms of inquiry and representation—including, for instance, phenomenological teacher inquiry (see Knoblauch and Brannon, *Critical*). I am not suggesting that we have moved past certain forms of research—quantitative empirical studies of writing, for instance. I am not interested in supplanting one narrative of progress with another. My claim is rather simpler: the forms and functions of our disciplinary knowledge are multiple and constantly changing. As North notes, we have moved to include work in diverse forms as part of the discipline: *Ways with Words,* Shirley Brice Heath's ethnography; *Lives on the Boundary,* Mike Rose's autobiography; *Home of the Wildcats,* Joan Cutuly's teacher narrative ("Death"). (We might also add Jane Maher's biography of Mina Shaughnessy.) North goes on: "It is not hard to imagine a future in which not only these three variations on narrative but indeed straight fiction will serve—with equivalent if not identical value—this companion/commentator's role in one or another context and in doing so equally warrant the designation 're-search'" ("Death" 204). Some will surely scoff at this prospect.[2] But it is difficult to deny North's claim that we are already seeing the acceptance among many compositionists of new genres and ever-diversifying forms of publication. And because these projects have developed under the aegis of the academy, it is fair to say that disciplinary knowledge itself has rapidly diversified in recent years and is sure to be under continual revision in coming years.[3]

To be sure, changing what counts as disciplinary knowledge in Composition and Rhetoric will not necessarily change business as usual in the academy at large; we might finally be talking here about simply another kind of grist for the academic mill. Ultimately, though, I believe that as an institution, the academy would be a very different place if pedagogy—the process of shared, reflexive inquiry—truly were at its center. If its resources were marshaled for the benefit of "ordinary people" within and beyond its own walls, it could positively affect the lives of many, many more people than it does today. It could build productive coalitions with P–12 teachers as well as community literacy workers. It could help teachers, students, and community members radically rethink who is capable of making knowledge, whose knowledge counts, and how that knowledge gets used. In so doing, it could become a crucial vehicle not only for educational reform, but also for social reform—as Dewey once dreamed.

Perhaps all this is, in fact, a dream. Perhaps the "prophets of regress" are right, and the academy is inevitably and merely an arm of capitalist social and economic reproduction. But at the risk of sounding prophetic myself, I confess that I'm holding out hope for the dream, and working, in whatever ways I can, in its service. Pedagogical progressivism, if it is ever to come into being, demands no less, and so I devote the balance of this book to showing what it might mean for Composition and Rhetoric to pursue the version of disciplinarity I have outlined here by reimagining our work both within the university (Chapter 5) and beyond it (Chapter 6).

# On Curriculum (and) Development

We're calling our panel at the CCCC Convention in Minneapolis a "collaborative case study." At the center of the study is Krista Stock, an undergraduate who has moved through three years of the Writing Sequence at SUNY–Albany. Krista, one of the first students to graduate from our program, is joining us, and we will speak from our positions relative to her: Amy Lee was writing director; I was Krista's teacher for her first workshop; Shari Stenberg was Krista's teacher for an advanced writing workshop; and Steve North, who founded the sequence, was Krista's teacher for a 300-level reading-intensive course.

Our initial goal for the panel was to explore the ways in which the undergraduate Writing Sequence supported undergraduates' writing development over a series of courses. As we developed our panel presentation, however, we realized that we wanted to talk as much about how students helped us develop the curriculum as about the reverse. Indeed, our revised aim is to represent the interaction of student, teacher, and curriculum development.

We bring several documents to provide context. The 1998 Writing Sequence brochure introduces the program as a series of mostly workshop courses that provide practice and study of rhetoric and poetics (see Intralude 4). We also bring a handout of the requirements for the sequence, including summaries of the courses we will discuss:

- ◆ **202: Intro to Rhetoric and Poetics:** 15-seat workshop exploring the relationship between "rhetoric" and "poetics"; emphasizes students' writing.

- ◆ **303: Forms of Rhetoric:** 15-seat workshop focusing on rhetoric as it functions in disciplinary, academic, and public contexts; emphasizes students' writing.

◆ **350: Contemporary Writers at Work:** 120-seat course focusing on analysis of texts across a range of genres; media; styles; and social, intellectual, and aesthetic contexts. (Adapted from "Proposal for a Writing Sequence")

Finally, we bring a packet of artifacts from the sequence: newsletters, writing prompts, and excerpts from Krista's writing. Amy will speak first. We are ready to begin.*

---

**Amy Lee:** The most striking feature of the Writing Sequence takes place outside the classroom, although it builds on classroom work. It takes place beyond the traditional scope of either teacher or student, but asks them to participate by expanding their roles. It certainly takes place beyond the purview of the director. For me, the *communities* that we came to enact—communities that promoted our collective ongoing development as writers, teachers, students, and colleagues—were quite extraordinary. These communities were not simply enforced or mandated, but there was an expectation that people committed to working within the sequence, teachers and students, would be interested in promoting a thriving program. We created opportunities for involvement that did not exist elsewhere in the English major, for either teachers or students. We instituted a teachers' development group, organized readings for students at local cafés, and produced a semesterly newsletter and an annual anthology. Inviting people to become involved beyond requirements or skeletal expectations taught me that, given the chance, people want to be and will be active participants. Here, I want to focus on the teachers' community because I believe it is most relevant to the other presentations.

This community building was possible in part because the curriculum was not built exclusively around teachers' interests,

---

*The following material is a representation of a presentation delivered at the 2000 CCCC Convention. Panelists have edited their comments. Italicized sections are excerpted from a packet we shared with the audience.

but rather around students' articulation of needs and interests as English majors. Therefore, we drew teachers into courses that, while related to their areas of interest, were not necessarily their declared specialties. This unsettling of our expertise, this working in new terrain, contributed to our ability to become learners, rather than allowing us to remain "masters." And, because the program was new and we were new to the program, the teaching development group formed to help teachers make the transition and to attempt to create a more coherent experience for students as they moved through these disparate courses. Our goals were fairly simple:

- ◆ We sought to understand and work out this curriculum that existed only on paper.

- ◆ We aimed to understand the place of our individual classes in the program.

- ◆ We hoped to further our understanding of what writerly development—across courses, across genres, across literature-oriented and writing-oriented classes—should look like as students made their way through the major.

We simply began meeting every other week, with facilitation rotating amongst participants. We did not have a set agenda beyond the goals listed above, and I am not even sure we understood those to be our goals at that time. We did make explicit that the group would value and discuss the practical (response, assessment, portfolios, assignments) and the theoretical (writing development, meaning of genres and formal boundaries/conventions, reading-writing continuum). Because everything—from the major, to the classes, to many of our teachers—was new, we were in a position to give an identity to our sequence. This meant we were not working from an already entrenched set of habits or assumptions. Our biggest challenge was enacting the principle that all of us, faculty and students, were students of our program. This meant working against the master-apprentice model that is so familiar in graduate programs.

In fact, the graduate student teachers were much better at taking on the role of learner without being underlings. Faculty seemed to have more difficulty forfeiting the master-teacher status and being open to discussions rather than moving to "fix" their "problems" by prescribing solutions. Graduate students were also better at expanding their sense of their disciplinary terrain, as they seemed to have less essential identification with a subject area. Some faculty felt their being to be essentially wrapped up in an area: "I am *in* composition"; "I *am* a poet"; and so on. But over time, and with much negotiation, these groups came to resemble a writing workshop in which teachers come together as learners to reflect on their individual and collective assumptions, practices, and products.

In addition, undergraduate students identified a need for more opportunities to get involved in the program, as well as for taking their work into more public contexts. As a result, we began organizing poetry/fiction/nonfiction readings at a local café. We instituted a newsletter and an annual anthology of selected works to both promote and celebrate our writers' community. These contributions were written, selected, edited, and designed by undergraduates. As an administrator, I learned an important lesson from the sequence: don't assume people are looking to do the minimum to get by; instead, invite them to participate actively, to contribute. When given an invitation, as our program demonstrated to me—because we were not an exceptional group but rather a typical group of interested and committed teachers and students—people will respond.

---

*Excerpt from Chris's English 202 Creative Writing Prompt, Spring 1998:*

*This piece will have two parts. The first will be a piece of original "creative" writing—in whatever form and on whatever topic you choose. This can be anywhere from 2–6 pages, poetry or prose. The second will be a reflective piece on what makes the first part "creative" (or "poetic," if you prefer) and its strengths and weaknesses as creative work (this part should be 3–5 pages). What makes creative writing **creative** (or poetic writing **poetic**)?*

*What is the relationship between "creative" writing and "rhetorical" writing? Is this a difference of kind, or degree, or emphasis? Do these terms name kinds of writing, or forms/genres of writing, or strategies or functions of writing—or something else altogether? Are they opposites? Do they complement each other? Can a single piece of writing be both creative and rhetorical?*

---

**Chris Gallagher:** The aims of the 202 course that Krista took with me were:

- to introduce and begin to develop shared language about writing and reading

- to introduce and begin to explore the terms/concepts "rhetoric" and "poetics"

- to introduce and begin to explore academic/cultural ideas about writers/writing

- to have students begin to consider themselves writers of rhetoric and poetics

- to have students begin to form a productive community of writers and readers

My goals for the course derived from my understanding of the trajectory of the program. This was not new for me: I had taught in several first-year writing programs in which the aim was to introduce students to the academy. In the sequence, however, the charge was very different, in three ways:

1. I was not introducing students to already-worked-out conversations. I was not *giving* them rhetoric and poetics; rather, I wanted them to begin to see themselves as *doing* rhetoric and poetics. By contrast, the first-year writing programs I had worked in were aimed primarily at acculturating students into preexisting conversations to which they would not contribute in any significant way.

2. These students formed a loose cohort and would move through our courses more or less together. Relationships formed among students, and between students and the program, would live on beyond the course. In contrast, the first-year writing students would likely never see each other (or a writing class) again.

3. The intellectual work begun in 202 would be extended in later courses. By contrast, I was to equip first-year students with transportable skills, strategies, and self-awareness that they could draw on and execute in any writing situation.

Teaching in the sequence, then, took pressure off of me. The expectations were no longer once-and-for-all, get-it-or-don't. Previously, I had considered student development only within a course; now my vision of development *within* the course was informed by a vision of development *beyond* the course. I once asked: Are they ready to write in the academy or the "real world"? I now asked: Have they begun to develop shared language? To explore rhetoric and poetics? To explore constructions of writers/writing? To consider themselves writers? To form productive relationships?

But while the sequence took pressure off me in this way, it also ratcheted up the pressure in another—because I now understood myself to be part of a collective enterprise aimed at developing writers over the long term. Perhaps I can illustrate this paradox through discussing the project that Krista and I have decided to focus on today.

When I handed out the creative writing prompt, many of the students were chilled at the prospect of writing creatively. All the constructions of The Writer that we had been discussing reared their heads: the mad genius, the tortured soul, the cool beat poet . . . . And for the most part, these cultural constructions were more disabling than enabling. For instance, one of Krista's peers claimed that he couldn't get the image of Jack Nicholson's character in *The Shining* out of his head and that this image was denying him the status of "writer." And he was not alone: on the first day of class, when I asked students to conjure a prototypical writing scene, almost none of them imagined themselves in those scenes.

Perhaps this accounts for their first set of drafts—the familiar plots, the flat characters, the overwrought symbols, and the syrupy poems that *always* rhymed. At any rate, in conferences I learned a great deal about the identity struggle I was asking students to confront. My conference with Krista was especially useful. She seemed nervous. She was working on a lightly fictionalized account of the death of her track coach's son. It was a moving story: the coach—well intentioned but demanding—pushes the kid too hard and the son dies. The prose was competent, but a bit . . . well, flat. It was a more or less chronological rendering of events much, I suspected, as they had happened.

I asked Krista how she felt about the piece and to describe her plans for it. She expressed frustration, saying something was missing, but she didn't know what. She felt paralyzed. We talked about that for a while, and we decided that perhaps the piece hewed too closely to reality. It's good to write about what we know, we decided, but sometimes what we know can box us in to a story we don't really want to tell. So Krista walked out that day with a single piece of advice: dissociate the main character from his real-life model, starting with a new name. Not a bad piece of advice, but neither did I think our conference had been particularly successful. Perhaps Krista would breathe life into the piece, but what, I wondered, had she learned about "creative writing": what it was, how it worked, how it related to "rhetoric"—the stuff of the course?

You'll hear Krista's version of the conference in a moment; for my part, the conference turned out to be instructive both at the time and subsequently. I left that conference understanding that what many students needed was encouragement to articulate the choices they were making as writers, opening up moments in their texts where they chose one strategy or device over another. In addition to a chance to think and write through the cultural constructions of writers and writing that they brought with them, they needed to try their hand at *being* writers and confronting writerly choices.

Perhaps the most important point here, though, is that this work was the beginning of a long process of writing development. Krista's rendering of our conference—which I read a year after it took place—reminded me of the fourth major difference between my teaching in the sequence and my teaching in first-year programs: students would not only extend but also revisit their work in this course as they moved through the program. This is why the pressure in 202 was both lower and higher than it had been in other programs; this work would be mined in later classes. Krista's representation of our conference has helped me recognize what is for me the most important idea we offer today: that learning how to listen to narratives such as Krista's may be the key to understanding not only student development, but also teacher and curriculum development.

---

*Excerpt from Krista's English 202 Portfolio Cover Letter, Spring 1998:*

*To My Future Professor,*

 *Throughout my life I have considered myself a reader. If I had any previous experience with writing, it was that I read it. I had never tried to write anything in addition to the assignments I was given in school. These assignments required little thought or creativity. It didn't occur to me that my experience with writing was limited until I got to college. It never occurred to me that I should **have** an experience as a writer at all.*

 *. . . [Now] I view my writing differently. I'm no longer convinced that writing is a God-given talent. It may be, but it may not be. I'm not so sure there is this great division between the **Writer** and the rest of us. Certainly some people are more gifted than others when it comes to writing. But you can still play even if you're not an All-Star. . . . That's what I mean when I say I'm at a different location. I'm no **Writer,** but I do feel that writing is a skill that can be improved and involves a process that can be fine-tuned. More important, I can picture myself in that endeavor.*

---

**Krista Stock:** I began the sequence with little experience in writing or talking about writing. For much of the first half of the semester, I struggled with two things: producing original texts and developing a vocabulary with which to talk about writing.

My session with Chris was important because it gave me insight into how a writer develops and presents an idea. Through brainstorming, and then making decisions regarding narrative style, voice, characters, and so on, I was engaged in the process of creating a text. Exploring my options, and what those options would allow me to do as a writer, modeled the kinds of decisions all writers make. What Chris introduced, although I don't think I fully understood it until much later, was that the writing I am accustomed to reading, writing by Writers, is crafted throughout a process that can be learned. Learning how one goes about producing a piece of writing made it much easier to then enter into conversations that involved issues like the blurred line between rhetoric and poetics, and the cultural work being accomplished in a text.

As I said, I also struggled with developing a vocabulary with which to talk about writing. The basic terms and concepts that are used throughout the sequence are introduced in 202. Chris had the challenge of introducing and using these terms in a way that would help students get comfortable with them. He invited us into the ongoing conversation that was taking place in the sequence as a whole. By the end of 202, I understood what it meant to study writing. Furthermore, I felt a sense of ownership of my education, especially when Chris asked us to write a letter to our next sequence teacher regarding what we expected from the class. Later, Shari's approach to my 303 class would allow us to take the conversation begun in 202 and build on it.

––––––––––––

*Shari's English 303 Workshop Reflection Assignment, Fall 1998:*

*For Wednesday please write about a good or bad workshopping experience. . . . Describe it in detail: What were your expectations prior to this experience and how did they relate to this experience? What were the results and what was your response? Did you attempt to alter the situation? Why or why not, and if so, what were the effects? How do you now understand the experience differently than you did at the time?*

### Excerpt from Krista's Response:

*I ran to class and approached my professor, Chris Gallagher. "I need an appointment NOW!" Sensing my obvious tension, he made time for me to meet with him that day. I walked into his office and explained my situation. I needed help. I didn't know where to go with this paper but I couldn't think of another story. Thankfully, Chris didn't ask to read my first draft. Instead, he offered to workshop the idea as if I had yet to put pen to paper. I told him my coach's story as I remembered it.*

*Chris's first suggestion was to make the main character, my coach, just that, a character, not my coach. This was extremely freeing to me. If I just changed the name, I could explore the character. Then we began to discuss different ways to present the story. I could use a flashback or tell it in first person. Make it dreamlike or leave it open-ended. I could even, dare I say, write it as a poem. Once I started talking about the piece, ideas started rushing into my head.*

*I left Chris's office feeling confident that I could conquer this assignment. Workshopping my paper had been a great help in opening my mind to different possibilities. The experience of working with my professor in a workshop setting undoubtedly helped facilitate that writing process, but just as important, I was able to take what I learned from this experience and apply it to my in-class workshops. In class I was open to all suggestions and tried to ask questions that would draw out the ideas of my classmates. I also tried to elaborate as much as possible on my thoughts. In fact, those are my three ground rules for a workshop: ask questions, be open, and elaborate.*

---

**Shari Stenberg:** Between the fall of 1998 and spring of 1999, I moved—along with Krista—from 202, Introduction to Rhetoric and Poetics, to 303, an advanced workshop in rhetorical and persuasive writing. I'd now have to determine how to build and extend the practices, issues, and questions of 202 into 303. Because I always felt there was so much we didn't get to in 202, I struggled a great deal with what it meant to make 303 more advanced, to make it more challenging, to make it a step up from 202.

As I prepared to venture into the new territory of 303, Chris facilitated a teacher meeting concerning these very issues. The meeting encouraged us to consider the aims of our individual classrooms, as well as how these aims fit into the curricular goals as a whole. We each wrote about what we hoped students would leave our individual classes knowing or being able to do. Interestingly, when Chris asked us to read them, many of us—whether teaching the advanced courses or the intro course—articulated similar goals.

This was important, for sure, but I was impatient. I needed to know—soon!—what should make 303 a different course than 202. Should students be doing more writing? Different kinds of writing? Should the readings be different? Should the workshops change? In focusing on rhetorical considerations, could students still write within poetic forms? And how about my role as teacher? Should that change as I worked with advanced students? We didn't come up with any final answers in that meeting or in the meetings that followed. But what we did come up with was perhaps more important: we began to realize the challenges that this curriculum posed for us. First, we came to see that we needed to think more carefully about our conception of student development: not only how we expected students to develop as readers, writers, and thinkers as they moved through the sequence, but also how we understood development in the first place. Perhaps the fact that we had so many shared goals in each of the classes told us something. In other words, perhaps there was a reason that we could not exactly quantify how one course should differ from the other.

Quite often the relationship of introductory courses to advanced courses is understood thus: intro courses provide skills and advanced courses provide content. Underlying this model is the assumption that acts of reading and writing can be finally mastered in those early courses, and that these skills can later be deployed in the "real," advanced classrooms. This also means that advanced teachers are somehow excused from teaching reading and writing, activities thought to have been already acquired. But in the sequence, where writing and reading are not understood as skills that can be mastered but rather as acts that are "endlessly negotiated and discovered anew" (Seitz 17), it made sense that we would be engaging these activities in all classes.

Responding to each other's writing, workshopping, entering new rhetorical contexts, reflecting on pedagogy—these are all activities that require ongoing learning. So instead of thinking only of what I would do differently in this advanced class, I began to think about what I would do the same. I tried to think about the relationship between 202 and 303 as dialogical rather than hierarchical.

In addition to reminding me what should be taught and engaged in all sequence classes, this meeting also helped me to see what sequence students had already begun in 202. As I looked at the list I'd constructed, reflection on learning stood out as one of the most crucial activities in which 202 students engage. For instance, many of us ask students in 202 to reflect on their histories as writers. In addition to examining what it is about our conceptions of The Writer that usually excludes students, such an exercise also encourages students to reflect on their histories as learners. How have past pedagogies helped or prevented them from seeing themselves as writers? This practice helps them, hopefully, make visible how they have learned, and gets them started thinking about how they are currently learning.

This reminded me that I might ask my current students, now at the end of their 202 course, to continue this kind of reflexive work. I might ask them to reflect on our class, to consider how they hoped to continue the work they'd started as they moved into 303. I was surprised at how much they had to say. They raised thoughtful ideas about what should change—more sustained assignments, more time for revision—and for what should remain in every workshop: revision, process accounts, "reading as writers," etc.

This conversation—in which students could reflect as (or more) adeptly on our class as they could on their written texts—also reminded me to build into 303 opportunities to reflect on

202—a course all of them would have taken. I wanted them to do what Chris calls "mining," revisiting their experiences from 202 to consider what and how they learned in that site, as well as how that learning could be continued in this new, but connected, context.

Reflective assignments have been important in two ways. First, they've enabled students to see the pedagogy the way they see their texts: as a series of choices that can be intervened in. Students are able to look at the classroom and at the curriculum and consider what aspects of their learning are enabling them as writers. Second, these assignments have been an important way for me to learn from the students about how to teach the courses, to enact the curriculum. Krista's reflection on the workshop with Chris is just one of the many that helped me think about these issues, and that has reminded me that our most crucial knowledge about what our courses should do, and how they should work in relation to each other, comes from the students.

---

*Excerpt from Krista's English 303 Final Portfolio, Fall 1998:*

*Part I—Myself as Writer: How would you describe yourself as a writer? This is for me an endlessly frustrating question. The learning kind? My current goal as a writer is quite simple: learn as much as I possibly can. "One on whom nothing is lost." So I guess I would describe myself as a writer-in-progress. I've come far enough that when people ask me what I'm studying I say writing, but not so far as to tell them that I want to be a writer when I grow up.*

*Part II—Myself as Reader: In my reading this semester I have become increasingly aware of the story the author is choosing not to tell. Knowing how much information I chose to leave out of my piece in order to further my own purposes, I am curious as to how much other people have left out of their work. I am not only referring to other student work but to all that I read. This has led me to be a bit of a more cynical reader. Even in journalis-*

*tic pieces I wonder what facts have been left out for spatial or other reasons and how that might change the perspective of the piece.*

---

**Krista:** The account of my workshop with Chris that I wrote for Shari's class is typical of the reflection students are asked to do in the sequence. Whether we are reading a text, workshopping, or writing, incorporated into all these activities is a conversation in which we evaluate what we are doing. For example, if I'm working on a piece for one of my classes, at various points during its development I'll write about my process, how it may be different from past projects, evaluating any new ideas or techniques.

Reflective writing serves to connect what we read, discuss, and write in a way that makes clear associations among them, which dissolves those reading-versus-writing, teaching-versus-learning divisions. A group can evaluate a workshop, or with the teacher evaluate the progress a class is making, in order to make the necessary adjustments (revisions).

---

*Steve's English 350 Assertive Reading Prompt, Spring 1999:*

A. *Some Principles for Assertive Reading (adapted from* Textual Intervention, *Rob Pope)*

*A general maxim: Do not cooperate with every text you meet. Refuse to be simply (made over as) its ideal reader/viewer. In fact, where you have cause and/or occasion, be distinctly uncooperative or, more positively, assertive:*

1. *Figure out whose words and worldviews are being represented in a text as it operates in a given context—and, therefore, whose words and worldviews are thereby being misrepresented, underrepresented, or simply not represented.*

   2. *Figure out whose interests (economic, political, cultural, aesthetic) a text in a given context is serving—and then whose economic, political, cultural, and aesthetic interests it is **not** serving.*

   3. *These words and worldviews featured in a text operating in a given context can be understood to express certain preferences, certain sets of values. Figure out what preferences those are, and then figure out what other preferences, what other values, are thereby being suppressed, oppressed, or repressed. And then determine this: do you support the preferences expressed in the text as it is, or do you prefer others?*

B. *Writing (toward) an Assertive Reading: Textual Intervention*

   1. *Intervene in and in some way transform the text.*

   2. *Consider what light these changes throw on the structures, meanings, values, and functions of the base text (this is best done in collaboration with others and in light of changes they too have made).*

   3. *Try to arrive at a final act of explicit preference, however provisional. (This can include features presented in the base text. For our purposes, though, it would be more useful to identify and articulate genuine differences of opinion—conflicts of interest—than to opt for any bogus consensus.)*

   4. *Be ready to read more—and/or more widely—and thereafter to alter the provisional preference expressed in #B3.*

---

**Steve North:** My part on this panel is to talk about a course called English 350: Contemporary Writers at Work. The course was designed to enroll approximately 120 students, thereby helping the sequence achieve an average number of seats/sections comparable to the English department's literature track. In essence, sequence students paid for the small-class opportunities offered by workshop courses of 15 by enrolling in this upper-division lecture class (taught without TA assistance).

Two features of this course have made economic necessity into an educationally defensible, if not absolutely desirable, curricular practice. First, we located this required large-section course at the upper division partly because it generates a greater FTE (full-time equivalency) return at that level, but also because self-selected, upper-division majors would be much better equipped to learn in such a setting than the generally more tentative lower-division students usually assigned to such courses in the usual university curriculum. In addition, however, we found that because the sequence involves a maximum of only fifty new students a year, taught by a core of perhaps twelve instructors, a substantial number of the students who enrolled were likely not only to know one another and the instructor from previous classes, sequence readings, service learning projects, etc., but also to have a strong sense of the sequence as a shared enterprise. In other words, English 350 had an even greater head start than we had expected in overcoming the tendencies toward anonymity and passive learning that frequently bedevil large classes.

In the section Krista took, we focused on the rhetoric and poetics of witness. My interest in this area began with Carolyn Forché's anthology *Against Forgetting,* in which Forché tries to articulate what it has meant to be a poet of witness in the twentieth century. In the course, however, our concern was somewhat broader: what did it mean for any writer to serve as a "witness"? Forché zeroes in on poets who write about the worst atrocities in a century sadly replete with them, but we considered a broader range of writers and a broader spectrum of events. In addition to Forché's poets, for example, we read *I, Rigoberta Menchu,* a book which has been enormously influential because of its claims to empirical truth, and controversial because that truth has been called into serious question; and Tracy Kidder's *Home Town,* a book which purports to be a nonfiction account of life in Northampton, Massachusetts, but which features any number of techniques—including the attribution of "thoughts"—usually associated with fiction. The stakes are perhaps not as high in the latter text as in the former, but both projects nevertheless raise interesting questions about what it means for a writer to serve as a witness.

The centerpiece of the course, however, was a six-week examination of texts dealing with the events tied historically to Schindler's list. We read Thomas Keneally's novel of that title; read portions of Steven Zaillian's screenplay; studied the Steven Spielberg film; and, last, read a set of interviews Elinor Brecher did with Schindler survivors after the film was released *(Schindler's Legacy)*. As Krista will explain, our broadest purpose was to examine these four texts as writers: to treat them, in other words, as made things—the kinds of things sequence majors would aspire to make themselves.

Our more particular concern, though, was with this business of witnessing. Given the enormous gravity of the events involved, what were a writer's or a filmmaker's responsibilities, and to whom? And one means by which we tried to get at such questions was to use a technique borrowed from Rob Pope's *Textual Intervention*. I asked students to take some particular portion of a target text—in the example Krista will offer, the opening of Keneally's novel—and to revise it, intervene in it, put it (as Pope says) "off balance." We compared our results (or did subsequent versions), and then asked critical questions about whose interests each of these various versions served, how so, and to what ends. Krista will illustrate the process by drawing on her interventions.

---

*Excerpt from Krista's English 350 In-Class, First-Draft Assertive Reading:*

*From Keneally's Prologue, Schindler's List:*

    *In Poland's deepest autumn, a tall, young man in an expensive overcoat, a double-breasted jacket beneath it and—in the lapel of the dinner jacket—a large ornamental gold-on-black-enamel Hakenkreuz (swastika) emerged from a fashionable apartment building on Straszewskiego Street, on the edge of the ancient center of Cracow, and saw his chauffer waiting with fuming breath by the open door of an enormous and, even in this blackened world, lustrous Adler limousine.*

### From Krista's In-Class Revision:

*In Poland's darkest autumn, a tall, arrogant opportunist in an overpriced double-breasted suit with a glinting, jeweled gold and onyx swastika on the lapel—close to his flask of cognac— stumbled out of a ritzy apartment building onto Straszewskiego Street on the edge of the cursed city of Cracow, and glared at his chauffer who waited anxiously to open the door of the pretentiously shining black limousine.*

---

**Krista:** A good illustration of how reading, writing, and revision intersect is Steve's exercise in assertive reading. Engaging the text in a way that changes it is comparable to a mechanic learning about engines by taking one apart. By rewriting (revising) the first paragraph of *Schindler's List*, we as readers were able to see how Keneally constructed Schindler's character. It became obvious that by changing the language we could change (revise) a reader's perceptions of the same event.

Revision is probably the most important concept I've learned. In the sequence, writing gets revised, ideas get revised, classes get revised. The concept of examining something, determining in what ways it can be changed, and predicting the effect of those changes, is critical. I have come to apply revision to almost everything.

CHAPTER FIVE

# *Toward Pedagogy-Centered Curricula*

In Chapter 4, I suggested that Composition and Rhetoric is moving in two directions simultaneously: toward traditional disciplinarity and away from it. This chapter takes the latter trend as its point of departure. Specifically, I am interested in compositionists' critiques of traditional disciplinarity as endorsing the notion that disciplinary knowledge is made only by "theorists"— specialized experts who consult primarily with one another— and then "trickles down" to teachers and, eventually, to students. In this view, teaching consists merely of passing on already-worked-out bodies of knowledge, and curricula are accordingly constructed around the imparting of those specialized studies. On the contrary, as I have suggested, many compositionists insist that pedagogy and curriculum should be considered acts and sites of disciplinary knowledge-making. In this view, we ought to think of disciplinary knowledge as deriving from the work that students and teachers do together, not the other way around. (In addition to those cited in Chapter 4, see Connors, "Rhetoric"; Ohmann, Foreword, "Professionalizing"; Phelps, *Composition;* Schuster.)[1]

In other words, compositionists are pointing the way toward what I term "pedagogy-centered curricula," a notion that helps us imagine what it would mean to place pedagogy at the center of our work in the academy. (Chapter 6 explores what it would mean to place pedagogy at the center of our work beyond the academy.) But we must also understand the historical and contemporary forces working against such an endeavor. Thus, I begin here by showing how the disciplinary and administrative constraints I have discussed throughout this book push against the very notion of pedagogy-centered curricula.

## Teaching Our Passions

John Trimbur uses the term "entrepreneurial" to describe the prevailing model of academic work: "each of us figures as a small start-up enterprise where we function as the owners and operators, seeking our market share and our piece of the action" (Foreword x). Similarly, Louise Wetherbee Phelps suggests that the academy functions on an "ethic of radical individualism" ("Practical Wisdom" 866). These principles translate in curricular terms into a scheme organized around professors' ever-narrower areas of expertise. That is, we are granted market share according to our ability to establish a niche in the academic marketplace. We are, it is true, allied in a loose confederation with other start-ups, but we are still expected to act independently. This confederation is more or less permanent, protected by academic freedom and—again, in curricular terms—the right to "teach one's passions." Even in most teaching-oriented colleges and universities, curricula tend to be organized not around pedagogy but around professors' (usually scholarly) passions.

This arrangement, of course, derives from the nineteenth-century confluence of the research-oriented German university and the business-minded new U.S. university. But, as North shows, a more recent moment has ratified the "primarily personnel-centered" English curriculum (*Refiguring* 32). After a Great Expansion after World War II and a Great Contraction beginning at the end of the 1960s, according to North, English studies found itself in quite a quandary by the late 1980s:

> [D]epartments found themselves having to decide again and again what it meant to "cover the field" when, on the one hand, that field—conceived in terms of both the constituent areas of expertise *and* the bodies of those who populated it—had diversified beyond anyone's experience, and, on the other hand, the resources available for carrying out any such coverage either remained the same or became scarcer. (59)

The Wye and Wayzata Conferences of 1987 bear this out: the primary message emerging from both groups seemed to be that the discipline was not "coverable," and that (for better or worse) we had lost whatever tenuous sense of coherence English studies had been able to achieve (see, for instance, Lunsford, Moglen, and Slevin; Elbow, *What?*).[2]

North suggests that English studies had three options in 1987. The first was "dissolution": the constituent fields within the discipline could go their own ways, each mustering as much institutional support as they could (*Refiguring* 69). The second option was "corporate compromise": "holding the conflicted enterprise together, however loosely, and then—for curricular purposes—finding some way to present *and* preserve all of its competing interests" (71). The final option North calls "fusion": "bringing disparate elements together under sufficient pressure and with sufficient energy to transform them into a single new entity, one quite distinct from any of the original components" (73).

As it turns out, "corporate compromise" has proven to be the option of choice for most English departments. Although much has changed demographically and doctrinally in the field of English studies in recent years, English curricula have generally absorbed these changes by developing what we might think of as the "rambling mansion" approach. In this approach, each theoretical innovation is accommodated by adding a new wing to the mansion, without making structural changes to the existing wings. Want a postcolonialist? Add a wing. Want a queer theorist? Add a wing. Want an ethnic lit person? Add a wing. The principle of growth and development here is simple accretion: the mansion continues to grow—and the wings, incidentally, keep getting farther and farther apart. Under the corporate compromise model, however, this is not a problem: the inhabitants of each wing simply agree to inhabit the same general structure and, for all practical purposes, to leave one another alone. (There are passions to be pursued, after all.) What's more, departments following this model can claim to be "progressive," having expanded to include "diverse" faculty members and expertise. (That "include" does not mean *engage* or even *take seriously* rarely seems to tarnish such claims.)

What results from this arrangement in curricular terms is typically a loosely confederated set of courses, sometimes organized into "tracks" or "concentrations." Under this arrangement, students may linger longer in one of the wings. But even in such instances, students are still asked to put in an appearance in several of the more established wings (just long enough, that is, to fulfill their core requirements). At any rate, students are likely to encounter difficulty navigating the mansion and seeing how the wings fit together (if, indeed, they do).

Even as the coverage model has become more difficult to defend intellectually, we have seen an erosion of economic support for a traditional, personnel-centered curriculum. In institutions across the country, the lines of departed or retired colleagues are not being returned as programmatic hires, institutional resources are becoming scarcer, and student enrollment is often on the rise. One need not be a "prophet of regress" to recognize that this is a formula for lean times (see Berubé; Berubé and Nelson; Readings).

Increasing institutional reliance on disturbing labor practices provides one index of our disciplinary dire straits (see Gilbert et al.; Association of Departments of English; "Statement from the Conference"). Composition and Rhetoric is of course particularly vulnerable to this trend since it is still fairly widely held in many institutions, and in the general public, that just about anyone can teach writing. So while the field has been professionalizing and becoming more "disciplined," the teaching of lower-division courses, and specifically required first-year writing, has been increasingly handed over to adjuncts, who are neither viewed nor treated (as their title suggests) as "real" professionals.[3] In this context, it is perhaps not surprising that compositionists scramble with as much verve as any of our colleagues for scarce institutional resources. We struggle to staff first-year writing courses with reliable, responsible teachers; we struggle to secure funding for writing centers; we struggle to build and maintain graduate programs; we struggle to fulfill our service roles in our departments (administering first-year courses, overseeing assessment programs, training TAs, etc.) *and* in other programs (Teachers Colleges and writing-across-the-curriculum programs, e.g.); we struggle to develop, and to obtain resources and intellectual support for, writing beyond the first-year course. As a result, the composition "curriculum" at many institutions often amounts to little more than the first-year course and perhaps a handful of upper-division courses (Advanced Composition, Expository Writing,

Argument and Persuasion) for students who sustain an interest in writing beyond their first year of college. Sometimes, a track or a concentration is developed within the English major; sometimes writing programs split from English departments altogether and become their own administrative unit. In any event, as I suggested in Chapter 4, as compositionists we often find ourselves participating in the institutional and disciplinary economy by engaging in the very acts of entrenchment and protectionism that have for so long marginalized our work. Well aware that scrambling for institutional resources and protecting our academic turf perpetuate a problematic status quo, we are nonetheless at a loss: What else can we do? What would be the use of giving up hard-won institutional resources, space, and authority? What choice do we have but to protect (and try to increase) our market share? What can we do but safeguard *our* passions?

## Refiguring English Studies, Reclaiming Curriculum

These are not, it turns out, merely rhetorical questions. A number of compositionists—sometimes taking their cue from the economic "crisis" many English departments and writing programs are facing—have begun to turn their energies to rethinking curriculum as a means of "refiguring" the field/discipline. At the risk of repeating a well-worn progressive cliché, I think of this shift as a move from "teaching our passions" to "teaching our students." There appears to be a growing awareness that—for both economic and intellectual reasons—we can no longer simply teach what we know and love; the personnel-centered curriculum has not held, and corporate compromise is alienating us from each other and from our students. We cannot continue to work in isolation from other teachers, counting on students to connect the disciplinary dots. Instead, we must hash out different visions of curriculum—and different visions of our disciplinary work.[4]

As I turn to examples of this thinking, it is important to recognize that compositionists have fellow travelers in this endeavor; indeed, some visible teacher-scholars in literary studies have also turned their attention to "refiguring" English studies. Although literary studies has traditionally been reluctant to discuss pedagogy at all—satisfied instead to rework the "content" of the discipline and then to assume that curriculum and pedagogy would take care of themselves—we have seen some evidence in recent years of what David Downing calls a "pedagogical turn" (xiii; see Berlin and Vivion; Cahalan and Downing; Downing; Graff, *Beyond;* Jay; Kecht; Pope; Smithson and Ruff). One of the most important features of this work is that much of it calls teachers out of their individual classrooms to work together on curriculum development. Literary scholars have paid a good deal of attention, for instance, to the curricular possibilities of culture/cultural studies (see, e.g., Balsamo; Foreman and Shumway; Kennedy; Mailloux; Straub). Instead of assuming that each teacher will teach his or her own passion in isolation, and that students will develop a sense of the discipline simply by moving from course to course, these new curricular reforms ask teachers to negotiate a shared and always evolving vision of the discipline.

Two particularly visible examples recommend themselves here. First we have Gerald Graff's widely known "teach the conflicts" model (*Beyond,* "Teach"). Graff proposes an "integrated" model of English studies to replace what he calls "cafeteria counter" curricula that tend either to isolate professors or to offer a watered-down version of consensus (*Beyond* 177). This integrated model puts the conflicts and disagreements of the discipline at the center of the curriculum; indeed, they become the primary object of study (see *Beyond,* "Teach"; see also Jay). Graff's model is limited—it is, in fact, an updated version of corporate compromise—in that it constructs a spectator rather than a participant role for students. But his curricular ideas are important here because while they may not put the work that students and teachers do together—pedagogy—at the center of the curriculum, they do disrupt the individualistic, entrepreneurial model of academic work.

The second example from literary studies goes a step further. While Graff imagines students as spectators of a performed disciplinarity-as-ritual-combat, Robert Scholes envisions a more active role for students in the curriculum and in the discipline. In fact, Scholes's "textual studies" model asks us to "rethink our practice by starting with the needs of our students rather than with our inherited professionalism or our personal preferences" (*Rise* 84; see also *Textual Power*). Scholes's principal contribution to the re-formation of English studies is the notion that the English curriculum and the discipline of English studies ought to be organized not around texts themselves, or even the debates that inform their inclusion in or exclusion from the curriculum, but around textual *practices*, including students' reading and writing.

A full treatment of Graff's and Scholes's ideas is beyond the scope of this chapter, but it should be clear enough even from this brief outline that these reform efforts—especially the latter—mark something of a departure from the "teaching our passions" tradition. Graff calls teachers out of their individual classrooms to forge a vision of dissensus to share with students; Scholes goes a step further and calls teachers *and students* out of their individual classrooms to produce knowledge together—to engage, that is, in pedagogy. Thus, these thinkers help us begin to clear some intellectual ground for pedagogy-centered curriculum.

But it is the recent work of compositionists that best suggests the possibilities for pedagogy-centered curriculum. Here, I focus on two writers whose projects, it seems to me, best position us to imagine curriculum with pedagogy at its heart. First, I return briefly to Stephen North's "fusion-based" curriculum.

North's primary concern is doctoral education, but his ideas about graduate curriculum are relevant to (and obviously would have an effect on) undergraduate education as well. Recall that North imagines three models for English studies: dissolution (each of the constituent specializations within English studies splinters off), corporate compromise (the constituent specializations are held together in loose confederation, thus preserving competing interests), and fusion, which he defines as

> bringing disparate elements together under sufficient pressure and with sufficient energy to transform them into a single new entity, one quite distinct from any of the original components. Or, to put it in terms specific to English Studies: rather than ending the field's divisions by breaking it up along the lines of conflict (dissolution), or packaging those conflicts for the purposes of curricular delivery (corporate compromise), the object would be to harness the energy generated by the conflicts in order to forge some new disciplinary enterprise altogether. (73)

Although North favors fusion, he admits that it would be the most difficult approach to enact because it would require the most radical change in our disciplinary business as usual. Curricular coherence would derive less from "covering" periods, or authors, or movements, or nationalisms, than from a nexus of disciplinary interests, which would emerge through what North terms "the disciplinary and professional equivalent of a locked room for what amount to do-or-die negotiations" (73). Even more challenging, North (like Scholes) envisions students as participants in the disciplinary conversation, not merely spectators of it (74). Indeed, the feature that most clearly distinguishes this model from corporate compromise is its requirement that faculty "renegotiate their disciplinary and professional status vis-à-vis the doctoral students in their programs" (75).

Certainly, undergraduate students cannot be (and often will not be interested in being) brought into disciplinary and professional conversations in quite the way advanced graduate students can (and wish) to be, but it is nonetheless true that North offers a vision of a curriculum—and a discipline—that is less about simply teaching our passions than about teaching our students. Whatever specific form a fusion-based curriculum might take— and that, of course, would depend on the constituents of the program—the key principle is that programmatic coherence derives from the textual practices that the teachers and students engage in together (*Refiguring* 85). Although a fusion-based curriculum would continue to draw on faculty's strengths and interests as specialists—that is, it would still allow faculty to pursue disciplinary projects that are important to them—the curriculum would no longer be organized strictly around those narrowly conceived areas of strength or interest. "Intradisciplinary" courses—perhaps with names such as History of English Studies, The Rhetoric and Poetics of Political Writing, Contemporary Writers at Work, Race and Representation, Literacy and Community, and the like—would replace traditional period, author, and genre courses. Under this truly integrated approach, the conflicts *and* the shared features and practices of the discipline would become deliberate features of the curriculum not by presenting them to students, but by engaging students in them.

Like North, James Seitz envisions an integrated curriculum

that brings courses, teachers, and students into more useful relation by means of a focus on the textual practices of both teachers and students. His "metaphorical curriculum" is

> one in which courses would meet not merely to discuss their differences but to share practices ordinarily reserved for just one of them. Thus, a cluster of courses in, say, composition, Renaissance literature, and creative writing might ask that students compose a narrative essay, read a comedy by Ben Jonson, and write a poem at different moments during the semester, whereupon these otherwise separate courses would intersect, encouraging students to explore the similarities and differences in their various approaches to the assignments. Rather than waiting for their professors to describe the contours of a conversation that will go on whether or not students choose to join it, the students in these courses would participate in a conversation created by the work—the literate endeavors—in which they are involved as readers and writers. (200–210)

Like North's fusion-based curriculum, Seitz's metaphorical curriculum would be organized largely around students' writing since that is the primary (though not only) way they produce knowledge. Among other things, this means that teachers must be willing to "merge student texts with the official material of their courses, so that the disjunctive discourses of student writers and experienced writers can be investigated together, often in the same class meeting with the same set of terms" (202).

As Seitz suggests—and this insight applies as well to North's and to Scholes's curricular notions—this refiguring of the curriculum (and by extension the discipline) would require professors to reimagine their authority relationships with students. It would require us not only to pay serious and scholarly attention to student writing, but also to recognize that this writing may well exceed the specialized frames we have developed for it. That is, whether our courses are clustered, as in Seitz's model, or completely reconfigured, as in North's and Scholes's models, we must expect that students will be doing intellectual work that we could not do ourselves—that we, ensconced in our specializations, could scarcely have imagined (see North, *Refiguring* 230).

# Toward Pedagogy-Centered Curricula

In urging us to dignify the reflexive work that teachers and students do together as constitutive of, rather than witness to, curricular and disciplinary knowledge-making, North and Seitz encourage us to develop curricula—and indeed our discipline—not for or around teachers and students, but with them. In doing so, they point the way toward pedagogy-centered curricula.

Pedagogy-centered curricula are, by definition, context specific. In fact, resistance to prepackaging and commodification is one of their key features: because they are always enacted within (and sometimes against) local constraints and possibilities, and because they are always negotiated by their human actors, they cannot be designed from outside the pedagogical situation and then "given" to teachers and students. When we talk about pedagogy-centered curricula, then, we are talking about a vision. But it's a vision that can never be enacted the same way twice because any "version" will evolve out of local practice and the enactment of what I have called institutional literacy.

That said, we can identify the fundamental principle of such curricula, and we might do so by starting with that familiar term from Deweyan progressive education: "student-centered." The concept of pedagogy-centered curricula, while consonant with the best of Dewey's thinking, takes a step beyond student-centeredness. Specifically, it describes the act of developing curriculum out of the dialectic between students' and teachers' experiences, knowledge, and interests. It dislodges "teachers' passions" from the center of the curriculum, but instead of simply installing students there, it makes the reflexive work that teachers and students do together—pedagogy—the driving force of the curriculum (and, by extension, the discipline).

As I indicated in Chapter 4, it was never Dewey's intention simply to "give over" the curriculum to students. A Deweyan curriculum would foster a dialogue between teachers and students and would develop through an examination both of "what is known" and the experiences of the learners (*Experience*, "Progressive Education"). By definition, then, progressive curricula would refuse the familiar notion that the goals of establishing curriculum are stability and standardization, opting instead for flexibility and diversity. But—and this point is often lost in critiques of Dewey's thinking—this does not mean that Deweyan curriculum is content-less. On the contrary, in a progressive curriculum, "subject matter" would *develop* (would *progress*) over time. Dewey explains:

> In the first place, the material would be associated with and derived from . . . activities or prolonged courses of action undertaken by the pupils themselves. In the second place, the material presented would not be something to be literally followed by other teachers and students, but would be indications of the intellectual possibilities of this and that course of activity—statements on the basis of carefully directed and observed experience of the questions that have arisen in connection with them and of the kind of information found useful in answering them, and of where that knowledge can be had. No second experience would exactly duplicate the course of the first; but the presentation of material of this kind would liberate and direct the activities of any teacher in dealing with the distinctive emergencies and needs that would arise in re-undertaking the same general type of project. Further material thus developed would be added, and a large and yet free body of related subject-matter would gradually be built up. ("Progressive Education" 179–80)

I quote this passage at length because this point is crucial: in a progressive curriculum, subject matter is drawn from, organized, and *revised* around the experiences, knowledge, and interests of teachers and students. When constructing new courses or new curricula, progressive teachers don't simply read experts in their field—though that is certainly part of their work. They also talk to students and teachers who have undertaken similar studies, in order to develop a method defined by *how* the material might best be learned.

It is perhaps clear by now why I prefer the term "pedagogy-centered" to "student-centered." If "pedagogy" names the work that teachers and students do together—as I have proposed— then a pedagogy-centered curriculum by definition evolves not around students' or teachers' experiences, interests, or knowledge, but precisely from the meeting of these. The primary role of such a curriculum would be to place teachers and students in dialogue with one another.

## By Way of Example

But what might such curricula look like? How would they evolve? While the possibilities are nearly endless, and while such curricula are always local and in process, it may be useful to reflect on how one group of writing teachers, administrators, and students worked together to build a pedagogy-centered curriculum. I turn now to the work represented in Intralude 5, not in order to offer a model for others to emulate, but to provide what Dewey calls an "indication of intellectual possibilities."

### *Part I: Developing a Pedagogy-Centered Curriculum*

According to the "Proposal for a Writing Sequence through the English Major," written by Stephen North and passed by the Department of English at SUNY–Albany in April 1993, the writing program at SUNY had become "increasingly diffuse and unfocused" in recent years. This was the result of three recent institutional shifts: first, a writing intensive (WI) program had been designed to replace the university's first-year writing requirement; second, the number of English majors had grown enormously, putting great pressure on writing courses; and third, the university had been putting increasing pressure on the department to produce more seats, and so writing courses—smaller than most university courses—were viewed as a "quantitative liability." These pressures conspired to create a "program" that was not a program at all, but rather a small set of 100- and 300-level courses that did not offer any programmatic coherence even for those few students who took more than one writing course as undergraduates.

The primary aim of the Writing Sequence was to provide students with a set of coherent, sequenced writing courses that also met the administrative exigencies I have described. In the words of the proposal,

> The Writing Sequence offers students . . . a sustained focus on
> their own writing as informed by two venerable traditions, rhetoric
> and poetics. It balances the small classes students repeatedly con-
> firm that they value, and in which their reading and writing can
> be supervised in a way that only such classes will allow, with
> larger classes designed to examine in a more general way the
> historical and theoretical contexts that inform their developing
> practice. (3)

Under the proposal, a series of 200- and 300-level fifteen-student
writing workshops introducing students to rhetoric and poetics
would be, in numeric terms, counterbalanced by two larger upper-division courses: Contemporary Writers at Work and Special
Topics in Rhetoric and Poetics.

It is important to view this document—and this program—
in terms of what I have called "institutional literacy." The document and the program were created in response not only to the
three exigencies noted in the proposal, but also to a wide array
of constraints and possibilities, including the lack of a required
first-year writing program; a largely literature-based English faculty; an innovative doctoral program; a generally amiable relationship between writing faculty and those in other specializations;
a strong core of Composition and Rhetoric faculty; and so on.
While it would be impossible to untangle all of these constraints
and possibilities here, it is important to recognize that many of
the promises (or, viewed slightly differently, the challenges) in
the proposal—for instance, to bring poetics and rhetoric together,
to integrate faculty from various specializations, to staff courses
with teachers of various ranks, and to "pay for" small introductory courses with large upper-division courses—derived in large
part from a careful reading of, and writing back to, local institutional constraints and possibilities.

Moreover, once the program was approved on paper, the
teachers, administrators, and students who participated in it were
charged with making sense of what it would look like in practice. Because the courses were imagined as a sequence; because
participating faculty would work closely together in regular teaching meetings; because the program was what we might call
"intradisciplinary"; because students would move through the
curriculum in cohorts (more or less); because the program was

so new—the teachers and students who participated in this program were responsible not only for the work that happened *within* individual courses, but also *across* courses. For most of the teachers in the program, these challenges proved difficult to negotiate. We had to unlearn how we thought about our work. Specifically:

♦ *We had to learn to listen to and act on students' representations of their experiences in/of our courses and the program.* We built feedback mechanisms into our courses and used students' responses to guide our classroom decisions and to inform our discussions with one another in our teacher meetings. But we also built into our courses and into the curriculum moments of situated reflection *across* courses—a practice much less familiar to most of us. Krista tells us, for instance, that by the time she entered Steve's large upper-division course, she had gained confidence as a writer and had developed a wide range of writerly and readerly strategies (as well as a critical understanding of when and how and to what effect to use them). But she also tells us that she remained very much a *developing* writer who continued to experiment and (therefore) to make mistakes. This helped us develop our ideas about the purposes of lower- and upper-division courses, and reinforced our sense that devoting advanced courses to "content," under the assumption that students should have "mastered" writing at the introductory level, is bad educational practice (see Seitz; Stenberg).

♦ *We had to learn how to negotiate our pedagogies and our program together.* As teachers we did not inherit a fixed program; instead, we entered an ongoing intellectual project that would emerge in large part out of our dialogue with one another. For those of us steeped in the still dominant classroom-as-private-space and teacher-as-master traditions, this was a difficult challenge, as Amy makes clear in her presentation. Some teachers, in fact, could not—or would not—engage in this different kind of conversation and dropped out of the group. Those of us who stayed, on the other hand, learned how to enact the kind of community Amy discusses.

♦ *We had to learn to become more comfortable with the flexibility and evolving nature of the curriculum.* Most of us came to the Writing Sequence with a history of relying on curriculum as a stable guide, a standardized set of parameters and procedures. Here, that comfort was gone, and we were challenged to develop the curriculum as we went along, remaking it semester by semester, week by week. It's not that we didn't have any educational principles or aims—it's that these principles and aims were viewed as *in process*, a site of negotiation among teachers and students. In fact, if anything, our evolving principles and aims were *more* influential in our teaching and our curricular decisions precisely because they were always objects of our shared inquiry, and we felt personally invested in them. While many of us found the prospect of continually revising the curriculum—in practice and on paper—daunting, this practice was also the source of great energy for those who continued to participate in this ongoing intellectual project.

In short, we had to place the reflexive work of teachers and students at the center of the developing curriculum. The dialogue that developed between and among teachers and students is what drove not only student and teacher development, but also the development of the program (and the presentation). The experiences, knowledge, and interests of faculty were not irrelevant; on the contrary, Krista's work shows us that she needed a good deal of guidance from experienced writers and teachers. But the experiences, knowledge, and interests of students were hardly irrelevant, either; indeed, one of the primary aims of the program was to help Krista and her colleagues see themselves as experienced writers and teachers of each other—and of us.

## Part II: Death at an Early Age (a Brief Programmatic Autopsy)

Even as our group was giving its presentation at the 2000 CCCC Convention in Minneapolis, the Writing Sequence was being disenrolled. Despite the program's demonstrable successes—its students regularly won departmental and university awards; it was visible (through public readings and publications) in the university and community; its graduates were pleased with the education they received and well-prepared for the many kinds of work they wanted to do; and its teachers were similarly gratified by their work in the program and have subsequently published and spoken publicly about it—the sequence was being slashed by unfriendly departmental administration.

In fact, though, the causes for the disenrollment of the Writing Sequence are many, and it is not easy to determine which were most influential. It is certainly true that in the few years that the Writing Sequence was developing, the department saw a growing rift between writing-centered faculty (not all of them in Composition and Rhetoric) and faculty who wished the department to have a more "theoretically sophisticated" profile. It is also true that this rift led to (1) turf wars over the still-young and innovative doctoral program, which is described briefly in Intralude 4 and at length in North's *Refiguring the Ph.D. in English Studies;* (2) a proposal for a new Writing Studies program, separate from the English department; (3) an uneasy "receivership" period after the university denied the Writing Studies proposal; and (4) a new departmental administration that was unfriendly to the department's previous focus—at both the undergraduate and graduate levels—on writing. Also, as a result of these developments, several writing-oriented faculty left the university or found places in the university outside of English. Finally, the sequence's very success may have played an important part in its eventual disenrollment because it made faculty outside of the sequence nervous about their place in the department. (Indeed, leaders in the new departmental administration indicated as much to writing program administrators.)

At any rate, the developments at SUNY–Albany were, to say the least, idiosyncratic and hardly generalizable as lessons for others elsewhere. Even so, it is clear enough that we have here another example of the trend I have been discussing: the sacrificing of pedagogical values to administrative values. As in the Texas and New York cases profiled in Chapter 2, there has been no informed public claim that this program was pedagogically problematic. No one worried, that is, that the program didn't "work" for the students and teachers who participated in it. "The problem," rather, lay in those outside of the program who made life sufficiently uncomfortable for administrators that the program became an administrative liability.

But again, I am unwilling to accept the easy reading of this set of events as the inevitable triumph of administrative over pedagogical progressivism. The curricular experiments at SUNY–Albany did have, and continue to have, important consequences for a fair number of students and teachers who participated in them (I count myself in both categories), as well as significant implications for the discipline. The program described in Intralude 5, after all, did graduate scores of students, and it involved dozens of teachers over its short existence. Students and teachers who have gone on to work in other institutions will take with them what they learned about teaching and writing, and will effect changes in those institutions as a result. The SUNY experiments have also become a visible part of the field's work on curriculum revision. In his final book, James Berlin cites the doctoral program at SUNY–Albany as an innovative curriculum that offers a useful vision of "reformed" English studies *(Rhetorics)*. Judith Fetterley, Warren Ginsberg and Cy Knoblauch—all architects of the program—have also written about it. And again, perhaps most notably, Stephen North explores the history and principles of this program at length in *Refiguring the Ph.D. in English Studies*.

In short, I believe it is too simple to say that the innovations at the graduate and undergraduate levels at SUNY have been failures because they have been either disenrolled (the Writing Sequence) or may be transformed (the Ph.D. program). In my view, the short history of the Writing Sequence at SUNY–Albany teaches us both that a pedagogy-centered curriculum *can work* and that making it work will not be enough. We will need to develop and deploy institutional literacy not only as we develop our pedagogy-centered programs, but also—and just as important—to protect them. Again, because institutions are different, institutional literacy will need to be practiced in multiple and context-sensitive ways. The final section of Shamoon, Howard, Jamieson, and Schwegler's *Coming of Age* suggests various useful strategies for protecting writing programs from administrative vagaries. But each essay in this section demonstrates plainly that local constraints and possibilities will always condition how we develop and choose such rhetorical/political/institutional strategies.

Instead of offering my own set of institution-specific strategies here, then, I want to reflect on what I believe the Writing Sequence experience has to teach us about building and protecting programs like it. Most important, maintaining such programs over the long haul will require others in our departments and institutions to engage in the kind of unlearning and relearning that we experienced as teachers in the Writing Sequence. In other words, for pedagogy-centered curricula to succeed, we will need to work in our departments and institutions (and perhaps our communities) for a series of mind-set shifts:

> *1. We must change our understanding of students.* In traditional "teach our passions" English programs, students are "subject" to faculty expertise; they are passive recipients of the professor's knowledge and ideas. Programs such as the Writing Sequence ask us to stop thinking of students as merely students and to begin to think of them as writers, readers, and participants in our discipline. Among other things, this will require a shift from merely evaluating student texts to engaging and even studying student texts as pieces of "real" writing.

> *2. We must change our understanding of ourselves as "professors."* Teaching our passions means modeling for students what we love and hoping they love it, too. Programs such as the Writing Sequence ask us to move from teaching our passions to teaching writers and readers. They ask us to stop thinking of ourselves as passing on our discipline to students, and to begin to think of ourselves as engaging with developing writers and readers in the production of disciplinary knowledge—a sometimes passionate pursuit, to be sure.

> *3. We must change our understanding of curriculum.* A curriculum driven by professors' passions derives its organizing force from whatever loose connections can be divined among the assembled personnel's interests and expertise. Programs such as the Writing Sequence ask us to organize curriculum around pedagogy: the reflexive work that students and teachers do together. They shift the focus of curriculum from standardization and stability (whether derived from a set of texts, a historical period, or an organizing idea) to flexibility and process.

Each of these shifts entails a fundamental rethinking of authority relationships—between professors and students, between students and their departments/institutions, between student texts and "professional" texts, between writing and other "studies." They also ask professors to renegotiate their claims to private spheres within their departments. Having worked in several universities, I know that this will not be a simple task. But finally, the struggle for all of us who care first and foremost about learning is to restore that lost commitment of the German university system to *Lernfreiheit* (freedom to learn) as a necessary complement to *Lehrfreiheit* (freedom to teach). (See North, *Refiguring*.)

## Expanding the Conversation

Ideally, these mind-set shifts will come about not only in our writing programs, departments, and institutions, but also in our communities and larger culture. As I hope to have shown, traditional ways of thinking about teaching and writing are shaped by broad discourses on education and literacy. But, as I also hope to have shown, we must start with the local by "tinkering toward utopia" in our own institutions (Tyack and Cuban). In this grassroots vision, we cannot wait for some grand, revolutionary gesture; we must develop and employ institutional literacy, always, in our moment.

The project I have in mind is no less political for its "localness." While I want to avoid participating in what sometimes seems to me lefter-than-thou posturing in our field, I suggest that the mind-set changes enumerated above, if widely enacted, would provide a foundation for radical—pedagogically progressive—educational change. A pedagogy-centered curriculum does not, after all, allow us merely to espouse diversity and dialogue; it puts pressure on us to enact these by making students, in all their diversity, active participants not only in individual classrooms but also in curriculum development. Unlike teacher-centered curricula, in which we might lecture to students about empowerment, or student-centered curricula, in which empowerment means "giving" students freedom to do whatever they like, pedagogy-centered curricula are "progressive" in the sense that Dewey used the term: they *progress*, they evolve, *through* the dialogue between and among teachers and students.

Again, for Dewey, progress is not an inevitable march toward a better future; it is a constructive process aimed at expanding democratic possibilities in school and beyond. Progress of this kind pushes us beyond what Malea Powell calls a "tolerated margins" approach, in which "other" discourses—of teachers, of students, of entire communities—are merely endured or uncritically celebrated. It requires us to *engage* those other discourses, making them a central part of our evolving work as teachers, curriculum developers, and scholars. With the recent proliferation in pedagogies—critical, feminist, cultural, oppositional, etc.—we are in danger of forgetting that this is what pedagogy is in the first place: the mutual and reflexive engagement of learners and teachers.

In a pedagogy-centered discipline, disciplinary knowledge derives from these local efforts. Teachers and students are not imagined as subject to disciplinary knowledge, but are rather conceived as producers of it. This is the version of disciplinarity that James Slevin advocates: the opening up of disciplinary conversations to those who, under traditional versions of disciplinarity, are at best spectators of them. And this project is not confined to college classrooms. In fact, as I argued in Chapter 4, changing business-as-usual in the academy alone will not allow compositionists to (re)claim pedagogical progressivism; instead—and this is the subject of my final chapter—we will need to work with those beyond the academy to speak back to the reincorporation of the schools and the increasing commodification of teaching generally. In doing so, we will develop and represent knowledge that has traditionally been outside the realm of disciplinary knowledge-making. We will, in other words, reconnect with our radical roots in cross-institutional and community literacy work by placing pedagogy at the center of what we commonly—and I suggest problematically—term "service."

# On Risking Complexity

Writing grants, facilitating assessment projects, writing for local newspapers, sitting on state Department of Education committees, organizing roundtables and local conferences—this is not the professional life my department had imagined for me. It is not the professional life that will most easily move me up the academic ladder.

*Why interrupt the trajectory of your career?*

*Why work with the schools when you're pretenure?*

*Why spread the Composition and Rhetoric faculty even thinner?*

*Why take such risks?*

School-based reform; teacher-led, criterion-referenced assessment; local control; district portfolios—this is not the kind of accountability the experts had imagined for us. It is not the kind of accountability that will earn us the highest grades on state report cards. (See "Quality Counts.")

*Why interrupt the trajectory of the Accountability Movement?*

*Why take this on when people already think we're backward?*

*Why spread our limited resources even thinner?*

*Why take such risks?*

This is our answer:

"Chaos," as Ann Berthoff tells us, "is the source of alternatives" (75). And so learning the uses of chaos means surveying alternatives, entertaining possibilities, exploring options. But this requires risking complexity in an age when simplicity, clarity, and efficiency are the coins of the educational realm. Call it conservative commitment to local control. Call it backwardness. Or, like us, be defiant and call it progressive. The point is, Nebraska resists the simplest educational idea of them all: give them all the same test (see Gallagher, "A Seat"; Roschewski; Nebraska Board of Education).

This is why we're learning the uses of chaos. This is why we're risking complexity. Because education without alternatives, as the teachers who participated in a Goals 2000 local assessments project reminded me, is no education at all.

---

## Goals 2000 Nebraska Local Assessments Project

**Phase I:** *Summer 1999 workshop. Teachers share "milestone projects" and, under the intellectual leadership of experienced teachers Pat Roschewski and Sue Anderson, as well as representatives of the Nebraska Writing Project and the School at the Center rural education program, learn key assessment language and principles, study several models of classroom assessment and evaluation, and work with other teachers.*

*Day One:* They grumble; they groan. They see this workshop on creating local assessments as an exercise in administrative tedium. Another imposition. Thirty-five of the state's best educational minds—most of them well known across the state for their commitment to teaching and learning—and they're wary. Having recruited the strongest teachers we know from eight of the most innovative districts in our state, we now have to make "assessment camp"—as they are good-naturedly (but with a hint of resentment?) calling our workshop—worth their precious summer time.

We spend most of the day discussing their favorite classroom projects and defining assessment. Pat and Sue talk about assessment as something they've done for years. *Assessment is gathering information about student learning; good teachers do it all the time. Yes, we need to document that learning in the context of state standards. But at least we get to do it, not some remote expert or company looking to turn a profit on public education.*

The most important advice the facilitators offer—and this is at the very heart of this project, we say—is not to *design down* from the standards, but instead to *design out* from the classroom. Start, we say, with your teaching, not others' mandates.

They are confused. Anxious. Suspicious. We break.

*Day 3:* We take up two rooms at the conference center. A group of teachers in every corner. Noise, confusion, argument, laughter. I move from group to group, helping gather supplies, answering questions, asking my own. It is July 12 and I am energized.

An English teacher and a social studies teacher work on a Roaring Twenties project in which students will research a hero or heroine of that decade and perform a radio show in character. The teachers are working on a grading rubric, but they are also developing and refining the project itself as they discuss their goals.

A group of math teachers works on a Community Math project in which they and their students solicit real-life math problems from community members. They are creating a scoring guide that will help them explain to students the goals of the project.

A group of teachers from the same district but different disciplines and grades develops its Telling Our Stories project, which has students gather and create stories from their community. They are discussing ways to involve students in assessment.

A group of elementary teachers develops a performance rubric for Everything Grows in the First Grade, a gardening project that involves math, writing, science, technology, and library skills. They realize, with obvious relief, that this single project meets many of the state standards.

Each group is animated, passionate. It is chaos. It is good. The air is filled with newfound assessment lingo—"rubrics," "learning objectives," "performance indicators"—but at the heart of each conversation, each project, is teaching and learning.

*Day 5:* A teacher suggests that we end our final day with her favorite icebreaking activity. Index cards are handed around. On the top of each, we write, "Now I can . . .":

◆ Now I can communicate and articulate to other teachers a *much,* much clearer vision of standards and assessment. I can now talk to others with knowledge and confidence about vocabulary (assessment, evaluation, rubric types, etc.) and the future.

◆ Now I can connect my classroom place-based learning to the state standards.

◆ Now I can . . . see the Big Picture of State Assessment a little more clearly!

◆ Now we can return to our school district with the foundation for our school's assessment plan.

◆ Now I can go back and help write school curriculum guides much more effectively and efficiently. I can go back and work up some more creative classroom lessons for special ed classrooms. I think it will help make me a more effective teacher.

◆ Now I can share assessment ideas with peers.

◆ Now I can do projects in class and know how to assess them. I don't have to test, quiz, test, quiz—grade homework. I really feel energized as a teacher. I learned some things I can do to chart progress in a fun way for kids—I think learning will be more fun in my room this year!

-----

We were to choose projects that we were already using successfully in our classrooms and create assessment tools for them. . . . We intuitively knew that our projects were meaningful teaching and learning tools. Breaking the projects into measurable objectives validated what our intuition had already told us about the strengths of our projects.

Another benefit of participating in the Goals 2000 project was the sharing of teaching ideas and assessment tools with other teachers from around the state. Seeing the projects that other schools were doing served as inspiration and motivation for all of us. . . .

The most beneficial aspect of the process was that it reduced some of the anxiety that we were each feeling about the daunting task of assessment. Assessment has some fairly negative connotations at this point in the statewide process. Goals 2000 helped put assessment into perspective.

ZOE VANDER WEIL*

-----

*All quotations, unless otherwise noted, are taken from "Authentic Evaluation," a handbook created by the Goals 2000 Nebraska Local Assessments project.

## Goals 2000 Nebraska Local Assessments Project

**Phase II:** *Academic year 1999–2000. Teachers meet in teams and "clusters" of teams to develop projects, share ideas, and develop locally appropriate assessments.*

I pick up "Sarah" at 5:30. Looks tired; must be just home from the high school.

I ask her how she is, and by way of reply, she says, half-jokingly, "Why did I ever agree to facilitate this project?"

I know that she has her own students' papers to read, her own work to do, but I remind her again that she is a great mentor for other teachers.

"Labor of love," she sighs, and in her sigh I hear a familiar mixture of earnestness and irony.

What neither of us says, but both of us know, is that Sarah also needs the money. Like many teachers, she is constantly looking for ways to supplement her income. This facilitation work is better than our mutual friend's part-time job: she delivers newspapers to her neighbors before heading to school to teach their children.

The hour-long drive passes quickly as we discuss our classrooms, our students. As teachers do, we exchange success stories and failure stories with equal frequency and passion. As we pull into the unfamiliar school parking lot, we realize that we have no agenda for this cluster meeting. This does not worry us.

Two teams of teachers are already seated in the Media Room and are engaged in animated conversation. They speak of athletic rivalries, difficult administrators, challenging students. Sarah and I sit down, smiling.

At first I am hesitant. As a professor who is not subject to the same constraints and mandates that these teachers are, I wonder about my standing to speak. Will I say something that shows my privilege? That seems condescending? That doesn't account for the complexity of their lives? That sentimentalizes those lives or oversimplifies mine? But my anxiety is soon replaced by an excitement about the ideas, the stories, the commitments of these teachers. We are teachers talking about teaching.

Suddenly, our third team stumbles into the room, and I realize that they are the teachers who work in this building. We tease them about how long we had to drive and how nice it is for them to walk down the hall to join us.

We're not certain they even hear us. They continue talking to one another. *That was a **great** meeting. . . . This project is amazing. . . . When Mike said that about the Monarch butterflies. . . . Mary's work on the history of that building. . . . Jessica's poem on the nature preserve. . . .* We may not understand what they are saying, but we understand their enthusiasm, and we like being in its presence. We can wait.

Finally, after a full minute, "Karen"—clearly the team leader—stops, surveys her visitors as if seeing us for the first time, and says, "But we're here to talk about standards and assessments, aren't we?"

Her colleague "Mike" groans. I am surprised: Mike is typically quiet, shy.

"What's wrong, Mike?" I ask.

He shrugs, smiling a smile that is half-invitation and half-rebuff.

I bite. "What is it?"

"Oh," his eyes are fixed on the floor in front of him, "I just want to *teach.*"

The sentiment is familiar, and understandable. Mike, like so many teachers who know what they're doing, just wants to be left alone.

"But Mike," Karen says, "that's not true. You also want to learn, and to grow, and to share your teaching with the rest of us. None of us wants other people to control our classrooms, but I don't think that's what this whole assessment system is about."

"Oh, I do," says Mike.

I have heard this discussion before. And as always, I am torn.

This *is* an imposition. For the first time, they are told: document your students' learning for others; become assessment experts; conform to state standards—and do it all without a pay raise.

But they are also told: you are the ones who should assess your students; we trust your expertise; instructional choices will be made in the classroom, where they belong.

As Karen and Mike continue their argument, it repeatedly leads back to their projects and their students. As I listen to them discuss and debate and wonder and tell stories, I think, *This is how it sounds when teachers talk.*

I look at Sarah. We have no agenda. It is chaos.

We smile.

---

While working through these research projects, the children had discussions about the research guides [created during the first summer workshop] and how they could be improved to be more meaningful. . . . [O]ur students recommended that the research guides must read from the left to the right, with the highest score quality indicators being read first by the students. "Why have us read what you don't want first?" commented the children. They also wanted to know what would happen if a student went above and beyond the highest indicator. So then we added a + column for the children who go above the expectations of the rubric. . . . Achieving beyond the expectations has become a real motivator and challenge for many of the students. And to think if the children had only taken a traditional test, they would have filled in the blanks and been done.

SUZANNE RATZLAFF

---

## Goals 2000 Nebraska Local Assessments Project

**Phase III:** *Summer 2000 workshop/"bazaar." Teachers reassemble to complete projects, share what they've done with peers, and show it off to invited guests.*

We have reserved the same two rooms at the conference center this year, but now the wall between them has been removed, and we have created one large display area. We are calling this a "bazaar" because, in addition to the fun wordplay it inspires, this term invites our visitors—teachers, administrators, district staff developers, representatives from the state Department of Education, politicians, community members—to wander through our teachers' exhibits.

Teacher-made displays fill the room; they have created poster boards, video and audio presentations, and handouts describing the assessment tools—rubrics, checklists, portfolios—they have developed with their colleagues. But the examples of student work generate by far the most excitement. Our guests are struck by the variety of ways in which students are asked to demonstrate their learning; they are surrounded by reports, charts, graphs, poems, stories, children's books, anthologies, photographs, audiotapes, videotapes, business plans, homemade products (corncob jam, lye soap), marketing campaigns, and some science projects that—if the visitors are anything like me—they can't even identify or understand without some help from the teachers.

At 10:00 A.M., it is time for one of our presentations. I call people to their seats, and they take them reluctantly. I assure them they will have more time to spend with the displays. I introduce the team from a recently consolidated district. This project has brought together six teachers, one principal, and scores of students from two towns, three grade levels, and several subject areas. I describe for the audience a scene from two months earlier: *On this warm spring evening, the large school auditorium is filled almost to capacity. Everyone, it seems, has come to see the children and their teachers share their work. They will not be disappointed.*

One of the teachers opens the presentation by reading from "Telling Our Stories: We Remember," the anthology the team has created:

> Stories are an important part of heritage; they define our families and our communities. Stories help students make connections to the past and can help them learn the skills that will be necessary for their futures. In the school year 1999–2000, several classes at [our schools] collected stories from diverse sources: interviews with family and community members; old autograph books; local and Nebraska historians; historical society resources. The formats used to retell these stories were varied as well—building a reproduction of an immigrant trunk; writing stories, essays, and poems; constructing charts and graphs; writing and performing plays; making books. ("Telling")

Then the teachers take turns describing their projects, as well as the community performance in which their students had shined. We hear about:

> fourth graders interviewing grandparents and community members about the autograph books they had created as children; choosing poems from those books; and writing introductions to the poems
>
> sixth graders researching and writing the history of local buildings, drawing on live interviews, historical documents, and the Internet
>
> high school Probability and Statistics and Information Processing students using a wealth of local resources to explore and document:
>
> - ◆ average local temperatures dating back to the 1920s
> - ◆ total local population for the past 120 years
> - ◆ track and field records dating back 35 years
> - ◆ bushels per acre of corn for grain harvested, 1939–1997
> - ◆ number of local businesses from 1890 to the present
>
> high school English students researching oral history and then writing stories, essays, poetry, and dialogue based on the collected stories
>
> high school English students researching and writing about the history of immigrant trunks and building their own immigrant trunk

All of these projects—whether poetry, charts, graphs, or carpentry—are presented as forms of place-based, historically conscious storytelling.

I watch the audience, and the response is identical to the one the group received in their own community: first, quiet amazement, then incredulous shakes of the head, and finally loud and appreciative applause. And I think: *This is it. No one needs an "assessment expert" to tell them that kids in this district are receiving a first-rate education. They have seen far more than any standardized test could ever show them because they have been invited into pedagogy, into the work that teachers and students are doing together.*

It is not easy to calm down the audience. But it is necessary; we have several presentations to go.

In completing this work, we came to realize certain truths: first, state standards need not drive curriculum. We were able to use curriculum that already existed. Second, paper-and-pencil testing is not the only way to assess student progress. Rubrics crafted to show student mastery of skills are equally as reliable a measure. Third, our commitment to using [our] community . . . as a learning-laboratory in a variety of ways was not diminished as we had feared it would be. Rather, we were able to reinforce and refine our community-based studies by coordinating the projects using state standards as the common denominator among them. Fourth, being able to see the projects of other schools as they developed helped us value our unique vision. Each school exists to serve the needs of the community that supports it. Consequently, even though we all started from the same "givens," all the schools in the Goals 2000 Workshop arrived at a different destination. Meeting state standards became the common denominator among us. The bottom line is that meeting state standards did not make us all "standard."

ELLEN KOHTZ

Gerry and I are scheduled to present on the Goals 2000 project at the 2000 Conference on College Composition and Communication Convention. Our topic: creating democratic cross-institutional alliances. Gerry, an experienced high school teacher, is excited. He has a few things to say to us college teachers.

But then, a few weeks before the conference, an e-mail: "Chris, I have encountered one of the largest constraints on democratic alliances: time." Student recommendations. District curriculum and assessment work. A demanding teaching schedule. New software to learn. Pep rallies. Blood drives. He just can't do it.

But he has a message or two for my university colleagues. First, he says, remember the reality of high school teaching: the complicated students of various abilities and attitudes, the pressures from administrators and parents, the lack of respect (and money) accorded to teachers by the general public and (sometimes) professors, the very fact that students are forced to be in a high school classroom. Don't pity us, Gerry says, but understand that these are very real impediments to forging democratic alliances.

Then there's our project. As always, Gerry is direct:

> [This project] was an honest start [toward democratic alliance]. You provided opportunities to dialogue. . . . Yet it seemed a one-way street in many ways to me. We all weren't sitting around the table together when it came to actual work groups. . . . We had to produce, you didn't. At least not in the same way. In that regard, we were not on equal footing. (McAndrew)

Gerry's assessment becomes the cornerstone of my—of our—presentation. But it also helps me rethink what it means to risk complexity. Pushing the academic envelope by asking my department and college to support a professional life they had not envisioned for me seems at times—when I think of my tenure file, for instance—a considerable risk. And yet Gerry's words teach me that I didn't take an even more important and complex risk: I didn't put anything—my teaching or my beliefs—on the table *within* the project. For teachers such as Gerry, risking complexity and learning the uses of chaos are far from luxuries; they are survival skills, job requirements. I am grateful to Gerry for this reminder. And I am grateful to him for the challenge he posed to me, which I brought to my university colleagues at the CCCC Convention:

> How can 6 speakers achieve much in [75] minutes? Cynical high school teachers would say this is just a topic to enhance college instructors' resumes. They would question the sincerity of the task. What about partnerships? Team teaching? Old ideas, but maybe might work. . . . If we really do believe that post-secondary learning is a continu[ation] of the K–12 experience, then we have to work at this as equals. What are you teaching today? How are you doing it? [You know] some of the things that constrain me. What are you dealing with? What do we share in common? How can we plan together? (McAndrew)

# CHAPTER SIX

# Toward Pedagogy-Centered Outreach

Compositionists seem to be increasingly aware of the political and pedagogical virtues of "going public," of "expanding the conversation," to use my phrase from Chapter 5. We have seen an explosion of interest in extending our teaching into the public sphere, largely through service learning (e.g., Adler-Kassner, Crooks, and Watters; Deans; Herzberg; Schutz and Gere). We have also seen a number of calls to take our scholarship more public (Cushman, *Struggle*; Ervin; Mortensen; Wells). The most recent editor of *CCC* has even opened up our flagship professional journal to a broader audience:

> I am . . . especially concerned that articles published in *CCC* speak to the diverse readers of the journal, including teachers of writing in a variety of positions (full-time and part-time faculty, staff, tutors, graduate teaching assistants) and at a variety of institutions (two-year, four-year, and liberal arts colleges; research universities; community literacy centers), as well as graduate students in rhetoric and composition programs and (sometimes) undergraduate students, administrators of writing programs, department chairs, and (sometimes) upper-level administrators, community literacy workers and literacy program developers, and even (sometimes) legislators, employers, parents, and alumni. I think it is necessary for us to communicate our perspectives on writing pedagogy to a broader readership if we hope to develop and gain support for more inclusive and effective writing and communication programs. (Cooper 364)

Although this statement might strike us as remarkably broad in scope—as indeed it is—it's important to note who is *not* mentioned among Cooper's vision of a "broader readership": P–12 teachers. To be sure, I don't want to suggest that this is anything more than an oversight. Still, I see this omission (inadvertent or not) as symptomatic of the invisibility of public school teachers to our field at the present moment. After all, CCC and College English do not generally run articles on working with public school teachers, much less articles that speak to them; only a handful of the hundreds of panels at any of the last several CCCC conventions have taken up this kind of work; and historically strong partnership programs—most notably, the National Writing Project—have been spottily represented at the conference in recent years.

This is a curious, and in my view unfortunate, feature of the recent evolution of our field. After all, unlike most academic enterprises, composition has a long history of productive (if often fraught) alliances with teachers in the schools, dating back to the very founding of NCTE, as we have seen. We also have much to learn from our colleagues in the public schools—about teaching, about learning, about writing, and (maybe especially, at this political moment) about developing institutional literacy to combat reductive understandings of our work.

Such, at least, is the claim of this final chapter, which follows roughly the same pattern as that of Chapter 5. I begin by describing this apparent retreat from making P–16 (prekindergarten through college) connections a visible part of our disciplinary self-representation. I then sketch in some history of alliances between P–12 and university faculty in English, and in Composition and Rhetoric specifically. Next, I explore some useful thinking about "outreach" in the field, thus clearing some intellectual space for pedagogy-centered outreach. I close with reflections on a project that attempts, with mixed results, to enact the principles of pedagogy-centered outreach: the assessment project described in Intralude 6.

## Going Public . . . without Public Schools

The 1996 Watson Conference on the history of Composition and Rhetoric (and the book that emerged from it, *History, Reflection, and Narrative* [Rosner, Boehm, and Journet]) provides one index of the invisibility of P–12 writing teachers in our field today. Although modern composition began in the academy as a response to worries about writing instruction in the schools (see Chapter 1), very few speakers at this conference (and writers in the book) even mention schoolteachers. Rather, the essays in *History, Reflection, and Narrative* generally leave one with the impression that Composition is a fairly recent—circa, say, the 1960s—and exclusively postsecondary enterprise. As Irvin Peckham, a former high school teacher, makes clear, this star-studded conference told "only part of the story [of Composition's development]—the college part" (253). In his useful critique of this literally history-making event, Peckham observes:

> This miswriting (or overwriting) of the history of Composition is not surprising: histories are generally the histories of the upper classes. . . . Only the upper classes are textualized: they are the ones who, like college teachers, have time to write, and they are the ones who are written about. So they are the ones whom histories trace. Working-class people (and high school teachers) are left on the margins or off the page. (257)

As I discuss in Chapter 4, it is important to note that this class-based academic economy is shaped by Composition and Rhetoric's vexed place/space within English studies and the academy generally. Working with P–12 teachers simply has not become a significant feature of the disciplinary work of English. Consider, for instance, two recent professional efforts designed to address teacher education in English.

The first example is the MLA Teacher Education Project and the publication it produced, *Preparing a Nation's Teachers* (Franklin, Laurence, and Welles, 1999). While ostensibly aimed at identifying and describing "model" teacher education programs, this project turned out to produce a series of reflections on the obstacles to developing such programs. The most significant obstacle, as the book makes clear, is English professors' marked lack of interest in P–12 education. On the whole, we learn, English professors see themselves as concerned with the "content" of the discipline, rather than the teaching of their subject. Donald Gray captures this self-perception with a series of questions:

> Why should we, trained to explore and talk to one another about questions of literature and culture that we sometimes think too recondite to take even into our undergraduate classrooms, make it part of our profession to attend to questions about the reading and writing of high school students? Our higher educations took us into the MLA and the company of literary critics and scholars. Why should we—indeed, why should the MLA—connect with a community of teachers in the schools, with students who aspire to be teachers, and with colleagues whose profession is the education of teachers? (1–2; see also Franklin, Laurence, and Welles, "Preface"; the Indiana University and University of Virginia reports; Broad; Marshall).

Indeed, this attitude, this disciplinary orientation, is so entrenched that the book becomes largely a collective lament about the state of the discipline.[1]

Considering that the second example was sponsored by NCTE and its Conference on English Education (CEE), its similarly distressing portrait of English studies is perhaps even more striking. To be sure, the authors of the introduction to *Teaching College English and English Education* are more sanguine than most of the participants of the MLA project about the common ground shared by English professors and English education professors (McCracken and Larson). But the book in many ways belies this optimism. Though often engaging and sometimes even inspiring, the assembled stories are, to be blunt, all over the map: although most are in one way or another "about" becoming an English teacher, as McCracken and Larson promise, some are not (e.g., Donahue; Monseau). Some focus primarily on writing (e.g., Elbow, "Illiteracy"), some on reading or literature (e.g., Tompkins), some on teaching (e.g., Foster). But strangely, few explore connections between English and English education; most essays are "about" one or the other.[2] In the end, even the editors seem to have trouble representing the bigger picture of the volume. Larson focuses mainly on the influences on the authors' growth, and takes up the relationship between English and English education only in a coda focused primarily on divergences between these fields. McCracken, meanwhile, does point to some potential common ground between the fields, but his overarching point seems to be that "[m]ore tension exists between English studies and English education than one might be led to believe by publications on college teaching" (369). Thus, this CEE effort leaves us with much the same impression as the MLA project: that English professors—even those interested in their own development as teachers—are prepared to leave the teaching of teaching to others.

Perhaps the most important conclusion we might draw from these two projects is that even where there is strong English education presence, teacher preparation is rarely a significant or visible part of English curricula. Indeed, Dilworth and McCracken report, on the basis of a survey of English faculty whose departments include active CEE members, that "44 percent of English professors do not know which of their students are prospective teachers, and many do not want to know. Almost 24 percent believe that those who seek certification to teach English are inferior students" (359). I suspect that in English departments without CEE presence, these numbers might be even higher.

## Composition Connections

Of course, when English departments do devote attention to working with prospective and practicing teachers, compositionists are likely to be heavily involved. In my own department, compositionists teach the only two Teachers College courses currently run through English (and one of them is a reading course). We also work with P–12 teachers through the Nebraska Writing Project, as well as special projects such as the assessment initiative described in Intralude 6. Moreover, we are responsible for training all new teaching assistants, by means of a summer workshop and a course called Teaching College English. We also teach pedagogy courses at the graduate level. And, not surprisingly, we are oversubscribed for advice, consultation, and letters of recommendation regarding teaching. While professors in other areas of English do work with teachers within and beyond our institution, it is fair to say that the Composition and Rhetoric faculty do the bulk of this work. And, as the MLA and NCTE projects attest, such an arrangement is far from unique.

Compositionists' heavy engagement with teachers and teacher development makes the general invisibility of our work with teachers in the schools all the stranger. It is no doubt true that postsecondary writing teachers face considerable and perplexing issues of their own, and it is laudable that the field has been involved in a struggle to confront the plight of overworked and underpaid adjunct teachers in higher education.[3] In focusing narrowly on issues facing part-time and adjunct faculty in the academy, however, the field forgoes an opportunity to develop a broader critique that would serve as a counteroffensive to the attacks launched daily against teachers, and especially teachers of writing, at *all* levels of education. "Commonsense" assumptions about teaching and writing as sets of "functional," lower-order skills, after all, underwrite the derogation of teaching writing at all—whether in elementary or secondary schools or in colleges and universities. Until we recognize that the plight of adjuncts in the university and that of teachers in the schools are ideologically and materially connected, we will continue to suffer the kind of containment I described in Chapter 2.

Recall that research conducted by the Hopkins committee nearly a century ago demonstrated the similar working conditions of writing teachers in the schools and those in colleges and universities (Chapter 1). Indeed, the Hopkins report reminds us that during the Progressive Era, the term "composition" signaled a pedagogical (and political) enterprise that was by definition cross-institutional. Composition, in fact, was central to "progressive" efforts by NCTE and its journal to address the secondary-postsecondary issues that emerged just after the turn of the twentieth century. And as I showed in Chapter 4, composition was also instrumental in the midcentury school reform movement that identified articulation as a major priority of the discipline. Indeed, the 1958 Basic Issues conference led to the creation of NCTE's Committee on High School-College Articulation and the College Board's Commission on English. Along with an infusion of funds from the expanded National Defense Education Act, these professional bodies provided the impetus for a great deal of interest in, and activity toward, high school-college articulation.

As the 1960s wore on, however, this interest waned, in part because campus enrollments and politics encouraged college teachers to focus on "immediate campus needs" (Fortune x). In the 1970s, with the advent of the reinvigorated "literacy crisis," as well as open admissions and remedial writing programs, interest in articulation resurfaced. This was the decade that saw the emergence of the Bay Area Writing Project (1974), which has led to perhaps the most successful cross-institutional English program to date: The National Writing Project (NWP). This momentum carried into the 1980s, spurred on by the 1983 publication of the alarmist *Nation at Risk* and a number of national organizations and programs, including the Coalition of English Associations, the Yale-New Haven Teachers Institute, the NEH's Summer Institutes for Teachers, and of course the rapidly growing NWP. In 1986, Ron Fortune compiled a collection of school-college collaborative programs from some of the nation's leading universities—and leading compositionists (e.g., James Gray at Berkeley; Max Morenberg at CUNY; Jay Robinson and Patricia Stock at Michigan; James Slevin at Georgetown). A year later, the Wye Conference brought together teachers from all levels of education to discuss their visions of the field; in fact, the conference included more P–12 than college teachers. Peter Elbow reported in his 1990 book on the conference that communication and learning across grade levels was a strength of that gathering *(What)*.

What, then, has happened to school-university partnerships, specifically in composition, over the past decade and a half? Why has such work become a less integral, less visible part of the work of Composition and Rhetoric? First, it may be that we saw in the 1990s something like what Fortune claims we saw in the 1960s: a refocusing on postsecondary issues as a result of "immediate campus needs." As I have suggested, the academy is indeed facing an economic crunch that has left many English departments depleted: lines are not being replaced when faculty retire; programmatic hires are scarce; economic support for outreach is dwindling; and faculty are stretched thin. Although the number of faculty positions in Composition and Rhetoric has risen dramatically in recent years, campus demands on faculty time—again, largely as a result of depleted resources and, in Composition and Rhetoric, our responsibilities to the universally required first-year course—continue to rise, siphoning off the bulk of our resources and energies, and encouraging institutions to rely more and more heavily on adjunct and graduate student labor. All of these factors may be contributing to the current lack of attention to cross-institutional partnerships.

I have also suggested a second possible explanation for Composition and Rhetoric's apparent retreat from alliance building with schoolteachers: that this kind of work does not fit neatly into the field's evolving disciplinary and institutional identity. After all, this work *is* going on—cross-institutional partnership programs such as NWP endure, and compositionists continue (albeit with what seems to be growing reluctance) to participate in them. This work has not come to a screeching halt; rather, it has simply not been a visible feature of our disciplinary self-representation. Even the important work that compositionists do in preparing public school teachers is confined almost exclusively to specifically designated education journals such as *English Education*. As Peckham suggests, our work with the schools has been written out of our official story, perhaps because its yield is so low in the academy: service of this kind, especially at research institutions, is typically not highly valued or rewarded.

Finally, it may be that school-college partnerships have come to be viewed by a new generation of compositionists, weaned on critical pedagogy and critical theory, as a relic of "old-school" expressivism, a product of 1970s-style process pedagogy. NWP, especially, is often viewed by younger faculty as espousing passé politics and a commitment to an outmoded, uncritical pedagogy. In this way, school-university alliances may be viewed as part of a historical movement that we've "progressed" past. (I return to this notion below.)

I suspect all three of these explanations contain some truth. Campus demands *are* consuming; it *is* often difficult to justify (much less celebrate) this kind of work in disciplinary and institutional terms; younger compositionists *do* tend to work from different pedagogical and political assumptions than do projects such as NWP. And yet, as I have suggested, we seriously limit our educational and political effectivity by focusing exclusively on the postsecondary teaching of writing.

# From Missionary "Service" to Pedagogical "Outreach"

The irony here is that compositionists generally do acknowledge that the academy is too narrow and insular an arena to take as our strict purview. Despite our field's waning attention to cross-institutional partnerships in recent years, Marilyn Cooper's editorial statement quoted earlier suggests that many compositionists *are* interested in exploring how their work can function outside the walls of the academy. At the same time, they understand that the academy's track record in "going public" has been problematic. Specifically, they warn that if we are to go public, we need to avoid the "public service" ethos that easily lends itself to condescension, paternalism, and missionary zeal. Framed in terms I have been using in this book, the fear is that we (and our students) will think of service as something that we do for and around the public, not with them. Here, I turn briefly to examples of this work in an effort to write toward a broader conception of "outreach"—one that would encourage and highlight cross-institutional alliances.

Schutz and Gere, first of all, reflect carefully on the dangers implicit in relationships between university representatives (whether professors or students) and community members. Specifically, they worry that when university students tutor community members, "tutoring often fails to change college students' visions of their tutees as lacking a free-floating 'expert' knowledge that they [the students] can provide" (135). Students, that is, often reenact an authoritarian teacher-student relationship, "professing" their knowledge and derogating that of community members. According to Schutz and Gere, the task is to move from a consensus- and caring-based notion of public space to one in which students are encouraged to view community members as equals and therefore to value their differences (141). That is, students must *create* public spaces with community members by developing a healthy respect for local history and social realities and by forging collective action in "a local, messy, and complex context" (142). This requires that they take a learner's stance as well as a teacher's stance (145, 146).

If we take Schutz and Gere's advice seriously, we move service learning out of the realms of liberal do-goodism and into the realm of pedagogy, the reflexive inquiry that teachers and learners undertake together. Similarly, Ellen Cushman argues that when academics engage in "service work" outside the academy, we must become learners as well as teachers—we must engage in pedagogy rather than missionary work. Instead of viewing service as a kind of noblesse oblige or, worse yet, self-marketing to "middle and upper class policy makers, administrators, and professionals" ("Public" 328), Cushman urges an "interactive" approach to outreach:

> When public intellectuals not only reach outside the university, but actually interact with the public beyond its walls, they overcome the ivory tower isolation that marks so much current intellectual work. They create knowledge with those whom the knowledge serves. Dovetailing the traditionally separate duties of research, teaching, and service, public intellectuals can use the privilege of their positions to forward the goals of both students and local community members. ("Public" 330)

For those accustomed to "professing," Cushman makes clear, this will involve humility and a willingness to engage the ideas of those who may indeed be very different from themselves (334). Like the theorists who will need to reimagine and renegotiate their authority relationships with teachers in order to create pedagogy-centered disciplinarity (Chapter 4), and like the master teachers who will need to reimagine and renegotiate their authority relationships to students in order to create pedagogy-centered curriculum (Chapter 5), academics will need to reimagine and renegotiate their authority relationships with community members in order to create pedagogy-centered outreach. In other words, like pedagogy itself, this kind of outreach evolves from the dialectic between the interests, experiences, and knowledge of all of its participants. Academics negotiate with community members to develop mechanisms whereby all participants have a voice in how projects will develop.

The work of scholars such as Cushman and Schutz and Gere helps us conceptualize pedagogy-centered outreach. But, as I have suggested, this notion must not exclude the participation of teachers in other sites, particularly those in P–12 schools. Pedagogically and politically, the vitality of our profession may well hinge on our ability to forge creative and mutually respectful alliances with our P–12 colleagues.

And yet here the move from missionary service to pedagogical outreach becomes especially fraught. University-school partnerships, after all, historically have been marred by just the kind of paternalism that Schutz and Gere and Cushman warn against. As Knoblauch and Brannon observe, it is not difficult to find university faculty who

> blame the schools for inadequate preparation of college students, who mistrust the competence as well as the dedication of practitioners (as opposed to scholars), who believe unself-consciously in "trickle-down" theories of educational change, and who would be shocked at any suggestion that elementary school teachers might have the same authority to address them that they have to speak in the schools. (*Critical* 177–78)

Even when we have worked in favor of teachers, Knoblauch and Brannon suggest, university faculty generally have been complicit in the cultural derogation of teachers' work: "ultimately everyone wants to do something 'for' teachers rather than relinquish the control that denies teachers power to construct their own professional lives" (179).

For support of Knoblauch and Brannon's claim, perhaps we need look no further than what remains the most common model of university-school interaction: inservices. In this model, university "experts" visit a school—sometimes for a day, often for an hour—to share their specialized knowledge with teachers, who presumably take good notes and think hard about how to apply the experts' theories to their own work. In this top-down transmission model, teachers are understood as passive technicians rather than as active participants in a professional conversation (Meyer et al. 9). One teacher I know describes this as the "popping in, popping off, popping out" model.

Even "innovative" programs that go well beyond this traditional staff development model run the risk of authorizing professors' expertise at the expense of teachers' expertise. Consider, for instance, the ambitious Center for Liberal Arts (CLA) project, as described by Harold H. Kolb Jr. in *Preparing a Nation's Teachers*. Although the CLA has much to recommend it—its premise that teachers are "professional colleagues in a community of learners" (336), for instance—it becomes clear that the program is predicated on a service-oriented, information-delivery model rather than on one that would truly engage teachers in democratic colleagueship. Here, for instance, is how Kolb describes CLA's vision of the future: "We envisage . . . ongoing colloquia at the university led by department chairs and senior scholars that update schoolteachers on issues and trends in the disciplines and keep them informed about developments in undergraduate and graduate studies" (342). In this example of trickle-down reform, those "in the know" keep those not "in the know" current so that the latter can disseminate this information to their students. CLA has even established an "Ask the Professor" Web site for this purpose.[4]

Pedagogy-centered teacher alliances, on the other hand, would promote nonhierarchical, democratic, truly collegial relationships with teachers. They would require professors to give up the still prevalent notion that they are the experts and the teachers are the laypeople. Instead, professors would learn to engage in pedagogy with teachers rather than handing pedagogy to them or theorizing it for them.

Compositionists who have been involved with the National Writing Project will recognize these as some of the chief aims of that program. And yet, as I have suggested, this organization has begun to fall out of favor, especially among newer members of the professoriate. How has this come to pass? Although I hardly have space here for a full history of NWP, it is instructive to reflect briefly on the possibilities and limitations of what is widely regarded as the most influential P–16 reform in writing instruction in the past thirty years.

## The National Writing Project: Reimagining Cross-Institutional Work

NWP began in 1974 as the Bay Area Writing Project (BAWP), a school-university venture aimed at developing teacher expertise in the teaching of writing at all levels of education (J. Gray). The idea: bring together good teachers from all educational levels to write together and to share their "best practices" with one another. Simple though it was, this idea turned inservicing on its head: instead of bringing an "expert" into the school, NWP brought teachers out of their schools to meet together as experts. And instead of the traditional top-down model of university-school projects, this partnership would assume the expertise of all participants from all grade levels (J. Gray 38). As a celebration of effective local practice and teacher-centered school reform, NWP aims to empower teachers both through offering them this expert's role and through putting them in conversation with other teacher-leaders (Gray and Sterling).

NWP has been remarkably successful. Three years after the founding of BAWP, NWP had fourteen sites and strong support from the National Endowment for the Humanities. Since then NWP has expanded to forty-eight states (plus Washington, D.C. and Puerto Rico), with multiple sites in several states and a number of sites overseas. Tens of thousands of teachers enroll in NWP's institutes each year with the help of funding from private donors, educational institutions, and state and federal governments.

But while both NWP and Composition and Rhetoric have grown enormously during the past thirty years, they have also grown, to some extent, apart. Specifically, NWP is largely failing to attract newer members of the profession. It is difficult to know with certainty why this is so; there has been no public backlash against NWP in the field's publications. Rather, we are witnessing what seems to be a silent withdrawal. The conspiring forces already mentioned—the immediacy of campus needs, the view that NWP is the product of "old-school" expressivism, and our inability or unwillingness to reconcile this work with the "disciplining" of our field—may go some way toward explaining this apparent professional schism. It is also true that NWP is sometimes experienced and criticized as a closed community that is unfriendly to critique and that, as a result, is not evolving. Despite its claims to "openness" (J. Gray), NWP has been faulted for being too rigid and structured—even dogmatic.

My own take on NWP is that despite the very good work it does for individual teachers, it is limited as a reform effort. Specifically, it is an individualistic enterprise, one that has been reluctant to develop or act on a broad-based cultural critique. Bonnie Sunstein, in her ethnography of the New Hampshire Writing Project, observes that NWP is aimed at "[n]either curriculum change nor institutional transformation," but rather teacher change (7). It aims to "empower" individual teachers by offering them an expert's role and putting them in conversation with other experts. This is, as Sunstein claims, an affirmative, rather than transformative, enterprise (233).

While a program that seeks teacher change has much to recommend it, David Wilson's longitudinal study of Writing Project teachers who try to implement NWP-inspired pedagogies teaches us that it is not enough. In *Attempting Change,* Wilson issues the following conclusion: "Results of this study support the assertion that participation in the Writing Project had a strong influence on the beliefs and practices of the secondary English teachers of this study, but also indicate that the contexts of schooling served as an impediment to the implementation of their beliefs" (xi). Too little time, too many students, preestablished curricula, outsiders' expectations, old habits—all of these negatively affected teachers' ability to implement the kinds of pedagogies they imagined for themselves in the Writing Project. Wilson's study suggests that teachers working alone cannot sustain meaningful reform even of their own classroom practices. Moreover, lasting reform will require more than bringing good teachers together to share "what works" and to celebrate local knowledge. In its laudable effort to offer teachers the "expert" role, NWP commits itself to a talking-head, show-and-tell pedagogy. In NWP teacher demonstrations, there is typically—and by design—little critical examination or collaborative inquiry; rather, these demonstrations are viewed as a sharing and a celebration of what teachers deem their "best practice," and attempts to inquire critically into these practices are often seen as impugning the teacher's expertise.

But though NWP fails to articulate or advocate a politics or the kind of pedagogical reflection that I would fully endorse, I am not interested in the kind of self-serving liberal bashing that would have us write off expressivist projects such as NWP as "old-school." (Indeed, I regularly participate in the Nebraska Writing Project, where I have learned a great deal from my P–12 colleagues.) Thousands of teachers can testify to the salutary effects of NWP on their classrooms and their sense of themselves as writers and teachers. The guiding principles of NWP—that teachers are the best teachers of other teachers, that writing teachers should be writers, and so forth—are well worth protecting and nurturing. What's more, to write off NWP would be to write off the single most effective university-school partnership in the history of writing instruction. It would be to write off a structured opportunity to work with our colleagues in the schools to develop P–16 educational reform initiatives that fight the reincorporation of the schools. It would be to write off what is perhaps our best chance to write teachers back into the script for educational reform.

Perhaps NWP cannot be changed from within; perhaps the moment it moved to critical inquiry and collective action it would lose its funding and its widely held support among the educational mainstream. On the other hand, perhaps it can become a site for what Brian Lord calls "critical colleagueship": ongoing, reciprocal relationships in which teachers serve as "commentators and critics" of each other's work. According to Lord, critical colleagueship depends in large part on "[c]reating and sustaining productive disequilibrium through self-reflection, collegial dialogue, and on-going critique" (192). The kind of "collective generativity" imagined here rests not on uncritical celebration of local practice, but on ongoing inquiry into that practice (192). In my view, this is the kind of collective work, the kind of mutual support, that would prepare us all—whatever level we teach—to articulate and defend our work against the commonsense notions of administrative progressivism. It would help us work for change not only in our classrooms, but also in our institutions, our communities, and our culture. Finally, it would help us place pedagogy—the reflexive inquiry that teachers and learners undertake together—at the center of our alliance projects.

In the following example, I explore a project that builds on the resources and ideas of the NWP model but also encourages its participants to engage in critical colleagueship. Instead of merely offering teachers a stage for their pedagogical work, or "giving" teachers a pedagogy, it encourages teachers to develop their pedagogies collaboratively, through critical inquiry into their "best practices" and through building the rhetorical and political resources necessary to engage their colleagues and their communities effectively. For me, and for the other participating university faculty, then, this project was an attempt—though a flawed attempt, as it turned out—to enact pedagogy-centered outreach.

## By Way of Example

As I suggest in Intralude 6, the Goals 2000 grant project involved the development of a consortium of schoolteachers, administrators, Nebraska Department of Education (NDE) personnel, and university faculty representing two educational initiatives: the Nebraska Writing Project and the rural education program School at the Center. The state of Nebraska, drawing on a long tradition of commitment to local control, has decided to buck the national trend, opting for a statewide system of local assessments in lieu of a single, statewide test. Our task in this project was to help teachers become "assessment literate" and to develop teacher-designed assessments.

The design of the project was simple. At either end of the year-long project was a summer institute. The first institute brought teams of teachers and project facilitators together to share what we called "milestone projects"—classroom and curricular projects that teachers were already using with success, but that they would also like to develop further—and to design assessments from them. Then—phase two—each team met in its district bimonthly and with other teams in their regions monthly. They also visited each other's classrooms and collaborated across classrooms to build assessment tools. Then came the second summer institute (2000), during which the teams put the finishing touches on their assessments and presented them to invited teachers, administrators, politicians, staff developers, and NDE staff.

At the heart of the philosophy of the project is the notion of "inside-out" assessment, as opposed to top-down assessment. This means that assessment begins in the classroom, as an integral part of pedagogy, and then moves out in the documentation and reporting stages. This is in sharp contrast to the typical process, whereby outsiders mandate what happens inside classrooms by controlling the assessment process (see Chapter 2). This explains why we asked teachers to begin with those milestone projects: we hoped that their assessment tools would be derived from their classroom practice rather than the other way around.

With this principle in mind, representatives of the Nebraska Writing Project and the School at the Center program initiated the project with the hope that it would be pedagogy-centered—in other words, that it would evolve from the reflexive inquiry of the participating teachers and learners. Several features of the project emerged from this commitment:

1. The project was conceptualized through dialogue among facilitators and participating teachers. Although I was the primary grant writer, the document was collaborative; I drew on/in responses from prospective participants to such questions as "What elements of your programs and curricula would you want to preserve? What elements do you believe need clarification, elaboration, or reworking? What kinds of assessment would help you achieve these goals?"

2. The bulk of the intellectual leadership for this project came from experienced teachers, not university faculty or outside "experts." The two facilitators who conducted the lion's share of the training during our first workshop had fifty years of teaching experience between them. Of the six facilitators who were active throughout the project, four were experienced P–12 teachers.

3. The university faculty who did participate—four in all, though only two were active throughout the process—were truly *facilitators*: we helped organize the institutes; visited with the teams to which we were assigned; participated as interested observers; and served as resources (for example, helping teachers locate research on assessment). Each team controlled its own work, including setting schedules, running budgets, and designing and carrying out the intellectual work. And teams were never under any obligation to accept

the advice or guidance of their facilitators. Thus, facilitators were charged with helping the teams frame their project; they were to work with the teachers rather than for or around them.

4. Although this project was initially motivated by account-ability mandates, it was a pedagogical, not an administrative, project. None of the facilitators had any administrative power over the teachers. Indeed, one of our goals was to help teachers offer feedback to the state on the developing assessment and accountability process.

5. Our project encouraged the development of learning teams and collaborative teacher research—rather than, say, serial inservices. The idea, again, was that teachers would teach each other through "critical colleagueship."

While each of these features of the project was important to its overall success, the project was also limited in a number of ways. For instance, one of our teams spent almost the entire project merely aligning local learning objectives with state standards. Also, we didn't always communicate well with administrators to make the teachers' work visible. Moreover, students were not as involved as they might have been. And the list could go on. But the most important limitation, as Gerry reminded me (see Intralude 6), was that the university folk remained, for all practical purposes, outsiders. While the university faculty acted as sponsors for the teaching of others, we did not participate as teachers ourselves. Our fear of becoming another set of experts legislating the work of teachers kept us from engaging with them as teaching peers.

As university facilitators, we set out to enact the three key features of what Cushman calls "activist research"—reflexivity, dialogue, and reciprocity (*Struggle* 21–37). We were careful not to determine the work of the teams. We tried to be aware, always, of our privileges and our limited perspectives vis-à-vis the participants. And we tried to remember that the project was not after all "for" the teachers alone; we too benefited, in the form of stipends, increased visibility in state educational politics, departmental service credit, and—most important—increased knowledge about education and assessment. Still, this project never became a P–16 enterprise, and so we missed a crucial opportunity not only to engage in critical colleagueship with other teachers, but also to use the project to engender cross-institutional alliances, which are sorely needed in our state. As Gerry reminds me, there is a great deal of work to do in learning how to listen, talk, and work across institutional borders.

However flawed, though, this project did help teachers and students develop wonderful projects as well as locally appropriate assessments. It also fostered assessment literacy in our state, several important public engagement moments statewide and locally, articles in national and local forums, and a professional development handbook that is now being used across the state. Perhaps most important, the project helped teachers and the students who worked with them gain a political voice in educational politics. The participants of this project are educators in the truest sense of the word: they work together, in critical colleagueship, to develop responsible pedagogies and then to teach others about them. Like most projects of this sort, then, this one turned out to be a complicated affair with mixed results.

## Conclusion

I do not wish to make any grand claims for the revolutionary or transformative power of the projects described in these pages. In fact, I have chosen to represent these projects precisely because they show the messy and unpredictable work of transformative intellectuals—students and teachers—learning together to practice institutional literacy. When we think of pedagogy as the reflexive inquiry that teachers and learners undertake together, we are "risking complexity" and tolerating (if not embracing) ambiguity. We are exploring a human process, one that cannot be reduced to algorithms and predetermined outcomes.

As I have suggested throughout this book, we are also exploring a process that is necessarily collaborative; pedagogy is by definition a form of collective action. The work I represent in this book—both in the chapters and in the intraludes—is not, after all, "mine," even though I have made the rhetorical choice to represent it primarily from my perspective and for the most part in my own words. It is part of an ongoing project among many teachers and scholars to imagine and reimagine the possibilities that this field called Composition and Rhetoric, and this work called teaching writing, have to offer. For in the end, pedagogical progressivism is not a single idea or pedagogy; rather, it is a commitment to putting pedagogy—the reflexive inquiry of teachers and learners working together—at the heart of our work inside and outside the academy. The transformative intellectuals with whom I have worked teach me that this hopeful project is not, after all, pie-in-the-sky idealism, but a real possibility for the twenty-first century.

# NOTES

## Introduction

1. Throughout this book, I use the term "composition" to refer to the teaching of writing and reserve the term "Composition and Rhetoric" for reference to the disciplinary field.

2. Compare this version of "the story," which I wrote before reading Phelps's essay in *History, Reflection, and Narrative* (Rosner, Boehm, and Journet), to Phelps's own ("Paths" 41–42).

3. In fairness to Berlin, I should note that he claims to be building a taxonomy of "dominant" rhetorics, not a teleology. Still, it is not difficult to find moments of slippage. Consider the final paragraph in *Rhetoric and Reality:*

> Writing instruction has been dramatically transformed in the past twenty-five years—a transformation that is salutary and ongoing. We have begun to see that writing courses are not designed exclusively to prepare students for the workplace, although they certainly must do that. Writing courses prepare students for citizenship in a democracy. (198–99)

While recent work in the field *has* focused on purposes for writing that extend beyond workplace training, it is not true that we have just "begun to see" these purposes, as I make clear in Chapter 1.

4. Connors, for instance, complicates earlier, dismissive versions of nineteenth-century writing instruction in *Composition-Rhetoric*. Similarly, Tobin comments (half-)ironically on the triumphalist narrative of "the writing process movement" as an emancipation from "an age of disciplinary darkness and desolation, say about 1965 or so, [when] writing students were subjected to cruel and inhuman punishments" (2).

5. I am indebted to Amy Lee for the formulation "visions and versions." It is important to account for the effects of how people have *imagined*

progressive education (visions) *and* how people have *enacted* progressive educational reforms (versions).

6. In earlier versions of the manuscript, I interspersed the narratives throughout the chapters. Interestingly, while readers generally had little trouble working their way through each chapter, they found the trajectory of the manuscript as a whole difficult to follow. Readers interested in an example of the "spliced" version are directed to my essay "'Just Give,'" which combines earlier versions of Intralude 3 and Chapter 3. At any rate, my hope is that the present structure of the book will honor multiple forms of "scholarly" writing while allowing readers to navigate narrative shifts with little difficulty.

# Chapter 1

1. Although readers will find parallels between Applebee's work and the historical work of this book—both are guided by an interest in how English teachers took up the ideas and practices of progressive education—the projects are different in two ways. First, Applebee's scope is much broader; he covers English reforms and traditions from the mid-seventeenth century until the 1970s. Second, Applebee focuses almost exclusively on the literary side of English Studies, while my interest lies primarily (though not exclusively) in the relationship between progressive education and composition.

2. Alan Trachtenberg reports that "[i]mmigrants alone represented a third of the total population increase between 1860 and 1900" (88). Cremin notes that a 1909 study by the U.S. Immigration Commission reported that "57.8 per cent of the children in the schools of thirty-seven of the nation's largest cities were of foreign-born parentage" (72).

3. Of course, in the United States of the mid-nineteenth century, Mann's claims to inclusiveness were compromised by social arrangements that systematically disenfranchised many groups, including women, African Americans, Native Americans, the working class, and others. Bowles and Gintis argue persuasively that Mann's calls for "universal" education were inspired less by democratic sentiment than by his devotion to the emerging industrial order and his fear of the development of class consciousness.

4. Trachtenberg's fascinating historical study, *The Incorporation of America,* inquires into both the literal "incorporation" of industry and business, and the figurative "incorporation" of U.S. culture—that is, the myriad and often subtle ways in which literal incorporation informed

"the shape and texture of daily life, and the thinking of Americans" (4). Similarly, when I write of the "incorporation" of U.S. schools, I have in mind both the literal organizational structures applied to the administration of schools and the *ideology* of incorporation and its cultural effects.

5. John Dewey's Laboratory School, also in Chicago, was in many respects similar to Parker's school: it was designed as a model democratic community, and it engaged students in active, hands-on learning. Activities were organized around themes, and students were encouraged to engage in self-reflection both as individuals and as community members, thus strengthening their sense of both independence and interdependence.

6. Writing a year earlier, Ellwood Cubberley of Stanford captures this same idea in this description of the public schools:

> Our schools are, in a sense, factories in which the raw products (children) are to be shaped and fashioned into the products to meet the various demands of life. The specifications for manufacturing come from the demands of twentieth century civilization and it is the business of schools to build students to the expectations laid down. (qtd. in Newkirk 120)

7. In fact, a national organization of English teachers was originally proposed by James Hosic as part of the National Education Association's Round Table Committee on College Entrance Requirements. The committee had been formed in protest against the uniform reading lists for high school English. Hosic's request was granted, and NCTE was formed in 1911; Hosic became the organization's first executive secretary (now called executive director).

8. I consider only the first ten volumes of *EJ* for demographic purposes, both to keep the numbers manageable and because beginning in 1923, *EJ* discontinued its practice of identifying its contributors by town and institution in bylines. I do not include committee reports (unless a single author is identified), round tables, reviews, or editorials. If institutions were not named in the byline, or were not made clear in the opening of the article, I do not include these when tabulating for institutional affiliation, though they are included in geographical tabulations as long as the town was identified in the byline.

9. Although almost all of the contributions from "schools" came from high schools, I use the former term because a handful of contributions came from teachers of earlier grade levels, especially toward the end of

the decade, when junior high schools began to emerge. It's worth remembering that while four-year high schools became the minority of secondary schools after World War II, 94 percent of all secondary schools in 1920 were four-year institutions; only 0.4 percent were junior high schools; and the remainder were combined junior-senior high schools (Tyack and Cuban). Also, despite repeated calls by *EJ* editors, it appears that elementary school teachers simply did not submit many articles (Hook).

10. In fact, issues of race and class, too, were routinely suppressed or ignored in the pages of *EJ*. Consider the Americanization movement, which aimed to enact the "melting pot" myth by extracting or suppressing difference in favor of a homogenous "Americanness." At South Philadelphia's diverse High School for Girls, for instance, Mary Moriarty taught American values through outside reading: "Think of it! 16000 books, largely by English and American writers, 16000 books dealing with Anglo-Saxon ideals, Anglo-Saxon institutions, Anglo-Saxon modes of thought, Anglo-Saxon attitudes toward life, brought to the very heart of the foreign colony!" (580). (See also Ale; Gibbs; Henderson; Poole; and Thorngate on Americanization.)

11. In fact, Helen Sand Hughes in 1922 wrote that "the course in Freshman English in colleges has been turning more and more into an inexpert forum in politics and economics: an Introduction to the Study of Society for the amateur by the dilettante" that includes endless discussions of "Americanism, Socialism, and 'the woman question'" (563). Readers might compare Hughes's argument to Maxine Hairston's more recent complaints about first-year writing courses as sites of political indoctrination.

12. Berlin claims that after World War I, "the progressives" shifted their emphasis from social reform to individual development, and that the latter was pursued "without regard for social or practical ends" (*Rhetoric* 60). But while we do see rising interest in depth psychology, creative arts, and expressionism in *EJ* during the 1920s (A. H. Gilbert; O. C. Johnson; Osgood, "Humanism"; Reeve), these influences did not have the effect of bracketing off "social or practical ends." On the contrary, those associated most closely with composition retained their devotion to the practical, the utilitarian, throughout the Age of Efficiency. Further, *EJ* provides no evidence that "creative writing" became a full-blown movement during the 1920s; indeed, as late as 1929, *EJ* editor H. D. Roberts suggested that "the creative writing movement is not yet sufficiently developed" (345). At any rate, as D. G. Myers makes clear, the creative writing movement, with its emphasis on personal expression, developed largely as a separate enterprise from composition, which was almost exclusively concerned with narrowly practical forms of writing.

13. The report, written primarily by John Clapp, was not strictly business oriented—its focus was on "the demands actually made upon the adult American today with respect to his use of language and what are the difficulties which he experiences" (110)—but this emphasis is certainly pronounced, perhaps in large part because its chief author was a leader in the "better business letters movement" (see Clapp).

14. Miller also writes about the "feminization of Composition" in *Textual Carnivals,* where she explores prevalent images of the composition teacher as a maid or a mother. Schell similarly demonstrates that the work of writing instruction remains organized around professional inequities that exploit women's labor ("Costs," *Gypsy*).

# Chapter 2

1. Standardized tests were used widely after World War II for placing men who were taking advantage of the GI bill. The availability of computer technology also aided a renaissance of standardized testing between the late 1950s and early 1970s. This period saw the rise of the SAT, the ACT, the National Merit Scholarship Corporation, the 1958 National Defense Education Act (which made provisions for standardized assessment), and the National Assessment of Educational Progress (NAEP) (1965). In the 1970s, testing was challenged as unreliable, biased, and invalid, especially by the National Education Association (NEA), which, at the prompting of the NAACP, called a brief moratorium on standardized testing. With the 1980s backlash against the "liberalism" of the earlier decades, however, standardized testing has steadily taken a more prominent role in educational reform. See Baker and Stites.

2. Sacks, a journalist, notes that while antitesting forces have earned a kind of spotty public cachet in the last twenty years, it would be dangerous to "underestimate the near magical power that quantification, standardization, and the measuring of minds continues [sic] to have over Americans" (7).

3. Currently, such regional accreditation is voluntary. It is important to note, however, that although legally voluntary, compliance with accreditation procedures is fiscally necessary for many institutions (see the ADE Ad Hoc Committee on Assessment).

4. I am grateful to Stephen M. Foley for helping me develop this understanding of standardized testing.

5. I should note the important work carried out by educational reformers—some of them compositionists—who have labored to build better tests. Roberta Camp and Edward M. White, for instance, have helped the test developers, and specifically the Educational Testing Service, to see the value of portfolios and holistic scoring (see White, "Power," *Teaching*). Advocates of "authentic assessment" have also encouraged the development of kinder, gentler tests in California, Kentucky, and Vermont, among other states. (See Archbald and Newman; Darling-Hammond, Ancess, and Falk; and Wiggins on "authentic assessment.") But we also need to recognize the limitations of tinkering with tests and of participating, as White urges us to do, in "the assessment community" ("Writing"). White argues that writing teachers have only two choices with respect to corporate-generated tests: "we can ignore them in the vain hope that they will go away, or we can participate in them in an informed way to make them as good as possible" (103). But it isn't at all clear that teachers must either passively accede to their disenfranchisement or actively participate in it. In Intralude and Chapter 6, in fact, I offer a third alternative: that teachers might become assessors themselves. While tinkering with tests is not itself a corrupt practice, it is not our only viable choice; we must seek multiple paths to alternative assessments.

6. Patrick Shannon has argued that the movement for national standards is "part of a coordinated effort by corporate America to discredit public schools in order to reduce the costs of social services in the United States, and thereby significantly reduce the tax burden on business" (qtd. in Brannon). Of course, the adoption of national standards would also be a boon for the standardized testing industry.

7. Copperman's gathering and use of "evidence" to support this argument are odd. He confesses that he found it extraordinarily difficult to find any statistics on academic achievement. After much searching, he obtained a limited number of unpublished standardized tests results through "two evaluation experts I knew" (19). After that, he requested additional information from test publishers, with this result: "Although all of the major test publishers had refused our direct requests for historical statistics (including Harcourt and Houghton Mifflin), we were able to add the McGraw-Hill data to our file when Paul Kullman [a friend] moved there from Harcourt" (20). Thus, by "putting together all of the various pieces of information, I was able to develop an historical profile of academic achievement in the United States since the late 1800s, a profile which becomes increasingly accurate as it approaches the present" (20). Even if we did trust Copperman's ability to "put together all of the various pieces of information"—he is neither a statistician nor a psychometrician—we must wonder why these test publishers

refused to publish the results of the tests and then refused Copperman's request for information. Further, Copperman provides precious little "evidence" of correlation between these questionable test results and the pedagogies of the educational liberals. His modus operandi, rather, is simply to juxtapose the test results with descriptions of these "soft" pedagogies, presumably confident that his readers can draw no other conclusion than that the latter caused the former. For a very different and far more compelling look at educational achievement data, see Berliner and Biddle.

8. This is not to suggest that literacy is not useful for work, or that there should be no connection between school and work. Indeed, I believe, with John Dewey, that if schooling is meaningful, students are more likely to seek meaningful employment and to work reflectively in that capacity with an ongoing awareness of the consequences of their work not only for themselves but also for others. In other words, rather than simply "taking their place," they are more likely to work to make their place and the places of others more livable, more humane. See Dewey, *Democracy;* "Learning"; "Need."

9. Of course, as a quick glance at the education section of any local bookstore will confirm, E. D. Hirsch's notion of "cultural literacy" has also become wildly popular. I suspect that critiques of Hirsch's content-based program are familiar enough to many readers (see, for instance, Bizzell, *Academic Discourse,* and Brodkey, *Writing Permitted*). The point I would make here is that Hirsch defines his reformist program around the concept of literacy, even though it has little to do with processes of reading and writing. We might read this as an index of how elastic the term "literacy" has become, but it also provides an indication that the continuing education crisis, whatever else it may be, is most certainly a *literacy* crisis in the public imagination.

10. Lil Brannon makes a similar argument about standards in "The Problem of National Standards."

11. I am grateful to Peter Gray for his assistance in reconstructing these events; see also Gleason, "Remediation."

# Chapter 3

1. Although the writers don't use this term, they do name the impetus for their work as higher education's "failure to courageously address social issues and problems" (60).

2. Moreover, there is slippage in this essay between *an* institution and *the* institution (of higher education). In a note, the writers suggest that "[w]hat we say about our universities and our states could also be said about *any of the other ones that we have seen*" (Hurlbert and Blitz, "Institution('s)" 75, authors' emphasis). The suggestion here is that their analysis is generalizable because their universities are generalizable. The writers assume that all universities/states are the same—or sufficiently similar not to warrant a discussion of their differences. But even within many state systems of higher education, there are huge disparities in resources, support services, recruitment and retention practices, and so on. Certainly these are even more pronounced when one shifts funding systems, geographical location, socioeconomic backgrounds of students, and the like.

3. It is interesting to note that Hurlbert and Blitz's subsequent work— especially their book *Letters for the Living* (Blitz and Hurlbert)—offers a much richer and complicated representation of working within and against institutions. Perhaps we can account for this shift by noting that in *Letters*, which is narrative driven, the writers do not write from within the discursive framework of critical pedagogy, as they do in this earlier essay.

4. While my notion of institutional literacy has much in common with Porter et al.'s notion of institutional critique, I prefer the former term for two reasons. First, as the authors make clear, institutional critique is "a methodology." I am less interested in designing a single, systematized process or research design than in describing a more general mode of inquiry, which will be enacted in diverse ways depending on the site in which it is engaged. Second—a related point—Porter et al. appear to be describing a specialized method for compositionists. They suggest, for instance, that *disciplinary* critique is "important to institutional critique— perhaps even necessary to it" (620). While the implications of this state-ment are unclear, it would seem that students—particularly undergraduate students, who are typically more or less unaware of the methods of disciplinarity—do not (and for the most part could not) engage in institutional critique. By contrast, the less specialized notion of institutional literacy seeks to make visible the resistance work of stu-dents as well as teachers and researchers.

5. Indeed, as I have suggested, even Dewey's sympathetic critics often brand him a reformist whom we have moved beyond. In *Border Cross-ings*, for instance, Giroux claims that with Bowles and Gintis's *School-ing in Capitalist Society*, we transcended Dewey's "earlier critical tradition" (13). In Bowles and Gintis's account, Dewey is portrayed as a naive, ineffectual liberal whose ideas (even the good ones) never saw

the light of day because he didn't understand how capitalism really worked. Because he didn't advocate a "second American revolution" (282), Dewey's reforms "turned out to be little more than a Band-Aid remedy" (196).

# Chapter 4

1. Some readers will no doubt note that in publishing this book, I am participating in the very system I join Ferry and Vandenberg in critiquing (just as those scholars participated in this system by publishing their articles in *Under Construction*). And they are surely right. Vandenberg addresses this argument directly, conceding that we are unlikely to disrupt the class system of academic disciplinarity by calling for such a disruption in our published texts. Only through "physical and symbolic action *outside* the realm of academic publishing" will such a change be possible (29). But while I agree with Vandenberg that academic publishing in itself is likely to do little to interrupt disciplinary business as usual, I do think that those of us producing it can use our positions of privilege to work toward such change. As Vandenberg suggests, the academic class system persists largely because "the top-down relationship of 'research' to teaching appears natural, logical, or self-evident rather than historical, contingent, and economically determined" (29). Publishing scholars have a responsibility, I believe, to use their voices to denaturalize this class system. They can educate their readers about the working conditions of most writing teachers, and they can value teaching by representing it, not in the abstract, but in particular sites of practice. In fact, I see this work happening in the rich texts offered by a new generation of compositionists, including Amy Lee, Harriet Malinowitz, Richard Miller, and Nancy Welch.

2. Here is Sandra Stotsky, for instance: "I doubt that the 'methodological integrity' [North] believes future genres of research can display can be a meaningful concept outside of our empirical research traditions and the kind of studies they create" (210).

3. It is also true, though, that some writers take considerable risks in doing this work. In a recent tenure case, a well-known outside reviewer declared that a colleague's book was "useful" for teachers but not "a major contribution" to theoretical scholarship. The reviewer made it clear that the book was "important" for its attention to classrooms— and that he supported this colleague's tenure case—but he made his distaste for the pedagogical focus of the book clear enough in his letter.

# Chapter 5

1. One exciting feature of this line of thinking is an increased emphasis on the potential diversity of writing curricula. Shamoon, Howard, Jamieson, and Schwegler suggest that advanced writing curricula are just now "coming of age," as compositionists begin to pay significant attention to pedagogy outside of the required first-year course. Their edited collection—*Coming of Age* (2000)—is among the first significant pieces of Composition and Rhetoric scholarship to represent a diverse range of what Sharon Crowley calls "vertical" writing curricula. In a similar vein, see Goggin and Miller. I regret that these publications appeared too late for me to assign them the kind of attention they deserve in the context of this project. Perhaps it is enough for my present purposes to recommend them to readers as examples of what I see as a hopeful trend in the field—and perhaps even as a step toward a reinvigorated pedagogical progressivism in Composition and Rhetoric.

2. In fact, as Hutcheon documents, dissensus has been a feature of English studies from its very beginnings.

3. For historical views of this development, see Connors, *Composition-Rhetoric*; S. Miller, *Textual Carnivals*; North, *Refiguring*; Schell, *Gypsy*; see also Chapter 1.

4. I choose to treat writers who offer integrative models of English studies because, while I am not convinced that English departments are always the best place for composition/Composition and Rhetoric, and while we are seeing more and more freestanding composition programs (see Shamoon et al.; Petraglia), most college composition continues to be taught within English departments, and so it remains instructive to see how compositionists struggle to imagine their work within the context of English studies. Also, more simply, I believe that some of the most innovative work on writing curricula today is taking place within the context of these integrated models.

# Chapter 6

1. This is not to say that none of the participants developed useful curricular innovations or reports; see, for instance, the Illinois State University and University of Iowa reports.

2. One could make a case for Milner, Foster, and Entes as exceptions since they do invoke English-English education tensions. Even these

essays, though, do little more than pose this familiar tension: Milner ends with an admission that his thinking is "inconclusive"; Foster essentially embraces the tension; and Entes concludes with a declaration that she will continue to connect reading, writing, and speech in her own classroom "regardless of whether I can coordinate my teaching with that of other faculty" (287).

3. The CCCC has formed the Task Force on Improving the Working Conditions of Part-Time and Adjunct Faculty and boasts an active Non-Tenure-Track Special Interest Group. See also Gilbert et al.; Association of Departments of English; "Statement from the Conference"; NCTE, "Statement"; Harris, "From."

4. Kolb does indicate a "reciprocal" move: "we need to send faculty members out to the schools to discuss texts and ideas in specific disciplines and to participate as well in on-site conversations about adopting texts, instituting new curricula, creating interdisciplinary courses, and coordinating programs between colleges, high schools, and middle and elementary schools" (342). But he gives no indication that the university "expert" would take on a truly collegial role in these "conversations," and project leaders seem unconcerned that such an expert might not be entirely welcome in such discussions.

# WORKS CITED

Adler-Kassner, Linda, Robert Crooks, and Ann Watters, eds. *Writing the Community: Concepts and Models for Service Learning.* Urbana, IL: NCTE, 1997.

Ale, Ida G. "Teaching the Foreign-Born." *English Journal* 9 (1920): 13–19.

Apple, Michael. *Education and Power.* 2nd ed. New York: Routledge, 1995.

———. *Official Knowledge.* New York: Routledge, 1993.

Applebee, Arthur. *Tradition and Reform in the Teaching of English.* Urbana, IL: NCTE, 1974.

Archbald, D. A., and F. M. Newman. *Beyond Standardized Testing: Assessing Authentic Academic Achievement in the Secondary School.* Reston, VA: National Association of Secondary School Principals, 1988.

Arenson, Karen W. "Why College Isn't for Everyone." *New York Times* 31 Aug. 1997, sec. 4: 1.

Aronowitz, Stanley, and Henry A. Giroux. *Education Still under Siege.* 2nd ed. Westport, CT: Bergin & Garvey, 1993.

Association of Departments of English. "Report of the ADE Ad Hoc Committee on Staffing." 24 May 2000 <http://www.ade.org/reports>.

Association of Departments of English Ad Hoc Committee on Assessment. "Report of the ADE Ad Hoc Committee on Assessment." *Profession 1997.* New York: MLA, 1997. 251–74.

"Authentic Evaluation: Nebraska Teachers Design Assessment through Active Classroom Learning." Lincoln: Goals 2000 Assessment Project. December 2000.

Babbitt, Irving. "English and the Discipline of Ideas." *English Journal* 9 (1920): 61–70.

Baker, Eva L., and Regie Stites. "Trends in Testing in the USA." *The Politics of Curriculum and Testing*. Ed. Susan Fuhrman and Betty Malen. New York: Falmer, 1991. 139–58.

Balsamo, Anne. "Cultural Studies and the Undergraduate Curriculum." Berlin and Vivion 145–64.

Baynham, Mike. *Literacy Practices: Investigating Literacy in Social Contexts*. New York: Longman, 1995.

Belanoff, Pat. "Portfolios and Literacy: Why?" Black, Daiker, Sommers, and Stygall 13–24.

Belanoff, Pat, and Marcia Dickson, eds. *Portfolios: Process and Product*. Portsmouth, NH: Boynton/Cook, 1991.

Belanoff, Pat, and Peter Elbow. "Using Portfolios to Increase Collaboration and Community in a Writing Program." Belanoff and Dickson 17–30.

Berlin, James A. "Rhetoric and Ideology in the Writing Class." *College English* 50 (1988): 477–94.

———. *Rhetoric and Reality: Writing Instruction in American Colleges, 1900–1985*. Carbondale: Southern Illinois UP, 1987.

———. *Rhetorics, Poetics, and Cultures*. Urbana, IL: NCTE, 1996.

———. "The Teacher as Researcher: Democracy, Dialogue, and Power." Daiker and Morenberg 3–14.

———. *Writing Instruction in Nineteenth-Century American Colleges*. Carbondale: Southern Illinois UP, 1984.

Berlin, James A., and Michael J. Vivion, eds. *Cultural Studies in the English Classroom*. Portsmouth, NH: Heinemann, 1992.

Berliner, David C., and Bruce J. Biddle. *The Manufactured Crisis: Myths, Fraud, and the Attack on America's Schools*. Reading, MA: Addison-Wesley, 1995.

Berthoff, Ann E. *The Making of Meaning*. Montclair, NJ: Boynton/Cook, 1981.

Berubé, Michael. *The Employment of English*. New York: New York UP, 1998.

Berubé, Michael, and Cary Nelson, eds. *Higher Education under Fire: Politics, Economics, and the Crisis of the Humanities*. New York: Routledge, 1995.

Bizzell, Patricia. *Academic Discourse and Critical Consciousness.* Pittsburgh: U of Pittsburgh P, 1992.

———. "Thomas Kuhn, Scientism, and English Studies." Rpt. in Bizzell, *Academic Discourse and Critical Consciousness* 39–50.

Black, Laurel, Donald A. Daiker, Jeffrey Sommers, and Gail Stygall, eds. *New Directions in Portfolio Assessment: Reflective Practice, Critical Theory, and Large-Scale Scoring.* Portsmouth, NH: Heinemann, 1994.

Blitz, Michael, and C. Mark Hurlbert. *Letters for the Living: Teaching Writing in a Violent Age.* Urbana, IL: NCTE, 1998.

Bloom, Allan. *The Closing of the American Mind.* New York: Simon and Schuster, 1987.

Bloom, Lynn Z., Donald A. Daiker, and Edward M. White, eds. *Composition in the Twenty-First Century: Crisis and Change.* Carbondale: Southern Illinois UP, 1996.

Bode, B. H. "Concerning the Teaching of English." *English Journal* 18 (1929): 381–89.

Bodziock, Joseph C., and Christopher Ferry. "Teaching 'Myth, Difference, and Popular Culture.'" Fitts and France 39–52.

Bowles, Samuel, and Herbert Gintis. *Schooling in Capitalist America: Educational Reform and the Contradictions of Economic Life.* New York: Basic, 1977.

Boyer, Ernest L. *High School: A Report on Secondary Education in America.* New York: Harper and Row, 1983.

Braddock, Richard, Richard Lloyd-Jones, and Lowell Schoer. *Research in Written Composition.* Champaign, IL: NCTE, 1963.

Brandt, Deborah. *Literacy as Involvement.* Carbondale: Southern Illinois UP, 1990.

Brannon, Lil. "The Problem of National Standards." *College Composition and Communication* 46 (1995): 440–45.

Brecher, Elinor. *Schindler's Legacy: True Stories of the List Survivors.* New York: Dutton, 1994.

Brereton. John C., ed. *The Origins of Composition Studies in the American College, 1875–1925: A Documentary History.* Pittsburgh: U of Pittsburgh P, 1995.

Broad, Bob. "Facing Our Professional Others: Border Crossing in Teacher Education." Franklin, Laurence, and Welles 373–79.

Brodkey, Linda. "The Troubles at Texas." *Writing Permitted in Designated Areas Only.* Minneapolis: U of Minnesota P, 1996. 181–92.

———. *Writing Permitted in Designated Areas Only.* Minneapolis: U of Minnesota P, 1996.

Bullock, Richard, and John Trimbur, eds. *The Politics of Writing Instruction: Postsecondary.* Portsmouth, NH: Boynton/Cook, 1991.

"Business English." Editorial. *English Journal* 2 (1913): 193.

Cahalan, James M., and David B. Downing, eds. *Practicing Theory in Introductory College Literature Courses.* Urbana, IL: NCTE, 1991.

Callahan, Raymond E. *Education and the Cult of Efficiency.* Chicago: U of Chicago P, 1962.

Camenisch, Sophia Catherine. "Some Recent Tendencies in the Minimum-Essentials Movement in English." *English Journal* 15 (1926): 181–90.

Camp, Roberta, and Denise Stavis Levine. "Portfolios Evolving: Background and Variations in Sixth- through Twelfth-Grade Classrooms." Belanoff and Dickson. 194–205.

Carter, Jean. "Contracts Socialized." *English Journal* 17 (1928): 544–49.

Certain, C. C. "Why Not Include Standardized Tests in Your Teaching Program This Term?" *English Journal* 12 (1923): 463–80.

Chamberlain, Essie. "Curriculum Building in English." *English Journal* 14 (1925): 1–12.

Clapp, John M. "The Better Business Letters Movement." *English Journal* 7 (1918): 237–44.

Clark, Fannie M. "Teaching Children to Choose." *English Journal* 9 (1920): 135–46.

Cody, Sherwin, "The Ideal Course in English for Vocational Students (Continued)." *English Journal* 3 (1914): 371–80.

———. "Organizing Drill on Fundamentals Like a Football Game." *English Journal* 6 (1917): 412–19.

Cohen, Ronald D., and Raymond A. Mohl. *The Paradox of Progressive Education: The Gary Plan and Urban Schooling.* Port Washington, NY: Kennikat, 1979.

College Composition and Communication Committee on Assessment. "Writing Assessment: A Position Statement." *College Composition and Communication* 46 (1995): 430–37.

Collins, Terence G. "A Response to Ira Shor's 'Our Apartheid: Writing Instruction and Inequality.'" *Journal of Basic Writing* 16 (1997): 95–100.

Condon, William, and Liz Hamp-Lyons. "Maintaining a Portfolio-Based Writing Assessment: Research That Informs Program Development." Black, Daiker, Sommers, and Stygall 277–85.

Connors, Robert J. "The Abolition Debate in Composition: A Short History." *Composition in the Twenty-First Century: Crisis and Change.* Ed. Lynn Z. Bloom, Donald A. Daiker, and Edward M. White. Carbondale: Southern Illinois UP, 1996. 47–63.

———. "Composition History and Disciplinarity." Rosner, Boehm, and Journet 3–22.

———. *Composition-Rhetoric: Backgrounds, Theory, and Pedagogy.* Pittsburgh: U of Pittsburgh P, 1997.

———. "Rhetoric in the Modern University: The Creation of an Underclass." Bullock and Trimbur, 55–84.

———. "The Rise and Fall of the Modes of Discourse." *College Composition and Communication* 32 (1981): 444–55.

Cook, Luella B. "Individualism in Our Composition Classes." *English Journal* 18 (1929): 31–39.

Cooke, John D. "Community English: A Means of Motivation for Oral and Written Composition." *English Journal* 9 (1920): 20–24.

Cooper, Charles R., and Lee Odell, eds. *Evaluating Writing: The Role of Teachers' Knowledge about Text, Learning, and Culture.* Urbana, IL: NCTE, 1999.

Cooper, Marilyn. "From the Editor: CCC 2000." *College Composition and Communication* 51 (2000): 363–65.

Copperman, Paul. *The Literacy Hoax: The Decline of Reading, Writing, and Learning in the Public Schools and What We Can Do about It.* New York: Morrow, 1978.

Courtis, S. A. "The Value of Measurements: The Uses of the Hillegas Scale." *English Journal* 8 (1919): 208–17.

Cremin, Lawrence A. *The Transformation of the School.* New York: Vintage, 1961.

Crowley, Sharon. *Composition in the University.* Pittsburgh: U of Pittsburgh P, 1998.

———. "Reimagining the Writing Scene: Curmudgeonly Remarks about *Contending with Words.*" Harkin and Schilb 189–97.

Cushman, Ellen. "The Public Intellectual." *College English* 61 (1999): 328–36.

———. *The Struggle and the Tools: Oral and Literate Strategies in an Inner City Community.* Albany: SUNY P, 1998.

Cushman, Ellen, and Terese Guinsatao Monberg. "Re-Centering Authority: Social Reflexivity and Re-positioning in Composition Research." Farris and Anson 166–80.

Cutuly, Joan. *Home of the Wildcats.* Urbana, IL: NCTE, 1993.

Daiker, Donald A., and Max Morenberg, eds. *The Writing Teacher as Researcher: Essays in the Theory and Practice of Class-Based Research.* Portsmouth, NH: Boynton/Cook, 1990.

Daiker, Donald A., Jeff Sommers, and Gail Stygall. "The Pedagogical Implications of a College Placement Portfolio." White, Lutz, and Kamusikiri 257–70.

Darling-Hammond, Linda, Jacqueline Ancess, and Beverly Falk. *Authentic Assessment in Action.* New York: Teachers College P, 1995.

Deans, Thomas. *Writing Partnerships: Service-Learning in Composition.* Urbana, IL: NCTE, 2000.

Dewey, John. *The Child and the Curriculum.* Chicago: U of Chicago P, 1902.

———. *Democracy and Education.* New York: Free, 1966.

———. *Experience and Education.* New York: Collier, 1963.

———. "Learning to Earn: The Place of Vocational Education in a Comprehensive Scheme of Public Education." *John Dewey: The Middle Works, 1899–1924.* Vol. 10. Ed. Jo Ann Boydston. Carbondale: Southern Illinois UP, 1980. 144–50.

———. "Logical Conditions of a Scientific Treatment of Morality." *John Dewey on Education*. Ed. Reginald D. Archambault. Chicago: U of Chicago P, 1964. 23–60.

———. "My Pedagogic Creed." *John Dewey on Education*. Ed. Reginald D. Archambault. Chicago: U of Chicago P, 1964. 427–39.

———. "The Nature of Aims." *John Dewey on Education*. Ed. Reginald D. Archambault. Chicago: U of Chicago P, 1964. 70–80.

———. "The Need of an Industrial Education in an Industrial Democracy." *John Dewey: The Middle Works, 1899–1924*. Vol. 10. Ed. Jo Ann Boydston. Carbondale: Southern Illinois UP, 1980. 137–43.

———. "Progress." *John Dewey: The Middle Works, 1899–1924*. Vol. 10. Ed. Jo Ann Boydston. Carbondale: Southern Illinois UP, 1980. 234–43.

———. "Progressive Education and the Science of Education." *John Dewey on Education*. Ed. Reginald D. Archambault. Chicago: U of Chicago P, 1964. 169–81.

———. "The Relation of Science and Philosophy as a Basis for Education." *John Dewey on Education*. Ed. Reginald D. Archambault. Chicago: U of Chicago P, 1964. 15–19.

———. *The School and Society*. Chicago: U of Chicago P, 1963.

———. "Science as Subject-Matter and as Method." *John Dewey on Education*. Ed. Reginald D. Archambault. Chicago: U of Chicago P, 1964. 182–92.

Dewey, John, and Evelyn Dewey. *Schools of To-morrow*. New York: Dutton, 1915.

Dilworth, Collett, and Nancy Mellin McCracken. "Ideological Crosscurrents in English Studies and English Education: A Report of a National Survey of Professors' Beliefs and Practices." McCracken, Larson, and Entes 349–61.

Dixon, Kathleen. "Making and Taking Apart 'Culture' in the (Writing) Classroom." Fitts and France 99–114.

Dobrin, Sidney I. *Constructing Knowledges: The Politics of Theory-Building and Pedagogy in Composition*. Albany: SUNY P, 1997.

"Doctor of Philosophy." SUNY-Albany English Department Web site. 25 June 2001 <www.albany.edu/english/grad/phd.html>.

Donahue, Patricia. "Falling into Narrative." McCracken, Larson, and Entes 251–59.

Donahue, Patricia, and Ellen Quandahl. *Reclaiming Pedagogy: The Rhetoric of the Classroom.* Carbondale: Southern Illinois UP, 1989.

Douglas, Lucile. "Teaching English on the Dalton Plan." *English Journal* 13 (1924): 335–40.

Downing, David B., ed. *Changing Classroom Practices.* Urbana, IL: NCTE, 1994.

———. Preface. Downing xiii–xv.

D'Souza, Dinesh. *Illiberal Education.* New York: Vintage, 1992.

Duddy, Edward A. "A Co-operative Course in English Composition for Students in Technical Courses." *English Journal* 10 (1921): 201–7.

Duncan, C. S. "A Rebellious Word on English Composition." *English Journal* 3 (1914): 154–59.

"The Efficiency Wave." Editorial. *English Journal* 1 (1912): 640–41.

Elbow, Peter. "Illiteracy at Oxford and Harvard: Reflection on the Inability to Write." McCracken, Larson, and Entes 91–114.

———."The Pedagogy of the Bamboozled." *Embracing Contraries: Explorations in Learning and Teaching.* New York: Oxford UP, 1986. 87–98.

———. *What Is English?* New York: MLA/Urbana, IL: NCTE, 1990.

———. "Will the Virtues of Portfolios Blind Us to Their Potential Dangers?" Black, Daiker, Sommers, and Stygall 40–55.

Elbow, Peter, and Pat Belanoff. "State University of New York at Stony Brook Portfolio-Based Evaluation Program." Belanoff and Dickson 3–16.

Ellsworth, Elizabeth. "Why Doesn't This Feel Empowering? Working through the Repressive Myths of Critical Pedagogy." *Feminisms and Critical Pedagogy.* Ed. Carmen Luke and Jennifer Gore. New York: Routledge, 1992. 90–119.

Emerson, Ralph Waldo. "The Poet." *Selected Writings of Ralph Waldo Emerson.* New York: Signet, 1983. 306–27.

Entes, Judith. "Connecting the Teaching of Reading, Writing, and Speech in Programs for Developmental Students." McCracken, Larson, and Entes 280–87.

Ervin, Elizabeth. "Academics and the Negotiation of Local Knowledge." *College English* 61 (1999): 448–70.

"Fact Sheet." Fairtest. 21 May 2001. <www.fairtest.org/facts>.

Faigley, Lester. *Fragments of Rationality: Postmodernity and the Subject of Composition.* Pittsburgh: U of Pittsburgh P, 1992.

Farris, Christine, and Chris Anson. "Introduction: Complicating Composition." Farris and Anson 1–7.

———, eds. *Under Construction: Working at the Intersections of Composition Theory, Research, and Practice.* Logan: Utah State UP, 1998.

Ferry, Christopher. "Theory, Research, Practice, Work." Farris and Anson 11–18.

Fetterley, Judith. "Dreaming the Future of English." *College English* 61 (1999): 702–11.

Fishman, Stephen M. "Explicating Our Tacit Tradition: John Dewey and Composition Studies." *College Composition and Communication* 44 (1993): 315–30.

Fishman, Stephen M., and Lucille Parkinson McCarthy. *John Dewey and the Challenge of Classroom Practice.* New York: Teachers College P, 1998.

———. "Teaching for Student Change: A Deweyan Alternative to Radical Pedagogy." *College Composition and Communication* 47 (1996): 324–66.

Fitts, Karen, and Alan W. France. Preface. *Left Margins: Cultural Studies and Composition Pedagogy.* Albany: SUNY P, 1995. ix–xvi.

———, eds. *Left Margins: Cultural Studies and Composition Pedagogy.* Albany: SUNY P, 1995.

Flesch, Rudolf. *Why Johnny Can't Read—And What You Can Do about It.* New York: Harper and Row, 1955.

———. *Why Johnny Still Can't Read: A New Look at the Scandal of Our Schools.* New York: Harper and Row, 1981.

Forbes, Cheryl. "Reading Portfolios Conversationally." Black, Daiker, Sommers, and Stygall 103–12.

Forché, Carolyn, ed. *Against Forgetting: Twentieth Century Poetry of Witness.* New York: Norton, 1993.

Foreman, Joel, and David R. Shumway. "Cultural Studies: Reading Visual Texts." Berlin and Vivion, 244–61.

Fortune, Ron, ed. *School-College Collaborative Programs in English.* New York: MLA, 1986.

Foster, Harold M. "English in Education: An English Educationist at Work." McCracken, Larson, and Entes 260–70.

Foucault, Michel. *Power/Knowledge.* Ed. Colin Gordon. New York: Pantheon, 1980.

Franklin, Phyllis, David Laurence, and Elizabeth B. Welles. "Preface: The School Reform Movement and Higher Education." Franklin, Laurence, and Welles ix–xiv.

———, eds. *Preparing a Nation's Teachers.* New York: MLA, 1999.

Freire, Paulo. *Education for Critical Consciousness.* New York: Continuum, 1994.

———. *Pedagogy of the Oppressed.* New York: Continuum, 1996.

Freire, Paulo, and Donaldo Macedo. *Literacy: Reading the Word and the World.* New York: Bergin & Garvey, 1987.

Fries, Charles C. "Educational Pressures and Our Problems." *English Journal* 18 (1929): 1–14.

Fulwider, James H. "Systematizing Instruction in Rhetoric." *English Journal* 11 (1922): 100–103.

Gallagher, Chris. "'Just Give Them What They Need': Transforming the Transformative Intellectual." *Composition Studies* 28.2 (2000): 61–83.

———. "A Seat at the Table: Teachers Reclaiming Assessment through Rethinking Accountability." *Phi Delta Kappan* 81 (2000): 502–7.

Gaston, Charles R. "The Notebook as an Aid to Efficiency in English Class." *English Journal* 4 (1915): 215–25.

Gibbs, Lincoln R. "Americanization and Literature." *English Journal* 9 (1920): 551–56.

Gilbert, Allan H. "What Shall We Do with Freshman Themes?" *English Journal* 11 (1922): 392–403.

Gilbert, Sandra M., et al. "Final Report of the MLA Committee on Professional Employment." *ADE Bulletin* (1998): 27–45.

Gilyard, Keith. "African American Contributions to Composition Studies." *College Composition and Communication* 50 (1999): 626–44.

———, ed. *Race, Rhetoric, and Composition*. Portsmouth, NH: Boynton/Cook, 1999.

Ginsberg, Warren. "Institutional Identity at the State University of New York at Albany: The New Ph.D. in English." Smithson and Ruff 157–66.

Giroux, Henry A. *Border Crossings: Cultural Workers and the Politics of Education*. New York: Routledge, 1992.

———. "Border Pedagogy in the Age of Postmodernism." *Journal of Education* 170 (1988): 162–81.

———. *Theory and Resistance in Education: A Pedagogy for the Opposition*. South Hadley, MA: Bergin & Garvey, 1983.

Giroux, Henry A., and Peter McLaren, eds. *Critical Pedagogy, the State, and Cultural Struggle*. Albany: SUNY P, 1989.

Giroux, Henry A., and Roger Simon. "Popular Culture and Critical Pedagogy: Everyday Life as a Basis for Curriculum Knowledge." *Critical Pedagogy, the State, and Cultural Struggle*. Ed. Henry A. Giroux and Peter McLaren. Albany: SUNY P, 1989. 236–52.

Glaser, Emma. "Eighth-Grade Composition by Project." *English Journal* 10 (1921): 520–25.

Gleason, Barbara. "Evaluating Writing Programs in Real Time." *College Composition and Communication* 51 (2000): 560–88.

———. "Remediation Phase-Out at CUNY: The 'Equity versus Excellence' Controversy." *College Composition and Communication* 51 (2000): 488–91.

Goggin, Maureen Daly, and Susan Kay Miller. "What Is New about the 'New Abolitionists': Continuities and Discontinuities in the Great Debate." *Composition Studies* 28 (2000): 85-112.

Goodburn, Amy. "It's a Question of Faith: Discourses of Fundamentalism and Critical Pedagogy in the Writing Classroom." *Journal of Advanced Composition* 18 (1998): 333-353.

Gordon, Lynn D. *Gender and Higher Education in the Progressive Era*. New Haven: Yale UP, 1990.

Gore, Jennifer M. *The Struggle for Pedagogies*. New York: Routledge, 1993.

———. "What We Can Do for You! What *Can* 'We' Do for 'You'? Struggling over Empowerment in Critical and Feminist Pedagogy." Luke and Gore 54–73.

Goswami, Dixie, and Peter Stillman, eds. *Reclaiming the Classroom: Teacher Research as an Agency for Change*. Upper Montclair, NJ: Boynton/Cook, 1987.

Graff, Gerald. *Beyond the Culture Wars*. New York: Norton, 1992.

———. *Professing Literature: An Institutional History*. Chicago: U of Chicago P, 1987.

———. "Teach the Conflicts." *South Atlantic Quarterly* 89 (1990): 51–68.

Graves, Donald H., and Bonnie S. Sunstein, eds. *Portfolio Portraits*. Portsmouth, NH: Heinemann, 1992.

Gray, Donald. "Introduction: What Happens Next? and How? and Why?" Franklin, Laurence, and Welles 1–11.

Gray, James. "University of California, Berkeley: The Bay Area Writing Project and the National Writing Project." Fortune 35–45.

Gray, James, and Richard Sterling. "The National Writing Project: A University-Based, Teacher-Centered Partnership Program." 6 June 2000 <www-gse.Berkeley.edu/Research/NWP/ nwparticle.html>.

Greenberg, Karen L. "A Response to Ira Shor's 'Our Apartheid': Writing Instruction and Inequality." *Journal of Basic Writing* 16 (1997): 90–94.

Guild, Thacher H. "Going Forth to the Philistines." *English Journal* 1 (1912): 412–18.

Gunther, Charles. "My Experience with the Hillegas Scale." *English Journal* 8 (1919): 535–42.

Gutjahr, Paul. "Constructing Art&Facts: The Art of Composition, the Facts of (Material) Culture." Fitts and France 69–82.

Hairston, Maxine. "Diversity, Ideology, and Teaching Writing." *College Composition and Communication* 43 (1992): 179–93.

Hamilton, Sharon J. "Portfolio Pedagogy: Is a Theoretical Construct Enough?" Black, Daiker, Sommers, and Stygall 157–67.

Hamp-Lyons, Liz, and William Condon. "Questioning Assumptions about Portfolio-Based Assessment." *College Composition and Communication* 44 (1993): 176–90.

Haney, Walter, and George Madaus. "Searching for Alternatives to Standardized Tests: Whats, Whys, and Whithers." *Phi Delta Kappan* 70 (1989): 683–87.

Haney, Walter, George Madaus, and Robert Lyons. *The Fractured Marketplace for Standardized Testing.* Boston: Kluwer, 1993.

Hansen, Allen Oscar. "Objectives Other Than English Skills." *English Journal* 13 (1924): 179–83.

Hargrave, Mary. "The Dalton Plan in Practice." *English Journal* 17 (1928): 372–80.

Harkin, Patricia. "The Postdisciplinary Politics of Lore." Harkin and Schilb 124–38.

Harkin, Patricia, and John Schilb, eds. *Contending with Words: Composition and Rhetoric in a Postmodern Age.* New York: MLA, 1991.

———. Introduction. *Contending with Words.* Ed. Patricia Harkin and John Schilb. New York: MLA, 1991. 1–10.

Harris, Joseph. "From the Editor: Copyright and Consent." *College Composition and Communication* 49 (1998): 7–8.

———. *A Teaching Subject: Composition since 1966.* Upper Saddle River, NJ: Prentice-Hall, 1997.

Hatfield, W. Wilbur. "The Clapp Report." *English Journal* 15 (1926): 153–54.

———. "A Nominal Change." *English Journal* 11 (1922): 118–20.

———. "Not Propaganda." *English Journal* 15 (1926): 716.

———. "The Project Method in Composition." *English Journal* 12 (1923): 173–79.

Healy, Patrick. "CUNY's 4-Year Colleges Ordered to Phase Out Remedial Education." *Chronicle of Higher Education* 5 June 1998: A26.

Healy, Patrick, and Peter Schmidt. "In New York, a 'Standards Revolution' or the Gutting of Public Colleges?" *Chronicle of Higher Education* 10 July 1998: A21.

Heath, Shirley Brice. *Ways with Words.* New York: Cambridge UP, 1983.

Heath, W. R. "The Demands of the Business World for Good English." *English Journal* 2 (1913): 171–77.

Henderson, Ruth Evelyn. "Sorting Them Out." *English Journal* 11 (1922): 554–62.

Henriques, Diana B., and Jacques Steinberg. "Right Answer, Wrong Score: Test Flaws Take Toll." *New York Times* 20 May 2001 <http://nytimes.com/2001/05/20/business>.

———. "When a Test Fails the Schools, Careers and Reputations Suffer." *New York Times* 21 May 2001 <http://nytimes.com/2001/05/21/business>.

Herzberg, Bruce. "Community Service and Critical Teaching." *College Composition and Communication* 45 (1994): 307–19.

Hill, Herbert Wynford. "The Problem of Harmonizing Aesthetic Interests with the Commercial and Industrial Trend of Our Times." *English Journal* 2 (1913): 609–12.

Hirsch, E. D. *Cultural Literacy.* New York: Vintage, 1988.

Hobbs, Catherine, ed. *Nineteenth-Century Women Learn to Write.* Charlottesville: UP of Virginia, 1995.

Hook, J. N. *A Long Way Together: A Personal View of NCTE's First Sixty-Seven Years.* Urbana, IL: NCTE, 1979.

Hopkins, Edwin M. "Can Good Composition Teaching Be Done under Present Conditions?" *English Journal* 1 (1912): 1–8.

———. *The Labor and Cost of the Teaching of English in Colleges and Secondary Schools with Especial Reference to English Composition.* 16th ed. Urbana, IL: NCTE, 1923.

———. "Wanted: A Bureau of Definition." *English Journal* 6 (1917): 131–45.

Horner, Bruce. *Terms of Work for Composition.* Albany: SUNY P, 2000.

Horner, Bruce, and Min-Zhan Lu. *Representing the Other: Basic Writers and the Teaching of Basic Writing.* Urbana, IL: NCTE, 1999.

Hosic, James Fleming. "Nationalization of Education." Editorial. *English Journal* 7 (1918): 468–69.

———. "The Policy of the *English Journal*." Editorial. *English Journal* 1 (1912): 375–76.

———. "Signs of Progress." Editorial. *English Journal* 1 (1912): 439.

Hudelson, Earl. "Some Achievements in the Establishment of a Standard for the Measurement of English Composition in the Bloomington, Indiana, Schools." *English Journal* 5 (1916): 590–97.

Hughes, Helen Sand. "English, Economics, and Literature." *English Journal* 11 (1922): 563–68.

Huot, Brian. "Beyond the Classroom: Using Portfolios to Assess Writing." Black, Daiker, Sommers, and Stygall 325–33.

Hurlbert, Mark C., and Michael Blitz, eds. *Composition and Resistance.* Portsmouth, NH: Boynton/Cook, 1991.

———. "The Institution('s) Lives!" *Pre/Text* 13 (1992): 60–77.

———. "Resisting Composure." Hurlbert and Blitz 1–8.

Hutcheon, Linda. "Introduction: *Plus Ca Change.*" *PMLA* 115 (2000): 1719–27.

Illinois State University. "Renewing the Nexus: Strengthening Connections Across the English Education Program." Franklin, Laurence, and Welles 17–48.

Indiana University, Bloomington. "Watch This Space; Or, Why We Have Not Revised the Teacher Education Program—Yet." Franklin, Laurence, and Welles 49–64.

Jacoby, Russell. *Dogmatic Wisdom: How the Culture Wars Divert Education and Distract America.* New York: Doubleday, 1994.

Janangelo, Joseph. "To Serve, with Love: Liberation Theory and the Mystification of Teaching." *Theoretical and Critical Perspectives on Teacher Change.* Ed. Phyllis Kahaney, Linda Perry, and Joseph Janangelo. Northwood, NJ: Ablex, 1993. 131–50.

Jay, Gregory S. *American Literature and the Culture Wars.* Ithaca: Cornell UP, 1997.

Jennings, John. *Why National Standards and Tests?* Thousand Oaks, CA: Sage, 1998.

Johnson, Oakley Calvin. "Higher Aims for Rhetoric." *English Journal* coll. ed. 17 (1928): 410–14.

Johnston, Peter H. *Constructive Evaluation of Literate Activity.* New York: Longman, 1992.

————. *Knowing Literacy: Constructive Literacy Assessment.* York, ME: Stenhouse, 1997.

Kecht, Maria-Regina, ed. *Pedagogy Is Politics: Literary Theory and Critical Teaching.* Urbana: U of Illinois P, 1992.

Keneally, Thomas. *Schindler's List.* New York: Simon and Schuster, 1982.

Kennedy, Alan. "Committing the Curriculum and Other Misdemeanors." Berlin and Vivion 24–45.

Keyes, Rowena Keith. "Self-Education in English." *English Journal* 18 (1929): 477–82.

Kidder, Tracy. *Home Town.* New York: Washington Square, 2000.

Kitzhaber, Albert R. *Rhetoric in American Colleges: 1850–1900.* Dallas: Southern Methodist UP, 1990.

Knoblauch, C. H. "The Albany Graduate English Curriculum." *ADE Bulletin* 98 (1991): 19–21.

Knoblauch, C. H., and Lil Brannon. *Critical Teaching and the Idea of Literacy.* Portsmouth, NH: Boynton/Cook, 1993.

————. "Pedagogy *for* the Bamboozled." Unpublished manuscript.

————. *Rhetorical Traditions and the Teaching of Writing.* Upper Montclair, NJ: Boynton/Cook, 1984.

Kolb, Harold H. Jr. "Connecting Universities and Schools: A Case Study." Franklin, Laurence, and Welles 332–52.

LaBrant, Lou L. "New Uses for Standardized Tests." *English Journal* 17 (1928): 299–302.

Lankshear, Colin, and Peter L. McLaren, eds. *Critical Literacy: Politics, Praxis, and the Postmodern.* Albany: SUNY P, 1993.

Larson, Richard L. "Interpreting the Reflective Stories: The Forces of Influence in Our Essayists' Lives." McCracken, Larson, and Entes 365–68.

Lather, Patti. "Post-Critical Pedagogies." Luke and Gore 120–37.

Lazere, Donald. "Teaching the Conflicts about Wealth and Poverty." Fitts and France 189–205.

Lee, Amy. *Composing Critical Pedagogies: Teaching Writing as Revision.* Urbana, IL: NCTE, 2000.

Lewis, W. D. "The Aim of the English Course." *English Journal* 1 (1912): 9–14.

Lord, Brian. "Teachers' Professional Development: Critical Colleague-ship and the Role of Professional Communities." *The Future of Education: Perspectives on National Standards in America.* Ed. Nina Cobb. New York: College Entrance Examination Board, 1994. 175–204.

Luke, Carmen. "Feminist Politics in Radical Pedagogy." Luke and Gore 25–53.

Luke, Carmen, and Jennifer Gore, eds. *Feminisms and Critical Pedagogy.* New York: Routledge, 1992.

———. Introduction. Luke and Gore 1–14.

———. "Women in the Academy: Strategy, Struggle and Survival." Luke and Gore 192–210.

Lunsford, Andrea, Helene Moglen, and James F. Slevin, eds. *The Future of Doctoral Studies in English.* New York: MLA, 1989.

Lyons, Marion C. "My Experience with Business English." *English Journal* 2 (1913): 312–17.

Magee, Helene B. "Inspiration in Freshman Composition." *English Journal* 7 (1918): 313–21.

Maher, Jane. *Mina P. Shaughnessy: Her Life and Work.* Urbana, IL: NCTE, 1997.

Mailloux, Steven. "Rhetoric Returns to Syracuse: Curricular Reform in English Studies." Smithson and Ruff 143–56.

Malinowitz, Harriet. *Textual Orientations: Lesbians and Gay Students and the Making of Discourse Communities.* Portsmouth, NH: Boynton/Cook, 1995.

Manchester, Frederick A. "Freshman English Once More." *English Journal* 6 (1917): 295–307.

Marsh, Alice Louise. "Socializing Influences in the Classroom." *English Journal* 5 (1916): 89–98.

Marshall, James. "Closely Reading Ourselves: Teaching English and the Education of Teachers." Franklin, Laurence, and Welles 380–89.

Mathews, David. *Is There a Public for Public Schools?* Dayton: Kettering Foundation, 1996.

McAndrew, Gerry. "RE: 4Cs." E-mail to Chris Gallagher. 3 Mar. 2001.

McComb, E. H. Kemper. "Social Motives for Composition. *English Journal* 3 (1914): 408–15.

McCracken, H. Thomas. "Interpreting Stories: Rebels in the Professoriate." McCracken, Larson, and Entes 369–74.

McCracken, H. Thomas, and Richard L. Larson. Introduction. McCracken, Larson, and Entes xiii–xviii.

McCracken, H. Thomas, Richard L. Larson, and Judith Entes, eds. *Teaching College English and English Education: Reflective Stories*. Urbana, IL: NCTE, 1998.

McLaren, Peter. "Schooling the Postmodern Body: Critical Pedagogy and the Politics of Enfleshment." *Journal of Education* 170.3 (1988): 53–83.

McWilliam, Erica. "Beyond the Missionary Position: Teacher Desire and Radical Pedagogy." Todd 217–35.

Medina, Noe, and D. Monty Neill. *Fallout from the Testing Explosion*. Cambridge, MA: FairTest, 1988.

Menchú, Rigoberta. *I, Rigoberta Menchú: An Indian Woman in Guatemala*. London: Verso, 1994.

Meyer, Richard J., et al. *Composing a Teacher Study Group*. Mahwah, NJ: Erlbaum, 1998.

Miller, D. W. "Scholars Say High-Stakes Tests Deserve a Failing Grade." *Chronicle of Higher Education* 2 Mar. 2001: A14+.

Miller, Richard E. *As If Learning Mattered*. Ithaca: Cornell UP, 1998.

———. "Let's Do the Numbers." *Profession 1999*. New York: MLA, 1999.

Miller, Susan. "The Feminization of Composition." Bullock and Trimbur 39–53.

———. *Textual Carnivals: The Politics of Composition*. Carbondale: Southern Illinois UP, 1991.

Milner, Joseph. "Living with Tension: Doing English and Talking Pedagogy." McCracken, Larson, and Entes 174–83.

Monseau, Virginia R. "Beyond the Obvious: Connoisseurs and Critics in the Classroom." McCracken, Larson, and Entes 139–45.

Moriarty, Mary L. "Making Americans." *English Journal* 11 (1921): 576–80.

Mortensen, Peter. "Going Public." *College Composition and Communication* 50 (1998): 182–205.

"Moving in the Margins: A Writing Sequence Anthology." Albany: State University of New York, University at Albany, 1998.

Murphy, Michael. "After Progressivism: Modern Composition, Institutional Service, and Cultural Studies." *Journal of Advanced Composition* 13 (1993): 345–64.

Murphy, Sandra, and Barbara Grant. "Portfolio Approaches to Assessment: Breakthrough or More of the Same?" White, Lutz, and Kamusikiri 284–300.

Myers, D. G. *The Elephants Teach: Creative Writing since 1880.* Englewood Cliffs, NJ: Prentice-Hall, 1996.

National Commission on Excellence in Education. *A Nation at Risk.* Washington, DC: U.S. Department of Education, Congressional Research Service, 1983.

National Council of Teachers of English. "English Teachers Pass Resolutions on High-Stakes Testing and the Rights of Test Takers." 15 June 2001 <http://www.ncte.org/news/2000resolutions>.

———. "Statement of Principles and Standards for the Postsecondary Teaching of Writing." 2 June 2001 <http://www.ncte.org/positions/>.

National Council of Teachers of English Committee on National Interest. *The National Interest and the Teaching of English: A Report on the Status of the Profession.* Champaign, IL: NCTE, 1961.

National Council of Teachers of English Committee on the Place and Function of English in American Life. "Report of Committee on the Place and Function of English in American Life." *English Journal* 15 (1926): 110–34.

National Council of Teachers of English Committee on the Scientific Study of the Teaching of English. "Scientific Standards in English Teaching." *English Journal* 4 (1915): 28–34.

Nebraska Board of Education. "State Board of Education Assessment Policy." Passed 1 Oct. 1998, Lincoln, Nebraska. 24 July 1999 <http://www.edneb.org/IPS/AppAccrd/assmntPOLC.html>.

Newkirk, Thomas. "The Politics of Composition Research: The Conspiracy against Experience." Bullock and Trimbur 119–35.

North, Stephen M. "The Death of Paradigm Hope, the End of Paradigm Guilt, and the Future of (Research in) Composition." Bloom, Daiker, and White 194–207.

———. *The Making of Knowledge in Composition: Portrait of an Emerging Field.* Upper Montclair, NJ: Boynton/Cook, 1987.

———. *Refiguring the Ph.D. in English Studies.* Urbana, IL: NCTE, 2000.

———. "Rhetoric, Responsibility, and the 'Language of the Left.'" Hurlburt and Blitz 127–36

Noyes, Ernest C. "Progress in Standardizing the Measurement of Composition." *English Journal* 1 (1912): 532–36.

Ohmann, Richard. Foreword. Parks xiii–xviii.

———. "Introduction to the 1995 Edition." *English in America.* Hanover, NH: Wesleyan UP, 1995. xiii–lii.

———. "Professionalizing Politics." Rosner, Boehm, and Journet 227–34.

Olson, Gary. "The Death of Composition as an Intellectual Discipline." *Composition Studies* 28.2 (2000): 33–41.

Opdycke, John B. "The English of Commerce." *English Journal* 16 (1927): 101–13.

Orner, Mimi. "Interrupting the Calls for Student Voice in 'Liberatory' Education: A Feminist Poststructuralist Perspective." Luke and Gore 74–89.

Osgood, Charles G. "Humanism and the Teaching of English." *English Journal* 11 (1922): 159–66.

———. "No Set Requirement of English Composition in the Freshman Year." *English Journal* 4 (1915): 231–35.

Palmer, Glenn E. "Culture and Efficiency through Composition." *English Journal* 1 (1912): 488–92.

Parker, Flora E. "The Value of Measurements: The Measurement of Composition in English Classes." *English Journal* 8 (1919): 203–8.

Parks, Stephen. *Class Politics: The Movement for the Students' Right to Their Own Language.* Urbana, IL: NCTE, 2000.

Peckham, Irvin. "Whispers from the Margin: A Class-Based Interpretation of the Conflict between High School and College Writing Teachers." Rosner, Boehm, and Journet 253–68.

Penticoff, Richard, and Linda Brodkey. "Writing about Difference: 'Hard Cases' for Cultural Studies." Brodkey, *Writing Permitted* 228–45.

Petraglia, Joseph, ed. *Reconceiving Writing, Rethinking Writing Instruction.* Mahwah, NJ: Erlbaum, 1995.

Phelps, Louise Wetherbee. *Composition as a Human Science.* New York: Oxford UP, 1988.

———. "Paths Not Taken: Recovering History as Alternative Future." Rosner, Boehm, and Journet 39–58.

———. "Practical Wisdom and the Geography of Knowledge in Composition." *College English* 53 (1991): 863–85.

Poole, Hazel B. "Americanizing the Teacher of English." *English Journal* 16 (1927): 705–10.

Pope, Rob. *Textual Intervention.* New York: Routledge, 1995.

Porter, James E., Patricia Sullivan, Stuart Blythe, Jeffrey T. Grabill, and Libby Miles. "Institutional Critique: A Rhetorical Methodology for Change." *College Composition and Communication* 51 (2000): 610–42.

Powell, Malea. "Blood and Scholarship: One Mixed-Blood's Story." Gilyard, *Race, Rhetoric, and Composition* 1–16.

Powell, Michael. "In N.Y., Putting Down Their Pencils." *Washington Post* 18 May 2001: A01.

"Proposal for a Writing Sequence through the English Major." Department of English. Albany: State University of New York, 1993.

Pryse, Marjorie. "Reading Regionalism: The 'Difference' It Makes." *Regionalism Reconsidered: New Approaches to the Field.* Ed. David Jordan. New York: Garland, 1994. 47–63.

Purpel, David E., and Svi Shapiro. *Beyond Liberation and Excellence: Reconstructing the Public Discourse on Education.* Westport, CT: Bergin and Garvey, 1995.

"Quality Counts '99." *Education Week on the Web.* 11 Jan. 1999 <http://www.edweek.org/sreports/qc99>.

Qualley, Donna. *Turns of Thought: Teaching Composition as Reflexive Inquiry.* Portsmouth, NH: Boynton/Cook, 1997.

Ravitch, Diane. *The Troubled Crusade: American Education 1945–1980.* New York: Basic, 1983.

Readings, Bill. *The University in Ruins.* Cambridge: Harvard UP, 1996.

Reese, William J. *Power and the Promise of School Reform: Grassroots Movements during the Progressive Era.* Boston: Routledge and Kegan Paul, 1986.

Reeve, Richard. "A Study in Dreams and Freshman Composition." *English Journal* coll. ed. 17 (1928): 835–44.

Reither, James A., and Russell A. Hunt. "Beyond Portfolios: Scenes for Dialogic Reading and Writing." Black, Daiker, Sommers, and Stygall 168–82.

Reynolds, George Fullmer. "For Minimum Standards in English." *English Journal* 4 (1915): 349–56.

Roberts, Holland D. "Method in Creative Writing." *English Journal* 18 (1929): 345–46.

Roemer, Marjorie, Lucille M. Schultz, and Russell K. Durst. "Reframing the Great Debate on First-Year Writing." *College Composition and Communication* 50 (1999): 377–92.

Roschewski, Pat, with Chris Gallagher and Jody Isernhagen. "Nebraskans Reach for the STARS." *Phi Delta Kappan* 82 (2001): 611–15.

Rose, Mike. *Lives on the Boundary.* New York: Penguin, 1989.

Rosner, Mary, Beth Boehm, and Debra Journet, eds. *History, Reflection, and Narrative: The Professionalization of Composition, 1963–1983.* Stamford, CT: Ablex, 1999.

Rothstein, Richard. "Lessons: Rebellion Is Growing against Required Tests." *New York Times* 30 May 2001: B9.

Royster, Jacqueline Jones, and Jean C. Williams. "History in the Spaces Left: African American Presence and Narratives of Composition Studies." *College Composition and Communication* 50 (1999): 563–84.

Russell, David R. "Romantics on Writing: Liberal Culture and the Abolition of Composition Courses." *Rhetoric Review* 6 (1988): 132–48.

Ruud, M. B. "Standard English in American Democracy." *English Journal* 11 (1922): 283–87.

Sacks, Peter. *Standardized Minds: The High Price of America's Testing Culture and What We Can Do to Change It*. Cambridge, MA: Perseus, 1999.

Salvatori, Mariolina. *Pedagogy: A Disturbing History: 1819–1929*. Pittsburgh: U of Pittsburgh P, 1996.

Schell, Eileen E. "The Costs of Caring: 'Femininism' and Contingent Women Workers in Composition Studies." *Feminism and Composition Studies: In Other Words*. Ed. Susan C. Jarratt and Lynn Worsham. New York: MLA, 1998. 74–93.

———. *Gypsy Academics and Mother-Teachers: Gender, Contingent Labor, and Writing Instruction*. Portsmouth, NH : Boynton/Cook, 1998.

Schilb, John. *Between the Lines: Relating Composition Theory and Literary Theory*. Portsmouth, NH: Boynton/Cook, 1996.

Scholes, Robert. *The Rise and Fall of English: Reconstructing English as a Discipline*. New Haven: Yale UP, 1998.

———. *Textual Power: Literary Theory and the Teaching of English*. New York: Yale UP, 1985.

Schrag, Peter. "High Stakes Are for Tomatoes." *The Atlantic* 286.2 (August 2000): 19–21.

Schuster, Charles. "The Politics of Promotion." Bullock and Trimbur 85–95.

Schutz, Aaron, and Anne Ruggles Gere. "Service Learning and English Studies." *College English* 60 (1998): 129–49.

Scott, Frank W. "The Relation of Composition to the Rest of the Curriculum." *English Journal* 7 (1918): 512–20.

Scott, Fred Newton. "Our Problems." *English Journal* 2 (1913): 1–10.

———. "Poetry in a Commercial Age." *English Journal* 10 (1921): 549–59.

Seitz, James. *Motives for Metaphor: Literacy, Curriculum Reform, and the Teaching of English*. Pittsburgh: U of Pittsburgh Press, 1999.

Shackford, Martha Hale. "A Partial Substitute for the Theme." *English Journal* 1 (1912): 208–13.

Shamoon, Linda K., Rebecca Moore Howard, Sandra Jamieson, and Robert A. Schwegler, eds. *Coming of Age: The Advanced Writing Curriculum*. Portsmouth, NH: Heinemann, 2000.

Sheldon, Kennon M., and Bruce J. Biddle. "Standards, Accountability, and School Reform: Perils and Pitfalls." *Teachers College Record* 100.1 (1998): 164–80.

Shor, Ira. *Culture Wars: School and Society in the Conservative Restoration 1969–1984*. Boston: Routledge and Kegan Paul, 1986.

———. "Educating the Educators: A Freirean Approach to the Crisis in Teacher Education." *Freire for the Classroom: A Sourcebook for Liberatory Teaching*. Ed. Ira Shor. Portsmouth, NH: Boynton/Cook, 1987. 7–32.

———. *Empowering Education*. Chicago: U of Chicago P, 1992.

———. "Our Apartheid: Writing Instruction and Inequality." *Journal of Basic Writing* 16 (1997): 91–104

———. *When Students Have Power*. Chicago: U of Chicago P, 1996.

Shor, Ira, and Paulo Freire. *A Pedagogy for Liberation*. South Hadley, MA: Bergin and Garvey, 1987.

Shumway, David R. *Creating American Civilization: A Genealogy of American Literature as an Academic Discipline*. Minneapolis: U of Minnesota P, 1994.

Simon, Roger I. *Teaching against the Grain*. New York: Bergin and Garvey, 1992.

Slevin, James F. "Disciplining Students: Whom Should Composition Teach and What Should They Know?" Bloom, Daiker, and White 153–65.

Smith, Mary Lee. "Put to the Test: The Effects of External Testing on Teachers." *Educational Researcher* 20.5 (1991): 8–11.

Smithson, Isaiah, and Nancy Ruff, eds. *English Studies/Culture Studies*. Urbana: U of Illinois P, 1994.

Sowell, Thomas. *Inside American Education: The Decline, the Deception, the Dogmas*. New York: Free, 1992.

Spellmeyer, Kurt. "After Theory: From Textuality to Attunement with the World." *College English* 58 (1996): 893–913.

———. *Common Ground: Dialogue, Understanding, and the Teaching of Composition.* Englewood Cliffs, NJ: Prentice-Hall, 1993.

———. "Response: Testing as Surveillance." White, Lutz, and Kamusikiri 174–81.

Spring, Joel. *The American School: 1642–1990.* 2nd ed. New York: Longman, 1990.

"Statement from the Conference on the Growing Use of Part-Time and Adjunct Faculty." *ADE Bulletin* 119 (1998): 19–26.

Stenberg, Shari. *Professing and Pedagogy: Learning the Teaching of English.* Diss. SUNY–Albany, 2000.

Stotsky, Sandra. "Research, Teaching, and Public Policy." Bloom, Daiker, and White 208–11.

Straub, Kristina. "Burning the Commodity at Both Ends: Cultural Studies and Rhetoric in the First-Year Curriculum at Carnegie-Mellon University." Smithson and Ruff, 167–79.

Struble, Mildred C. "A Big Business-English Project." *English Journal* 9 (1920): 463–66.

Sullivan, Francis J., Arabella Lyon, Dennis Lebofsky, Susan Wells, and Eli Goldblatt. "Student Needs and Strong Composition: The Dialectics of Writing Program Reform." *College Composition and Communication* 48 (1997): 372–91.

Sullivan, Patricia, and James Porter. *Opening Spaces: Writing Technologies and Critical Research Practices.* Greenwich, CT: Ablex, 1997.

Sullivan, Patricia, and Donna J. Qualley, eds. *Pedagogy in the Age of Politics.* Urbana, IL: NCTE, 1994.

Sunstein, Bonnie S. *Composing a Culture: Inside a Summer Writing Program with High School Teachers.* Portsmouth, NH: Boynton/Cook, 1994.

Sykes, Charles J. *Dumbing Down Our Kids: Why American Children Feel Good about Themselves but Can't Read, Write, or Add.* New York: St. Martin's, 1995.

———. *Profscam: Professors and the Demise of Higher Education.* New York: Regnery Gateway, 1988.

"Telling Our Stories: We Remember." Heartland, NE: Heartland Community Schools, 2000.

Thorndike, Edward L. "Notes on the Significance and Use of the Hillegas Scale for Measuring the Quality of English Composition." *English Journal* 2 (1913): 551–61.

Thorngate, Ella. "Americanization in Omaha." *English Journal* 9 (1920): 123–28.

Thurber, Edward A. "Composition in our Colleges." *English Journal* 4.1 (1915): 9–14.

Tieje, R. E., et al. "Systematizing Grading in Freshman Composition at the Large University." *English Journal* 4 (1915): 586–97.

Tobin, Lad. "Introduction: How the Writing Process Was Born—and Other Conversion Narratives." *Taking Stock: The Writing Process Movement in the '90s.* Ed. Lad Tobin and Thomas Newkirk. Portsmouth, NH: Heinemann, 1994.

Todd, Sharon, ed. *Learning Desire: Perspectives on Pedagogy, Culture, and the Unsaid.* New York: Routledge, 1997.

Tompkins, Jane. "Facing Yourself." McCracken, Larson, and Entes 3–9.

Trachtenberg, Alan. *The Incorporation of America.* New York: Hill and Wang, 1982.

Trainor, Jennifer Seibel, and Amanda Godley. "After Wyoming." *College Composition and Communication* 50 (1998): 153–81.

Trimbur, John. Foreword. Horner ix–xii.

———. "Taking the Social Turn: Teaching Writing Post-Process." *College Composition and Communication* 45 (1994): 108–18.

———. "Writing Instruction and the Politics of Professionalization." Bloom, Daiker, and White 133–45

Tyack, David B. *The One Best System: A History of American Urban Education.* Cambridge: Harvard UP, 1974.

Tyack, David, and Larry Cuban. *Tinkering toward Utopia: A Century of Public School Reform.* Cambridge: Harvard UP, 1995.

University of Iowa. "Educating Teachers of English." Franklin, Laurence, and Welles 104–25.

University of Virginia. "Fit Teachers Though Few." Franklin, Laurence, and Welles 126–42.

Vandenberg, Peter. "Composing Composition Studies: Scholarly Publication and the Practice of Discipline." Farris and Anson 19–29.

Villanueva, Victor. "On the Rhetoric and Precedents of Racism." *College Composition and Communication* 50 (1999): 645–61.

Walkerdine, Valerie. "Progressive Pedagogy and Political Struggle." Luke and Gore 15–24.

Webster, Edward Harlan. "Preparation in English for Business." *English Journal* 2 (1913): 613–17.

Welch, Nancy. *Getting Restless*. Portsmouth, NH: Boynton/Cook, 1997.

———. "Resisting the Faith: Conversion, Resistance, and the Training of Teachers." *College English* 55 (1993): 387–401.

Wells, Susan. "Rogue Cops and Health Care: What Do We Want from Public Writing?" *College Composition and Communication* 47 (1996): 325–41.

Welsch, Kathleen. Review: "History as Complex Storytelling." *College Composition and Communication* 50 (1998): 116–22.

White, Edward M. "Power and Agenda Setting in Writing Assessment." In White, Lutz, and Kamusikiri 9–24.

———. *Teaching and Assessing Writing: Recent Advances in Understanding, Evaluating, and Improving Student Performance*. San Francisco: Jossey-Bass, 1985.

———. "Writing Assessment beyond the Classroom: Will Writing Teachers Play a Role?" Bloom, Daiker, and White 101–11.

White, Edward M., William D. Lutz, and Sandra Kamusikiri, eds. *Assessment of Writing: Politics, Policies, Practices*. New York: MLA, 1996.

Wiggins, Grant. *Educative Assessment*. San Francisco: Jossey-Bass, 1998.

Williams, Edna. "How to Make English Literature Teaching Utilitarian as Well as Cultural." *English Journal* 1 (1912): 151–55.

Wilson, David E. *Attempting Change: Teachers Moving from Writing Project to Classroom Practice*. Portsmouth, NH: Boynton/Cook, 1994.

Wise, Christopher. "Pee-Wee, Penley, and Pedagogy, or, Hands-On Feminism in the Writing Classroom." Fitts and France 129–38.

"The Writing Sequence." Brochure. Albany: SUNY–Albany, 1998.

Yancey, Kathleen Blake, and Irwin Weiser, eds. *Situating Portfolios: Four Perspectives*. Logan: Utah State UP, 1997.

Yeomans, Mabel Ford. "Women and Public Speaking." *English Journal* 7 (1918): 377–82.

Zaillian, Steven. *Schindler's List*. Draft of Screenplay Based on Novel by Thomas Keneally. 31 Jan. 1993.

Zandy, Janet. "Human Labor and Literature: A Pedagogy from a Working-Class Perspective." Downing 37–52.

Zebroski, James T. "The Expressivist Menace." Rosner, Boehm, and Journet 99–114.

Zinn, Howard. *A People's History of the United States, 1492–Present*. New York: HarperCollins, 1995.

# INDEX

# AUTHOR

**Chris W. Gallagher** is assistant professor of English at the University of Nebraska–Lincoln, where he teaches undergraduate and graduate courses in writing, rhetoric, literacy, and English Studies. He is also conducting research with P–12 teachers on the effects of standards and assessment practices on teaching and learning, with emphasis on the teaching and learning of writing. His dissertation won the 1999 James Berlin Memorial Outstanding Dissertation Award from the Conference on College Composition and Communication, and his writing has appeared in *College English*, *Composition Studies*, *Phi Delta Kappan*, and *Writing on the Edge*.

*This book was typeset in Sabon by Electronic Imaging.*
*The typeface used on the cover was ITC Stone Serif.*
*The book was printed on 50-lb. Husky Offset by IPC Communications.*